Brazil Theme Issue

The Journal of Decorative and Propaganda Arts is published annually by The Wolfson Foundation of Decorative and Propaganda Arts, Inc. U.S. subscription rate (1 issue): individuals $19, institutions $25. Foreign subscription rate (payable in U.S. dollars): individuals $24, institutions $30. Back issues available at $25 U.S., $30 foreign (payable in U.S. dollars).

Send address changes to *The Journal of Decorative and Propaganda Arts,* 2399 N.E. Second Avenue, Miami, Florida 33137 U.S.A. Fax 305/573-0409.

For advertising rates and schedules, write to *The Journal of Decorative and Propaganda Arts* or call 305/573-9170.

Printed in Japan by Nissha Printing Co., Ltd.

Cover: Roberto Burle Marx, detail of plan for the terrace garden, Ministry of Education and Public Health, Rio de Janeiro, gouache on paper, 1938. (See page 170.)

1995

21

The Journal of Decorative and Propaganda Arts   1875–1945

Editor
Pamela Johnson

Managing Editor
Cathy Leff

Assistant Editor
Susan Campbell

Administrative Assistant
Natascha Otero-Santiago

Design Director
Jacques Auger

Designer
Frank Begrowicz,
Jacques Auger Design
Associates, Inc.

On-Press Consultant
Gaku Okubo
Okubo Design Studio

**Portuguese Supplement
Editor**
Berta M. Sichel

Assistant Editor
Mario Sergio Mieli

Acknowledgments

By Pamela Johnson

"... for everything will bear fruit

only in the supernatural atmosphere of poetry."[1]

The Brazil of our dreams was larger-than-life — a vision of gorgeous landscapes, intrinsic wealth, and culture drawn from the Indian, the African, the European. It was a Brazil governed by poets, peopled by Amazons and madonnas, artists and tycoons, scholars and beachcombers.

Such a myth begged to be shattered. But, astonishingly, it did not happen. Instead, our journey through the real Brazil — comprising more land than Australia, more inhabitants than Russia[2] — assumed mythic proportions. And those who helped us create this theme issue matched the archetypes we dreamed of (though we must admit, we did *not* meet an Amazon!).

To realize our goal, we sought the sanction of Brazil's cultural leaders, and they, too, materialized in ideal form.[3] We gratefully acknowledge the kind assistance of Luiz Roberto do Nascimento e Silva, Minister of Culture of Brazil; Celina Albano, Secretary of Culture of the State of Minas Gerais; Guilherme M. de La Penha, Secretary of Culture of the State of Pará; and Ricardo Ohtake, Secretary of Culture of the State of São Paulo.

For his interest and encouragement, we are indebted to His Excellency Paulo Tarso Flecha de Lima, Ambassador of Brazil to the United States.

Without the inspiration given us by Vera Barrouin Machado, Consul General of Brazil in Miami, Florida, this issue would not have been possible. She collaborated each step of the way, making introductions, providing research materials, and even bestowing a grant from the Brazilian Consulate General. In addition, she commended us to premier institutions in Brazil who subsequently became sponsors — first and foremost, Vitae Apoio à Cultura, Educação e Promoção Social, and the Safra Bank.

Vitae — funded by the Lampadia Foundation — fosters cultural, educational, and social projects. Their magnanimous contribution to the *Journal* was given to further international diffusion of Brazilian arts and culture. We would like particularly to thank Robert B. Glynn, Chairman of the Board of Lampadia; José E. Mindlin and his fellow Board Members at Vitae; and Regina Weinberg, Executive Director of Vitae, and her dedicated staff, for their unfailing help.

1. João Cabral de Melo Neto, "Poetry," in *Selected Poetry, 1937–1990* (Hanover, New Hampshire: Wesleyan University Press, 1994), 6–7.
2. *Rand McNally World Atlas* (1994), 197.
3. Please note that all titles referred to in these acknowledgments were in effect during the period of our research in Brazil, from November 1993 to July 1994.

An equally magnanimous contribution came to us from the Safra Bank through the Safra Cultural Project. Their aim is to maintain Brazil's historical and cultural traditions, and to promote Brazilian and international art in myriad forms. To this end they sponsor concerts, art exhibitions, and an ongoing series of books portraying Brazilian museums. The *Journal* owes special thanks to Jorge Visniauskas, our liaison with Safra in São Paulo.

Varig Brazilian Airlines was another major donor, underwriting our flights throughout Brazil. They substantially enlarged the range of our research and thus the scope of the issue. We are beholden to Marcelo William Bottini, Regional Manager; Graziella Cabrera; and all others at Varig who coordinated our complex itineraries.

The Maksoud Plaza Hotel generously provided rooms during our stays in São Paulo. Our appreciation goes to Roberto F. Maksoud, Managing Director, for his gracious hospitality.

The Copacabana Palace Hotel in Rio de Janeiro extended us many courtesies during our visits, for which we are most grateful.

As Brazil is vast and its people warm-hearted, we were welcomed in city after city. It would truly be impossible to acknowledge all those we were privileged to meet. Aware that any effort is inadequate, we mention only a few who were unstinting with time and advice.

In São Paulo, where we began our explorations, profound thanks to Emanoel Araújo, Director, Art Museum of the State of São Paulo; Marcelo Mattos Araújo, Chief, Department of Museology, Lasar Segall Museum; Ana Maria Belluzo; Aron Cohen; Maria Estela Segatto Corrêa, Cultural Advisor, USIS, American Consulate General; Agnaldo Farias, Curator, Secretariat of Culture; Isabella di Savoia Genova; Fulvia and Adolpho Leirner; Arlindo Mungioli, *Revista Projeto*; Carlos Perrone, Technical Director, Secretariat of Culture; José Roberto Pini and Mário Pini, Pini Editora; Barbara Scarlett, Cultural Affairs Officer, USIS, American Consulate General; Hugo Segawa, *Revista Projeto*; Philip Taylor, Consul General, American Consulate General; Irene Tourinho, Vice Director, Museum of Modern Art; and, above all, Barbara Starr and Wolf A. Wolf.

In Rio de Janeiro, obeisances to Sandra and Marcello Cattaneo Adorno; Julia and Mario Gibson Barboza; Lourdes de Brito e Cunha; Jorge P. Czajkowski; Gilberto Ferrez; Miriam Gaudenzi; Piedade Epstein Grinberg; Paulo Herkenhoff; Heloisa Helena Oliveira Buarque de Holanda; and Gilberto Velho.

In Belo Horizonte, remembrances to Angela Gutierrez; Roberto B. Martins; José Alberto Nemer; Conceição Piló, Curator, Liberty Palace; Paulo Roberto Rossi; and Eunice Vivacqua von Tiesenhausen.

In Belém, our gratitude to Célia Coelho Bassalo; Jussara da Silveira Derenji; and Antonio Carlos Lobo Soares.

In Brasília, we salute Wladimir Murtinho and Margarida Patriota, Ministry of Culture.

In Fortaleza, a tribute to José Liberal de Castro.

In Manaus, regards to Ana Lúcia N. S. Abrahim.

In Ouro Preto, our respects to The Honorable Angelo Oswaldo de Araújo Santos, Mayor.

In Porto Alegre, accolades to Andrea and Edson Mahfuz.

In Recife, bows to Neil R. Klopfenstein, Regional Director, USIS, American Consulate General; and Nehilde and Geraldo Gomes da Silva.

In Salvador, our very best to Sylvia Maria Menezes de Athayde, Director, Bahia Museum of Art.

In São Luís, salutations to Carlos Frederico Lago Burnett and Paula Ferguson Marques.

Among those in Buenos Aires who lent every aid were Jacqueline Rothschild; Edward Shaw; and Frances Switt, Cultural Attaché, USIS, American Embassy. In addition, we especially recognize Irma Arestizábal, Director of the Casa Rosada Museum, who first advanced the concept of a Brazil theme issue and made specific, useful recommendations.

Among those in Miami, Florida, who facilitated the planning and carrying out of the issue were Norah Aurélio, Vice Consul, Brazilian Consulate General; David Beaty; Jack Luft, City of Miami Department of Development; and Carlos Alfredo Teixeira, Deputy Consul General, Brazilian Consulate General.

In New York City, the devoted efforts of Berta M. Sichel, Editor of the Portuguese supplement to the *Journal*, deserve high praise. Also, we could not have completed our task without her diligent Assistant Editor, Mario Sergio Mieli.

To a cadre of fine translators — Paulo Henriques Britto, Izabel Murat Burbridge, Kim Mrazek Hastings, Elizabeth A. Jackson, David J. Jacobson, Elza B. de Oliveira Marques, Robert Myers, Edward Shaw, and Elizabeth Wynn-Jones — we give thanks for their excellent work, asking forgiveness for any editorial changes not to their liking. To Florence E. Irving, Leon H. Lehman, Duncan Lindsay, and William J. Shelton, who joined in earlier stages of translation, applause for their contributions.

Those not mentioned here are by no means forgotten. They are a living part of this book, and we will remember them always. □

L'EXPOSITION DE PARIS

DE 1889

Prix du numero : **50** centimes.

ABONNEMENTS. — PARIS ET DÉPARTEMENTS : **20** FR.

Adresser les mandats à l'ordre de l'Administrateur.

Journal hebdomadaire. — 3 août 1889.

N° 23

BUREAUX : 8, RUE SAINT-JOSEPH. — PARIS

Prix du numéro : **50** centimes.

ABONNEMENTS. — PARIS ET DÉPARTEMENTS : **20** FR.

Adresser les mandats à l'ordre de l'Administrateur.

LE PAVILLON DU BRÉSIL AU CHAMP DE MARS.

Fig. 1. Brazilian Pavilion, Paris World's Fair, 1889.

Stages in the Formation of Brazil's Cultural Profile

By Aracy Amaral

Translated by Kim Mrazek Hastings

Aracy Amaral is professor of art history in the Department of Architecture and Urbanism at the University of São Paulo. She was director of the Art Museum of the State of São Paulo from 1975 to 1979 and of the Museum of Contemporary Art at the University of São Paulo from 1982 to 1986. A scholar of Brazilian modernism, she has published widely on this subject and on Brazilian contemporary and colonial art. She has curated many exhibitions, most recently *Brazil—The New Generation* at the Museum of Fine Arts, Caracas, Venezuela (1991), and *Mirrors and Shadows* at the Museum of Modern Art, São Paulo (1994).

Photographs by Rômulo Fialdini except where noted.

Contemporary Brazil's cultural profile owes a great deal to changes that took place in the country's mentality during the second half of the nineteenth century and at the beginning of the republic (fig. 1).[1] Following the end of the Second Empire in 1889, Brazil emerged as a contradictory reality, with disproportionate wealth and poverty and flagrant regional differences in terms of development and quality of life, particularly between the South and the Northeast.[2] Not until the Vargas era (1930–1945) did Brazil begin to perceive itself as a unified whole; even then, there was a relative lack of communication among its diverse regions. This situation remained unaltered until the advent of mass communication in the 1950s.

Numerous events and initiatives occurring during this period also contributed to the configuration of modern-day Brazil: exploitation of Amazon rubber (the province was created in 1850) triggered sudden, intensive development of the North lasting through the end of the century; the mobilization of Brazil's armed forces for their first external conflict, the Paraguayan War (1865–1870), prompted pro-army sentiment and military interest in abolitionist and republican causes; an influx of foreign capital, especially from England, paved the way for construction of railroads, including the São Paulo Railway, which connected the cities of Santos and Jundiaí; newly formed Brazilian private capital went toward other railroads necessary for transporting coffee crops—the Companhia Paulista de Estradas de Ferro (1868) and Sorocabana (1870)—and the creation of São Paulo's industrial park. European immigration, primarily by Germans and Italians, began at this time, mainly to São Paulo and Brazil's southern states, as an alternative to slave labor, which would soon be abolished.[3]

1. Brazil achieved independence in 1822 after Emperor Pedro I succeeded in obtaining a huge loan from England—a condition set by his father, the King of Portugal, for recognition of the new nation. These funds were retained in London for payment of Portugal's debts. As a result, Brazil began her independent life in debt. Reaching 237.5 million pounds sterling between 1889 and 1930, the debt went down slightly from 1930 to 1945, following an economic crisis and the subsequent reduction of foreign investments. By 1943 Brazil's diminished dependence on England (to whom 65 percent was then owed) was balanced by the United States' emerging role as creditor. See Ovídio de Andrade Melo, "Reflexões/O Brasil de D. Pedro I a Itamar," in *Carta: falas, reflexões, memórias/informe de distribuição restrita do Senador Darcy Ribeiro*, no. 10 (Brasília: Gabinete do Senador Darcy Ribeiro, 1994), 90–91.

2. The Canudos rebellion against the liberal republic, which began in Bahia in 1893, exemplifies the political climate of the Northeast, steeped in both social and mystical problems.

3. The decree abolishing slavery in Brazil was signed in 1888 by Princess Isabel, daughter of Emperor Pedro II.

Fig. 2. Carlos Ekman,

Penteado family residence,

exterior view, São Paulo, 1902.

Photograph courtesy of the

University of São Paulo

Department of Architecture

and Urbanism.

The immigrants' arrival generated new energy and ideas and provoked social changes, although these would become more evident by the early twentieth century. Gradually immigration and industrialization fostered appreciation of new customs; traditional habits lost their value. According to the late American historian and Brazilianist Warren Dean, Brazil's upper classes "identif[ied] their interests not with their fellow countrymen but with their fellow whites from Europe, and...look[ed] to European immigration, to the 'bleaching' of the population, as the cure for the economic backwardness of the country. Hence the ready hospitality of the Brazilians, the partnerships, and the marriage alliances."[4] São Paulo, a town of only 31,385 inhabitants in 1874, underwent rapid and drastic transformation to become a full-fledged city of 130,775 in 1894. By 1900 this figure would reach 239,820.[5] Although São Paulo's conversion to a metropolis did not fully intensify until 1910, when urban remodeling was planned to alter the city's somewhat colonial image, the opening of Paulista Avenue (1893) remains a milestone in the city's history. Elegant *chácaras*, homes for Brazil's wealthy immigrants and coffee "barons," were built along this prestigious three-kilometer avenue, situated on one of the highest points of the São Paulo plateau. Best described as "villas," these eclectic homes featured an array of architectural styles: from Florentine to Mozarabic, from French with mansards and slate roofs to stately neoclassical.

Brazil's most impressive nineteenth-century architecture is concentrated in Rio de Janeiro, capital of the republic as of 1889. There the simplified neoclassical style brought to Brazil by French architect Grandjean de Montigny, the country's first professor of architecture, took root in a particular fashion. Examples still standing today include Grandjean de Montigny's own home in Gávea; the old Customs Building (now the Casa Brasil-França); the Ministry of Foreign Affairs,

4. Warren Dean, *The Industrialization of São Paulo, 1880–1945* (Austin: University of Texas Press, n.d.), 79.

5. This population explosion occurred all over the country, from 17.5 million in 1900 to 48 million in 1939.

Fig. 3. Victor Dubugras,

Mairinque Railroad Station,

state of São Paulo, 1906

project plan.

Fig. 4. Belmiro de Almeida,

publicity sketch for Restaurant

Madrid, India ink, 43 x 29 cm,

no date. Milton Guper

collection, São Paulo.

also known as the Itamarati Palace (1851); the Automobile Club Building (circa 1850) designed by Manuel Araújo de Porto Alegre; the Beneficência Portuguesa (1853); and the residence (1862) later transformed into the Catete Palace, seat of the federal government until Brasília's inauguration as capital in 1960.

Art nouveau could be seen in São Paulo's architecture—not only in grand houses (fig. 2) but also in the Santa Ifigênia Viaduct imported from Belgium, and in the "bungalows" imported and set up at the beach town of Guarujá, for instance, with their decorated lambrequins of cut wood. The style is widely found in other regions of Brazil as well, including Petrópolis in the state of Rio de Janeiro; the Manaus Market in the Amazon; and the shop called Paris na América in Belém, Pará. Of the many iron buildings imported from Scotland and erected in Brazil, the José de Alencar Theater in Fortaleza, Ceará, is an exceptional example. Actually, Brazil's first fully functionalist building, without ornamentation of any kind, was not built until 1907: the Mairinque Railroad Station in the interior of São Paulo, designed by Victor Dubugras (fig. 3). This same architect submitted award-winning *art-nouveau* plans for Rio de Janeiro's Municipal Theater, but the work he envisioned was substituted by another project, a Brazilian version of the Paris Opera House.

The *art-nouveau* style appealed to only a few plastic artists, among them Eliseu Visconti and, occasionally, Belmiro de Almeida (fig. 4). Visconti marked the transition to modernity in the plastic arts by showing himself to be sensitive to pre-Raphaelite trends (fig. 5) as well as to *art nouveau* and echoes of the impressionist movement, albeit belatedly.[6] Having studied at the Guérin School in France with Eugène Grasset, Visconti put together an exhibition upon his return to Brazil in 1900; there his concern with utilizing local traditions, as in the Marajoara-inspired decoration of ceramic vases, was made apparent.[7]

6. At the century's end, Visconti painted works—*Gioventù* and *Dança das Oréades* (Dance of the oreads) (1900)—revealing his familiarity with the British pre-Raphaelite movement. Commissioned to execute large-scale paintings for Rio de Janeiro's new Municipal Theater (1905), the artist created a pointillist stage curtain [see page 46], an innovation given the less than experimental art scene of the time.

7. Flávio Motta, "Visconti e o início do século XX," in Roberto Pontual, *Dicionário das artes plásticas no Brasil* (Rio de Janeiro: Editora Civilização Brasileira, 1968), n.p. See also Carlos Cavalcanti, "O predomínio do academismo neoclássico," in ibid.

65 x 49 cm, 1900. National

Museum of Fine Arts,

Rio de Janeiro.

During this same period of transition between political regimes and industrialization, Brazil awakened to nationalism.[8] Both the plastic arts and literature were framed by a context in which Brazil began to see itself with new eyes, without prejudices, as exemplified by José Almeida Júnior's canvases. A romantic-realist academic, his work toward the end of the nineteenth century gave emphasis to the *caipira*, or inhabitant of the interior of São Paulo. Although artists of the day, like Almeida Júnior, had the opportunity to travel to Paris and witness what the world's art capital had to offer, few were influenced by impressionism, the vanguard of Parisian art from 1870 on. In fact, after returning to Brazil, Almeida Júnior chose to settle in the interior of São Paulo, where he was originally from, and to devote himself to a national agenda, portraying regional customs and personae (fig. 6). [9]

Before Almeida Júnior, a landscape school arose in 1870 with Jorge Grimm, a teacher at Rio de Janeiro's Imperial School of Fine Arts. Like their São Paulo counterparts, these landscape artists had their interest sparked by the discovery of Brazil's readily accessible imagery, her environment. Antônio Parreiras, João Batista Castagnetto, and Vítor Meirelles figured among them; the latter, unquestionably influenced by photography, completed a number of "panoramas" first presented in Brussels, then at the 1889 World's Fair in Paris, and later in Rio de Janeiro, with exhibits open to the public. These works were vast paintings mounted cylindrically for appreciation by spectators standing at the center of the display.

◀

Fig. 6. José Almeida Júnior,
***O violeiro* (The guitar player),**
oil on canvas, 141 x 172 cm,
1899. Art Museum of the State
of São Paulo.

Images of black people first appeared in academic Brazilian painting toward the end of the century, and especially after abolition. Examples include works by Lucílio de Albuquerque, Abigail de Andrade, and, although ambiguously, Modesto Brocos's paintings (*A redenção de Cam* [The redemption of Ham], National Museum of Fine Arts, Rio de Janeiro). This imagery was also extended to cinema.[10] Dissent was stirring Rio's National School of Fine Arts. Republicans, influenced by Auguste Comte's positivist ideas, demanded that the institution be closed and total freedom be granted to all who wished to become artists. Modern artists headed by the brothers Henrique and Rodolfo Bernardelli and Visconti, according to historian Frederico Barata, also sought reform but not the school's dissolution. An agreement was signed in 1890 and went into effect during a wave of receptiveness to fresh ideas.[11] Artists who had had some tie to the emperor, such as Vítor Meirelles and Pedro Américo, were dismissed given the republican times.

The same aspiration toward nationalism could be heard in music. According to writer and critic Mário de Andrade, "although Brazil did not manage to move beyond religious music during the colonial period, by the second half of the nineteenth century profane music prevailed." Predominantly romantic,

8. The Paraguayan War offered academic painters a motif for official historical paintings; not just battle scenes, as in Pedro Américo's *Batalha do Avaí* (1877), but also recreations of history, such as Vítor Meirelles's *Primeira missa no Brasil* (1860).

9. The painting of Rio Grande do Sul native Pedro Weingartner reveals the same nationalism (although *La faiseuse d'anges* [1908] [Art Museum of the State of São Paulo] was influenced by Goethe's *Faust*).

10. Brazil's attraction to cinema seems to have been love at first sight. Two years after cinema was introduced in Brazil (1896), Alfonso Segreto made the first Brazilian film; shortly afterwards, the first halls for viewing cinematic "spectacles" were opened to the curious public (fig. 7).

11. Motta, "Visconti."

this music was marked by "two manifestations specifically characteristic of sexual sensuality: the *modinha de salão*, or love lament, and the melodrama," constituting "an escape valve for the passions."[12]

Romanticism coupled with nationalism also influenced the literature of the day. Brazil's roots were revealed through literature, especially nativist fiction —albeit with a European perspective. This description applies to Rodolfo Amoedo's *Marabá* (1887, National Museum of Fine Arts, Rio de Janeiro): the painting shows an indigenous woman in an absolutely European pose—what we call "romantic treatment." Operas such as *O escravo*, *O Guarani*, and *Moema* by composer Carlos Gomes of Campinas, in the state of São Paulo, were also inspired by nativist literary successes; the most prominent writers of this trend founded on Brazilian reality included Visconde de Taunay and José de Alencar.

The greatest literary figure at the turn of the century was, however, indisputedly the *carioca* (Rio native) Joaquim Machado de Assis. He captured the daily life of Rio de Janeiro's middle class in countless novels and short stories with exemplary realism—and a unique brand of pessimism. By the beginning of the twentieth century, writers like Lima Barreto and Graça Aranha, whose novel *Canaã* (1902) is about Espírito Santo's first German immigrants, consolidated the predilection for native subjects and produced works now considered classics of Brazilian literature. *Os sertões* (Rebellion in the backlands) (1902) by *Estado de S. Paulo* journalist Euclides da Cunha was the first literary work to depict the land and people of Brazil's rural Northeast for the industrializing South; it remains an ambitious and masterful profile of the country.

In the twenties, architecture, literature, and the visual arts were marked by a desire for formal renovation, making the early years of this century a time of cultural definition, particularly in São Paulo. The intellectual and art communities remained attentive to what was happening in Europe, especially in Paris, but emotional commitments lay with Brazil. Although educated in Europe, the Brazilian artists and writers who participated in the modernist movement— which had its historical beginning during the Week of Modern Art at São Paulo's Municipal Theater, 11 to 18 February 1922—gradually came to realize that Brazilian reality was as important as formal renovation.[13]

Nearly ten years before the Week of Modern Art, Oswald de Andrade, a young journalist and poet from São Paulo, returned from Europe with knowledge of Marinetti's futurist manifesto. In 1915 he began to write in favor of an art that would reflect Brazilian reality, not simply copy foreign schools.[14] By 1917 the young painter Anita Malfatti (fig. 8) had returned to São Paulo, after studying with Lovis Corinth in Germany and, during World War One, with Homer Boss in New York, and exhibited "fauvist" works showing total freedom of creation and expression. The show was attacked by the well-known nationalist writer José Monteiro Lobato. Both Mário and Oswald de Andrade (no relation despite their shared name) supported Malfatti, judging her a pioneer in the renovation of modern Brazil's arts. Two other young artists, the sculptor

12. Mário de Andrade, *Música do Brasil* (Curitiba: Editora Guaíra Limitada, 1941), 21.

13. Outside the realm of the arts, the twenties were marked by various events in the political and intellectual arenas: the Lieutenants' Revolt at Copacabana Fort and the founding of the Communist Party in Rio de Janeiro in 1922; the opposition movement against the federal government led by Isidoro Dias Lopes in São Paulo in 1924; and the awakening of Brazilian intellectuals to political problems with the creation of a Democratic Party in 1926.

14. A regionalist tendency emerged in literature of this period with writers Menotti del Picchia, Cornélio Pena, and later José Monteiro Lobato, among others. This phenomenon reflected the climate of World War One, with its campaign for mandatory military service headed by symbolist poet Olavo Bilac, and preparations to commemorate the centennial of Brazil's independence in 1922.

Fig. 8. Anita Malfatti, *Ritmo/torso* (Rhythm/torso), charcoal and pastel on paper, 61 x 46.8 cm, 1915–1918. Museum of Contemporary Art, University of São Paulo.

Fig. 9. Victor Brecheret, *Daisy*, marble, 59 x 56 x 30 cm, ca. 1920. São Paulo State Governor's Palace (Bandeirantes Palace).

Victor Brecheret (fig. 9) and the painter Emiliano Di Cavalcanti (fig. 11), also pledged their solidarity to the painter. Both had begun to incorporate stylistic innovations into their works; although somewhat hybrid in nature, these innovations shied away from the still dominant academic art.

It was this group that initially began preparations for the Week of Modern Art. Modeled after European events like that at Deauville, France, and somewhat futurist in spirit—though the modernists soon rejected all ties to Marinetti's movement—the Week featured conferences, art and architecture exhibits, poetry readings, and music (composer Villa-Lobos participated in the event). The artists chosen reveal the lack of orientation on the part of the event's organizers. The participants' primary goal at the time was to show themselves opposed to pretentious, conventional styles and in favor of change.

Fig. 10. Antônio Paim Vieira,

Maxixe, published in the

February issue of *Ariel*,

São Paulo, 1924.

Fig. 11. Emiliano Di Cavalcanti,

Sem título (Untitled), water-

color and crayon on paper,

33.4 x 22.8 cm, ca. 1927.

Museum of Contemporary Art,

University of São Paulo.

What came to light during the Week's exhibits was precisely this "desire for change," for movement away from academic tendencies. Diverse directions were taken: from postimpressionism to half-baked cubism, given a lack of direct contact with the school's leading artists. Traces of expressionism may be detected in artists such as the German Wilhelm Haarberg; in the Cézanne quality of Swiss-educated John Graz's paintings; and in works by those who mastered the movement's pictorial language through formal training, as Anita Malfatti had. All the Week's other artists, including Vicente do Rego Monteiro, Antônio Paim Vieira (fig. 10), and Di Cavalcanti, demonstrated, first and foremost, a desire to be modern. The architecture presented in drawings further reflected hybrid directions, as seen in works by the Polish Georg Przyrembel and in Antônio Garcia Moya's Hispanic stylizations. Moya already showed signs of the art-deco style that would define his later work.

And so went the Week. After trips and stints in Europe, Brazilian artists quickly comprehended the precepts of cubism, seen in 1923 in Tarsila do Amaral's paintings. Amaral, for her part, visited the studios of Lhote, Gleizes, and Léger that same year. Other artists who traveled or took up residence in Paris would present surprisingly mature works throughout the decade—Brecheret, Di Cavalcanti, Rego Monteiro, Antônio Gomide, and Ismael Nery. Art deco became part of the modernist vocabulary of all the aforementioned artists during the twenties, although Antônio Gomide (fig. 12) and Regina Gomide Graz were the first to introduce cubist concepts into applied arts in São Paulo interiors—just as architect Gregori Warchavchik would. As a client of Parisian dressmaker/cultural activist Paul Poiret, Tarsila do Amaral would also bring to Brazil fashions and styles discovered after the 1925 Decorative Arts Exhibition in Paris.

Fig. 12. Antônio Gomide, *Árvores* (Trees), watercolor, 51 x 32 cm, 1925.

Fernando Stickel collection, São Paulo.

Just months following the now famous Week, Amaral returned to Brazil and joined the modernist group. With her companion of that decade, Oswald de Andrade, Amaral would become without a doubt the most unique artist of the modernist movement (fig. 13). Her rediscovery of the colors of Brazil's interior, while traveling in Rio de Janeiro and Minas Gerais in 1924 with other modernists and French-Swiss poet Blaise Cendrars (who would make several subsequent trips to Brazil, given his great friendship with intellectual businessman Paulo Prado of São Paulo), vividly enriched her painting: constructive, contained, with an unmistakeable appeal to the elements of the Brazilian landscape from a chromatic point of view.

During this same decade Oswald de Andrade drafted his *Manifesto pau-brasil* (Brazil-wood manifesto) (fig. 14), advocating a Brazilian art for export; the work was followed in 1928 by his *Manifesto antropófago* (Cannibal manifesto). This second essay essentially demanded that Brazilian artists devour the enemy, or, more specifically, what comes from outside—European culture—in order to impose what is Brazilian. Andrade spoke of uniting Brazil's intense tropical creativity and her major technical advances—airplanes, elevators, television—thus accepting Brazil's paradoxes and heterogeneous traditions. That same year Mário de Andrade wrote *Macunaíma*, based on studies of indigenous legends of the Amazon and dialectically opposed tales of life and adventure in a big and modern city. The work is a genuine rhapsody on the contradictory Brazilian personality, fascinated when faced with the problems and populations of urban environments, where wealthy immigrants were surfacing. Other writers, including Antônio de Alcântara Machado and Oswald de Andrade, also wrote highly irreverent works of modernist prose during this period—*Brás, Bexiga e Barra Funda* (1927) and *Serafim Ponte Grande* (1933), respectively.

Fig. 14. Oswald de Andrade's

Manifesto pau-brasil,

book cover, 1925.

José E. Mindlin collection.

In the former work, Alcântara Machado documented with gusto the behavior and Italo-Brazilian speech of São Paulo. Modernist contributions may also be seen in the publication of magazines, including *Klaxon* (nine issues in 1922), *Terra Roxa*, *Verde*, and the *Revista de Antropofagia*.

Amid these ruptures in literature and the plastic arts, an architectural style known as "neocolonial" arose and gained acceptance in Brazil. Imbued with fantasy and desires of grandeur, it involved a return to the past as it sought colonial traditions in architecture—traditions that frequently had not been characterized by scale or decorative wealth in civil architecture. It was disseminated by architect Ricardo Severo in São Paulo, beginning in 1914, and soon after by José Mariano Filho in Rio de Janeiro.[15] Portuguese Ricardo Severo defended architecture that had to do with the inheritance of a Lusitanian "traditionalist" style; Mariano Filho defended the constructions of colonial Brazil, earlier adaptations of Portuguese styles. Their attitude reflected the concern of traditionalist architects who disapproved of international eclecticism, the blending of architectural types in one building—a solution rife in Brazil's southern region in particular, owing to the arrival of immigrants of various nationalities.

São Paulo's sudden growth during this century's first two decades led to a revised concept of residential urbanism introduced by the English Companhia City, which planned residential areas for an affluent population. Their "City Gardens" distinguished the emerging metropolis: Jardim América, Jardim Europa, Alto da Lapa, Pacaembu, and Alto de Pinheiros are made up of winding treelined streets and homes, from neocolonial to ultramodern, set in the midst of perfectly landscaped plots.

Today neocolonial architecture may be seen to anticipate modern trends in Brazil as it disconnected from Europe as a sole source of influence.[16] In São Paulo eclecticism was already becoming widely known, especially through the office of prestigious Belgian-educated architect Ramos de Azevedo.

Modern architecture, characterized in Brazil by functionalism, the search for purity of lines, absence of decorative elements, and Bauhaus influence (in the cases of Warchavchik and, after 1930, Le Corbusier), was born during these same restless years in São Paulo. In 1927 Warchavchik built his first modernist house; and architect, scenographer, and plastic artist Flávio de Carvalho entered a competition with an equally modern and bold plan for the State Governor's Palace.

In 1929, en route from Buenos Aires, Le Corbusier visited São Paulo and Rio de Janeiro and won over young architect Lúcio Costa with modern ideas. From then on the federal capital saw the beginnings of modern architecture sponsored by the Brazilian government.

Getúlio Vargas's coup in 1930 signaled a new era in Brazil. Following the crisis of 1929, which subjected Brazil to economic paralysis and unemployment, there was a swerve to the political left, even in cultural circles. Despite the traditional lack of communication among countries, the same was seen all over America—the product of *Zeitgeist*. Vargas's rise to power initially

15. Throughout the Americas neocolonial and neo-Hispanic styles appeared, representing a search for identity intensified by the centennials of many countries. See Aracy Amaral, ed., *Arquitectura neocolonial: América Latina, Caribe, Estados Unidos* (São Paulo: Fondo de Cultura Econômica/ Memorial da América Latina, 1994).

16. The California mission style, for example, was exported to Central and South America, especially through architectural magazines. See Amaral, *Arquitectura neocolonial*.

Fig. 15. Cândido Portinari, *Mestiço* (Mestizo), oil on canvas, 81 x 65 cm, 1934.

Art Museum of the State of São Paulo. (See page 22.)

Fig. 16. Flávio de Carvalho,

residence on Alameda Lorena

in São Paulo, detail, 1930s.

Photograph courtesy of the

University of São Paulo

Department of Architecture

and Urbanism.

brought hope of rupture with the First Republic (1889–1930) and its "coffee with milk" politics—a reference to the alliance between Minas Gerais and São Paulo, the two major producers of dairy products and coffee. To the peoples' dismay, however, Vargas joined with factions of the right just after conceding advanced labor laws. One-time revolutionary lieutenants joined his regime, which became a dictatorship by the middle of the decade.[17]

In the arts the climate shifted considerably. Following vanguard movements ceased to be a priority, in spite of events like the opening of Warchavchik's Casa Modernista (1930) to the public. The house, located in the new neighborhood of Pacaembu, was completely decorated with furniture, objects, and works of art integrated into the architecture in Bauhaus fashion; it also featured the first plans for tropical landscaping, authored by Warchavchik's wife, Ema Klabin.

Social concerns permeated literary circles as well as the plastic arts and architecture. The painter Cândido Portinari, returning from Europe in the early thirties (fig. 15), became Brazil's most celebrated artist through the forties. The creator of numerous panels and murals detailing Brazil's history and customs, Portinari showed the influence of Mexico's muralists, although not formally. Popular and regional themes also dominated the visual arts of this period, coinciding with the economic crisis that shook the country. Artists of humble origins banded together in groups and produced a type of painting frequently focused on work as a theme. Their concern lay not with the search for avant-garde languages but with refining painting as a craft. The Núcleo Bernardelli in Rio de Janeiro counted Quirino Campofiorito, Eugênio Sigaud, Milton Dacosta, and Yoshiya Takaoka among its members; the Família Artística Paulista in São Paulo linked artists of proletariat immigrant origin, such as Aldo Bonadei, Alfredo Volpi, Mário Zanini, Francisco Rebolo, and Fúlvio Pennacchi, for example.

Second generation modernist artist Flávio de Carvalho brought life to São Paulo's art scene in the thirties, an age of clubs, artists' groups, and art salons. An engineer, architect (fig. 16), and performer in 1931, Carvalho also wrote experimental theater (O bailado do deus morto [Dead god's dance]) (1933). Further, he founded the Modern Artists' Club and organized the Third May Salon in 1939. Foreign and abstract artists were invited to this event, anticipating the international biennials that would begin to take place in São Paulo in 1951, and indicating just how cosmopolitan the city had become.

Literature reflected the same politicization in the thirties with novels by northeastern writers committed to social issues—Jorge Amado, Rachel de Queiroz, Graciliano Ramos, and José Lins do Rego. In the fields of history, economy, and sociology, three books fundamental for the thirties generation, according to Luís Saia, former director of the Historic and Artistic National Patrimony in São Paulo, were published: Raízes do Brasil (Roots of Brazil) (1936) by historian Sérgio Buarque de Holanda, Evolução política do Brasil (Political evolution of Brazil) (1933) by Caio Prado Júnior, and Casa grande e senzala (The masters and the slaves) (1933) by sociologist Gilberto Freyre.

17. Vargas flirted with the extreme right and thus stalled in siding with the Allies in World War Two. No doubt war was declared against the Axis as a result of intense local campaigning and pressure from Brazil's intellectuals.

Fig. 17. Lúcio Costa and

Oscar Niemeyer, Brazilian

Pavilion, detail, New York

World's Fair, 1939.

(See page 24.)

Cinema, as a counterpoint, was based in Rio de Janeiro during the Vargas regime, with productions dominated by the Atlântida company.[18] The *chanchada*—a brand of spicy comedy—soared to great heights of popularity. There were few avant-garde films; Mário Peixoto's early work *Limite* (Limit) (1930), influenced by the Russian and French vanguards, was an exception. Mineiran Humberto Mauro achieved renown with *Lábios sem beijos* (Lips without kisses) (1930) and *Ganga bruta* (Brutal gang) (1933), "one of the undisputed masterpieces of Brazilian cinema."[19] Actress and producer Carmen Santos also deserves mention; regarded as a phenomenon within the Brazilian film industry, Santos owned Brasil Vita Filme, a company that produced *Favela dos meus amores* (Favela of my loves) and *Mlle Cinema*. In the latter film, Santos worked with actor Alex Orloff under the direction of Czech actor Leo Marten.

In architecture, Rino Levi surfaced in the thirties and forties as a great modern planner, along with Álvaro Vital Brazil, Elisiário Bahiana, and Mayor Prestes Maia with his urbanistic accomplishments for São Paulo. In Pernambuco,

18. Exceptions were two films made in São Paulo, one made in Minas Gerais, and one made in Pernambuco. See Adhemar Gonzaga and Paulo Emílio Salles Gomes, *70 anos de cinema brasileiro* (Rio de Janeiro: Editora Expressão e Cultura, 1966) on this subject. In the twenties and thirties there were various regional cycles. The Pernambucan cycle, for instance, saw thirteen films made in eight years; the same occurred in Campinas, and in São Paulo where close to fifty films were made between 1923 and 1933.

19. Ibid., 61.

in Brazil's Northeast, Luís Nunes evolved plans that modernized Recife's urban profile in the thirties. During the same decade in Rio de Janeiro, personalities like Affonso Eduardo Reidy, an exceptional architect within Brazil, appeared; in addition, the Ministry of Education and Public Health (1936–1943) was built. The preliminary designs were Le Corbusier's, but the work was completed by a group of young Brazilian architects, including Lúcio Costa, Oscar Niemeyer, Jorge Moreira, Carlos Leão, and Ernesto Vasconcellos, and marked the start of an official modern Brazilian architecture (fig. 17).

Architects Marcelo and Milton Roberto also authored projects that contributed to the federal capital's new image under Vargas: the Brazilian Press Association (ABI) Building (1936–1938) and Santos Dumont Airport (1937–1944) (fig. 18).[20]

Of this group, Niemeyer became the most prominent architect; the painter Portinari would eventually collaborate with him on a number of far-reaching projects. In the urbanization of Pampulha in Belo Horizonte, Portinari created a tile panel for the St. Francis of Assisi Church, and in Rio de Janeiro his large panels on different floors of the Ministry of Education depict Brazilian life and work scenes.

After World War Two Brazil's art climate would undergo rapid change. A number of museums were founded: the São Paulo Museum of Art (1947) by journalist Assis Chateaubriand; the São Paulo Museum of Modern Art (1948) by industrial manufacturer and patron of the arts Francisco Matarazzo Sobrinho, also the creator of São Paulo's International Biennials (1951); and the Rio de Janeiro Museum of Modern Art (1949) by Niomar Moniz Sodré. The Brazilian Comedy Theater, or TBC,[21] and the Vera Cruz motion picture production company also came into existence at this time; Vera Cruz was responsible for exporting Brazilian cinema in the fifties and sixties.

The onset of the fifties brought accelerated industrialization, especially of the automobile industry, and the building of a new capital, Brasília. As a result, Brazil would witness gradual development of regional cultural poles outside Rio de Janeiro and São Paulo. There is no denying that urban centers arising between 1875 and 1945 determined the course of the twentieth century in Brazil. Development often went unchecked—as in São Paulo, along with Porto Alegre, Recife, Belém, Belo Horizonte, Curitiba, and eventually Brasília. The country's cultural traditions continue to be most strongly felt in the Northeast and in Minas Gerais; the South is truly of international flavor. Regardless, Brazil's most invigorating art is perceived to reside in her two primary urban centers; in São Paulo, due to its cultural entities and universities, and in Rio de Janeiro, permanent storehouse of Brazil's identity and memory, and the nation's capital through 1960. □

20. See Nestor Goulart Reis Filho, *Quadro da arquitetura no Brasil* (São Paulo: Editora Perspectiva, 1970) and Yves Bruand, *Arquitetura contemporânea no Brasil* (São Paulo: Editora Perspectiva, 1981) regarding this period.

21. During the first two decades of the century, theater had presented mainly European prose and variety companies. More up-to-date experiments were undertaken by Eugênia and Álvaro Moreyra and their Teatro de Brinquedo (Toy theater) in the twenties in Rio de Janeiro. By the forties, groups like the Teatro de Estudante (Student's theater) directed in Rio by Paschoal Carlos Magno, and productions like Nelson Rodrigues's *Vestido de noiva* performed by Os Comediantes (The comedians) and directed by Zibgniew Ziembinski, signaled the beginnings of modern Brazilian theater (both playwriting and production). Furthermore, the foundation of São Paulo's Escola de Arte Dramática (Drama school) by Alfredo Mesquita during the late forties warrants mention. Today the EAD is part of the University of São Paulo.

Fig. 18. Marcelo and Milton
Roberto, Santos Dumont
Airport, detail of the interior,
Rio de Janeiro, 1937.
Photograph courtesy of
the University of São Paulo
Department of Architecture
and Urbanism.

Marc Ferrez: A Master of Brazilian Photography

By Pedro Vasquez

Translated by Robert Myers

Pedro Vasquez is a photographer, a poet, and an independent curator. He was responsible for creating the Brazilian National Institute of Photography for the National Foundation for the Arts, as well as the Department of Photography, Video, and New Technologies at the Museum of Modern Art, Rio de Janeiro.

Fig. 1. Broom peddler, Rio de Janeiro, ca. 1895. Gilberto Ferrez collection.

It is generally acknowledged that Marc Ferrez (1843–1923) was the finest Brazilian photographer of the nineteenth century. He devoted himself to an unprecedented personal project of documenting and valorizing the Brazilian landscape, photographing the country from north to south, from the state of Pará in the Amazon region to Rio Grande do Sul on the border with Uruguay, also focusing on the states of Pernambuco, Sergipe, Bahia, Espírito Santo, Minas Gerais, Rio de Janeiro, São Paulo, and Paraná.

While living in Rio de Janeiro, capital of the state of the same name, he completed a photographic ode in praise of the city (figs. 2 and 3) that finds its equal only in Eugène Atget's celebrated ode to Paris. While Atget was fascinated by the historical legacy of *vieux Paris*, Ferrez shared the spirit of North American pioneers and devoted himself to the celebration of the *nouveau monde*, of vast America, the land of infinite possibilities and dazzling promises, as much to the north as to the south of the equator. Ferrez was more akin to great North American photographers of the West, such as William Henry Jackson, Eadweard Muybridge, and Carleton Watkins, with whom the German historians Fabian and Adam correctly identify him in *Masters of Early Travel Photography*.[1] Furthermore, the inclusion of Ferrez in this volume, which goes beyond American pioneers to include equally renowned Europeans such as Frances Frith, Felice Beato, and Maxime Du Camp, proves that the Brazilian attained the same level of excellence as the greatest photographers of his day, even those who had the benefit of better technical resources and the cultural tradition of great European centers such as London (Frith) and Paris (Du Camp).

Ferrez was an extraordinary artisan who ordered the construction of panoramic cameras in Paris conceived especially to meet his personal requirements. From the Brandon firm he once ordered a camera which, as he explained in a booklet about his work,[2] was "expressly to obtain views of Rio de Janeiro that would be as important and beautiful as the splendid landscapes displayed in luxuriant and smiling nature." It is worthwhile to give a description of this camera because it conveys a sense of Marc Ferrez's fascination with photography's technical aspects: "This apparatus achieves an extension of a minimum of 120 degrees and a maximum of 190. It is perfectly automatic and functions by

Photographs by Marc Ferrez.

1. Rainer Fabian and Hans-Christian Adam, *Masters of Early Travel Photography* (London: Thames and Hudson, 1983).

2. *Exposição de paisagens photographicas, productos do artista brasileiro Marc Ferrez* (Exhibition of landscape photography made by the Brazilian artist Marc Ferrez). This booklet, published by Marc Ferrez himself, presumably in 1880, was rereleased in photographic facsimile by Gilberto Ferrez in 1983. Originally only ten copies were made, and they were not sold to the public. In spite of being extremely succinct (ten pages), the booklet is a precious document because it is the only statement by Marc Ferrez about his own work.

Fig. 2. Carioca Square,

Rio de Janeiro, ca. 1890.

Museum of Modern Art,

Rio de Janeiro.

Fig. 3. Lapa Square, Santa Luzia

Beach, Santa Luzia Church

(foreground), Rio de Janeiro,

ca. 1875. Museum of Modern

Art, Rio de Janeiro.

means of a clock movement. Its complete rotation can be effected in 3 to 20 minutes, depending on the light and the objects that have to be reproduced. It weighs 110 kilograms and uses plates of crystal [42 centimeters high and 8 millimeters thick, weighing] 8 kilograms each, giving panoramic images of one meter and ten centimeters in length."[3] He explains, furthermore, that it took three years to study and perfect this camera. Transporting it to the secluded locations and steep hillsides he chose as points of view for his panoramas required herculean determination.

His penchant for technical inventions led him to become the only Brazilian honored with the title of Photographer of the Imperial Navy. "He accomplished the feat of taking photographs on boats using large format cameras, for which the use of a tripod was obligatory. Anyone who has attempted to take photographs aboard ship, even with modern compact cameras and the technical means available today, has an idea of the degree of difficulty in obtaining well-composed images. This gives a sense, therefore, of the problems that confronted Ferrez, not only in framing but also in controlling the exposure, handling the camera with its fragile glass plates, and keeping it stable during exposure. Although no material proof remains in existence, it is known that a version of Ferrez's invention was constructed that was capable of absorbing the incessant movement of waves, thus neutralizing the oscillations that would inevitably compromise his shots."[4] Images of the Almirante Barroso (Admiral Barroso) (fig. 4) and of the Mindello (fig. 5) bear witness to his skill in this area. The former is the more beautiful and picturesque, with sailors perched on the masts of the ship, but the latter is more significant for Brazilian history because it was in this Portuguese corvette that some of the leaders of the Navy Revolt took refuge, causing a diplomatic incident between Brazil and Portugal.[5] In both photographs the perfect rendering of ocean water, rare for photographs of that time, should be noted.

3. Ibid.

4. Pedro Vasquez, "Marc Ferrez, fotógrafo da Marinha Imperial" ("Marc Ferrez, photographer of the Imperial Navy"), in *Fotografia: reflexos & reflexões* (Photography: reflections and reflections) (Porto Alegre: L and PM, 1987), 46–47.

5. The Navy Revolt was a *coup d'état* led by Vice Admiral Custódio José Coimbra against President Floriano Peixoto with an eye toward re-establishing the monarch deposed in 1889. The revolt lasted from 6 September 1893 to 13 March 1894, provoking untold material damage as well as loss of human lives in the cities of Rio de Janeiro, Niterói, and Magé.

Fig. 4. The cruiser Almirante Barroso as it set off on the second circumnavigation of the globe

Fig. 5. The corvette Mindello,

which sheltered leaders

of the Navy Revolt.

Rio de Janeiro, ca. 1894.

Gilberto Ferrez collection.

Marc Ferrez maintained an interest in technological innovations until the end of his life, even after he was no longer involved with professional photography. His final obsession was a stereoscopic camera, utilizing the Lumière brothers' positive color Autochrome plates which he introduced in Brazil in 1912. He was also a pioneer in the development and use of cinema for commercial purposes in Brazil, as representative of the French firm Pathé and as owner of the second movie house to open in Rio de Janeiro. His grandson Gilberto Ferrez relates that Marc Ferrez constantly utilized the stereoscopic camera (producing images that are still unreleased) and that on one occasion "he waited for rain for three days, and when the rain stopped he said to me, 'Let's go now. Everything will be clean.' And we went to photograph the construction of Niemeyer Avenue. This must have been in 1920. He didn't photograph anything without a careful study of the daylight, the best angle...for this reason his material has the quality that it does."[6] Having been put in charge of carrying the box holding unused glass photographic plates, Gilberto Ferrez, at age twelve, had a double initiation—into photography and the city of Rio de Janeiro. This apprentice-ship made him a leader in the study of the history of photography in Brazil (his celebrated and seminal essay, *A fotografia no Brasil* [Photography in Brazil], dates from 1946) and the premier specialist in *carioca* iconography.[7] He is author of more than a dozen books on the latter subject.

Much more than a skillful technician, Marc Ferrez was an esthete of uncommon talent and possessed a sophisticated visual sense that ran in his family. He was the son of sculptor Zeferino Ferrez and the nephew of Marc Ferrez, both members of the French Artistic Mission.[8] His visual sensibility was

6. Gilberto Ferrez, interview by author, Rio de Janeiro, 13 June 1994.

7. *Carioca* was the designation given by the Indians of the Rio de Janeiro region to European coloniz-ers and is still used to identify persons born in Rio, as well as things and sites pertaining to the city.

8. The French Artistic Mission was composed of painters, sculptors, and architects brought from France by King John VI of Portugal in 1816 with the intention of founding an academy of fine arts in Rio de Janeiro, and in so doing to promote the development of artistic activities in Brazil. The Mission, led by Joachim Le Breton, had as its greatest exponents the architect Grandjean de Montigny and the painters Nicolas Antoine Taunay and Jean-Baptiste Debret.

refined through an education in France (he completed preparatory studies in Paris under the guidance of Alphée Dubois, also a sculptor, in whose house he lodged) and renewed through a number of subsequent trips to Europe, which helped keep him attuned to the technical and esthetic evolution of international photography.

Ferrez won the recognition of his contemporaries in the form of prizes at the three National Exhibitions that took place in Rio de Janeiro in 1861, 1866, and 1873; at the Academy of Fine Arts Exhibition in 1879; at the Commemorative Exhibition of the Centenary of the Independence of the United States in Philadelphia in 1876; and at the Universal Exhibition of Paris in 1878. He also won prizes in Buenos Aires in 1882 and in Amsterdam in 1883 and was made a Knight of the Order of the Rose by Emperor Pedro II in 1885. In spite of all the approbation received in his lifetime, it is only now that the magnitude of his contribution can be appreciated. Of particular importance was his creation of an idealized photographic vision of imperial Brazil. Although he left no written document explaining this, it is as evident in his work as the similar project of valorizing Paris is in Atget's.

To accomplish this task, he turned his back on the only lucrative genre of the period—the portrait—and sought to finance his own photographs through those rare activities that permitted travel in Brazil, such as documentation of railroad construction, thanks to which he journeyed through the states of Minas Gerais (fig. 6), Paraná, and São Paulo. He also joined an expedition of the Geologic Commission of the Empire (1875–1876), headed by geographer and geologist Charles Frederick Hartt, during which he became the first person to photograph the Botocudo Indians in the interior of Bahia. The photographs of the *curumim* ("child" in the Tupi-Guarani language) from the Mato Grosso region (fig. 7) and the apparel of the Apiacá chiefs (fig. 8), both taken in improvised studios, date from this period. On another commercial commission—the documentation of mining—he pioneered the use of the

Fig. 6. Slaves leaving

for work in the field,

Minas Gerais, ca. 1882.

Gilberto Ferrez collection.

Fig. 7. Indian boy from the

Mato Grosso region,

1875. Museum of Modern

Art, Rio de Janeiro.

▶

Fig. 8. Apparel of the Apiacá chiefs, 1875. Museum of Modern Art, Rio de Janeiro.

Fig. 9. Miners extracting gold, Passage Mine, Minas Gerais, ca. 1890. Gilberto Ferrez collection.

magnesium flash. His photos of the Passage Mine (ca. 1890) are the first of this kind in Brazil (fig. 9), although his experience with a magnesium flash goes back to 1887 when he photographed the painter Belmiro de Almeida and Paul Ferrand, a French engineer and professor of the School of Mines in Ouro Preto, who was responsible for the innovative commission given to Ferrez. The next images, both taken in the state of Minas Gerais, are the first from the interior of mines in Brazil. One shows workers, the majority of whom are ex-slaves, extracting minerals from the deep tunnels of the Old Hill Mine (fig. 10), and the other shows workers in the Pary Mine washing gravel to separate gold from dross (fig. 11).

Ferrez's incursions into portrait-taking are exceedingly rare but certainly noteworthy. In addition to the ethnographic images for the Geologic Commission, he also produced family portraits for a very special client, Emperor Pedro II, whom we see here with the Empress Teresa Cristina during the inauguration of the great Mantiqueira Railroad Tunnel on 25 June 1882 (fig. 12). Distinct from the rigid and hierarchical portrait studies of the period, they show the royal

Fig. 10. Workers crushing stones to search for gold, Old Hill Mine, Minas Gerais, ca. 1890. Gilberto Ferrez collection.

family in intimate and natural poses, such as the beautiful portrait of Princess Isabel playing the piano in the company of the baroness of Muritiba in the Laranjeiras Palace. Even more interesting is the group of portraits Ferrez took of peddlers of European origin whose work replaced that performed by slaves on the streets of Rio de Janeiro around 1895. They offer their services as tinkers, basket weavers, knife sharpeners (fig. 13), and bottle dealers, selling everything from live chickens and brooms (fig. 1) to umbrellas, canes, sweets, breads, and other foods. In these extraordinary portraits Ferrez used a direct and innovative approach, isolating his subjects in front of a neutral background of fabric installed right out on the street, thus prefiguring the vision of such modern photographers as Diane Arbus, Irving Penn, and Richard Avedon.

However it was as a photographer of Brazilian landscapes and urban settings that Marc Ferrez achieved the level of mastery that placed him ahead of all his colleagues. Obviously there were other excellent landscape photographers in Brazil, such as Augusto Stahl, Revert Henrique Klumb, Camillo Vedani, Juan Gutierrez, and Guilherme Gaensly, but Ferrez had that indefinable something, that mysterious spark of creativity that distinguishes true masters and confers an aura of brilliance on everything they do. Moreover he was one of the very few photographers active in imperial Brazil who produced what today would be considered an *oeuvre*: a significant group of works endowed with its own distinctive organic quality.

The photography practiced in Brazil during the period being discussed was essentially utilitarian in nature. Contemporary estheticizing readings of this production run the risk of attributing contemporary intentions and desires to works generated from a totally different mind-set. A similar phenomenon would be if we were to consider indigenous artifacts—essentially utilitarian and/or ritualistic—as "indigenous art." There exists between our vision and that of the indigenous people an unbridgeable gap, as there is a kind of parallax

Fig. 11. Workers washing gravel to search for gold, Pary Mine, Minas Gerais, ca. 1890. Gilberto Ferrez collection.

Fig. 12. Emperor Pedro II and Empress Teresa Cristina at the dedication of the Mantiqueira Railroad Tunnel, Minas Gerais, 25 June 1882. Gilberto Ferrez collection.

between our contemporary interpretation and the real intentions of nineteenth-century photographers, as if we were observing an object under water. We believe we see it in correct perspective; however it is not where we believe it to be but rather a little nearer or farther as a result of refraction. Nonetheless, a restricted group of four photographers probably transcended the utilitarianism of the past century in Brazil, attaining superiority by virtue of the "intentionality" of their offerings: Victor Frond, Militão Augusto de Azevedo, Guilherme Gaensly, and Marc Ferrez.

Frond was creator of one of the first books of photography in the world: *Brazil pittoresco* (Picturesque Brazil). Published in 1861 from material produced between 1858 and 1859, it was the embryo of a larger project of photographing even the most recondite corner of the most far-off province of Brazil. De Azevedo, although technically inferior to the others, had the inspiration to produce *Álbum comparativo da cidade de São Paulo* (Comparative album of the city of São Paulo), tracing the evolution of the capital of São Paulo state from

1862, when he began his career, to 1887, when the aforementioned work was his swan song. Gaensly left no similar work, but he produced hundreds of excellent photographs—especially of Salvador and São Paulo, his principal bases of activity—that came out of a longing to create a significant, personal documentation of these cities. During the decades that he took photographs for the São Paulo Tramway Light and Power Company, he normally made duplicate shots of the most interesting views for his personal use or separated the negatives he preferred. It is not unusual to find photographs in the albums of the Light and Power Company with the notice "negative belongs to Gaensly," indicating that he had retained it for himself. Ferrez, whose output was more voluminous and expressive than any of those mentioned above, always searched for ways to adapt the professional jobs he did so as to produce photographs that interested him personally. Questioned about the personal goal of a photographic valorization of Brazil by Marc Ferrez, Gilberto Ferrez affirmed in a straightforward manner that his grandfather "was never interested in portraits, which was how one made money then. What he really intended was to show various aspects of the country. He felt all of the beauty of this country and wished to show it to others in a period when people only thought of portraits, portraits, portraits...."[9] The most compelling proof of the existence of such a personal goal comes from Marc Ferrez himself when, in describing his business, he says, "This establishment, *dedicated especially to creating views of Brazil,*[10] was founded in 1860. All the progress and improvements that the art of photography has achieved up to today have been studied and utilized in this establishment; no expense or labor has been spared to elevate it to first place in the industrial area to which it has been devoted and which it continues to pursue."[11]

If Marc Ferrez loved Brasil, he was truly passionate about Rio de Janeiro and focused on the city from varied viewpoints for more than forty years. The most impressive result of this passion was the *Álbum da Avenida Central* (Album of Central Avenue), which consumed three years of work and recorded the construction of the then principal avenue of city—known today as Rio Branco Avenue—from the first plans approved by the construction commission to the buildings after construction. Unfortunately, an edition of two thousand copies printed in Paris and Zurich was not distributed, since all copies were destroyed in 1913 by a flood that inundated the warehouse in which the books were stored.[12]

Gilberto Ferrez does not exaggerate when he asserts: "In every way, the work of Marc Ferrez is a landmark in the history of Brazilian photography. It is both a culmination and a point of departure. On the one hand, it marks the end of the long adventure set into motion by the daguerreotype demonstrations of Chaplain Louis Compte in Rio de Janeiro. On the other hand, his daring

9. Gilberto Ferrez, interview.

10. My italics.

11. Marc Ferrez, *Exposição de paisagens photographicas.*

12. "In its original edition, the album consists of a case containing three plans, 118 plates and forty-five loose pages, weighing around five kilograms. The case, measuring 52 x 42 centimeters, is covered with green cloth and has engraved on the cover the words 'Avenida Central, 8 March 1903–15 November 1906—Marc Ferrez, Rio de Janeiro.'" This description is from Gilberto Ferrez's *Registro fotográfico de Marc Ferrez da construção da Av. Rio Branco, 1903–1906* (Photographic record by Marc Ferrez of the construction of Rio Branco Avenue, 1903–1906), a catalogue of the exhibition held at the National Museum of Fine Arts in Rio de Janeiro when the album was released in book form by the João Fortes Engineering Company in 1982.

Fig. 14. Entrance of the Bay of Rio (Guanabara Bay), from the Santa Cruz fortress at Niterói, with Sugarloaf Mountain in the background, ca. 1880.

Gilberto Ferrez collection.

innovations herald the existence of paths that would be blazed somewhat later. His work is a bridge between Brazilian photography's past and present. His work is the reflection of the man in whom the artist and technician co-existed in harmony, both driven by the same ardent desire to attain perfection. Therefore, it should come as no surprise that his work has been rediscovered and that there is a growing interest in it today, both in Brazil and abroad. Neither is it surprising that a number of foreign scholars today place Marc Ferrez among the great photographers of his time."[13]

American historian Naomi Rosenblum does not hesitate to characterize Ferrez as the "most famous Latin American photographer of his time,"[14] an opinion confirmed in almost precisely the same words by H. L. Hoffenberg in his book *Nineteenth Century South America in Photographs*.[15] Fabian and Adam assert that "Ferrez was undoubtedly the most effective pictorial chronicler of Brazil in the second half of the 19th century. He photographed the imperial family, the Bay of Rio [fig. 14], Sugar Loaf Mountain [fig. 15], and Copacabaña Beach

13. Gilberto Ferrez, *A fotografia no Brasil, 1840–1900* (Photography in Brazil, 1840–1900), (1946; updated reprint, Rio de Janeiro: Fundação Nacional de Arte/Fundação Nacional Pró-Memória, 1985), 229.

14. Naomi Rosenblum, *A World History of Photography* (New York: Abbeville Press, 1984), 127.

15. New York: Dover Publications, Inc., 1982.

Fig. 15. Jurujuba Beach at Niterói, with Sugarloaf Mountain in the background, ca. 1890.

Gilberto Ferrez collection.

[fig. 16], still a deserted strip of sand. Indeed, Ferrez photographed whatever was worth looking at between Paraná and Bahia—churches, monuments, bridges, waterfalls, rivers, and ports. He accompanied geological expeditions and reported on the progress of the water lines and railways then being cut through the jungle."[16] Even the curator of the J. Paul Getty Museum, Weston Naef, says in his study: "For all their technical perfection, Ferrez's early photographs are not arid, as so often happens when technique dominates perception. Ferrez consistently posed figures in a delicate, often provocative way, never with the simple frontality of the sheer documentarian. Ferrez was thoroughly an artist, always more interested in the shapes of the buildings, the play of light, and the abstract forms in nature than his more human interest-oriented colleagues such as Frisch."[17] The photographs reproduced here bear witness to the fully justified posthumous acclaim of Ferrez's work and the irrefutable value of his contribution to the history of photography. □

16. Fabian and Adam, *Masters*, 161.

17. Gilberto Ferrez and Weston Naef, *Pioneer Photographers of Brazil, 1840–1920* (New York: The Center for Inter-American Relations, 1976), 115–116.

Fig. 16. Copacabana Beach,

Rio de Janeiro, ca. 1895.

Museum of Modern Art,

Rio de Janeiro.

Fig. 1. Rio Branco Avenue,

originally Central Avenue,

Rio de Janeiro. Photograph from

Impressões do Brasil no século

vinte (London: Loyd's Greater

Opera Houses

By Benedito Lima de Toledo

Translated by Elza B. de Oliveira Marques

Benedito Lima de Toledo is an architect and a professor of history of architecture at the University of São Paulo. He is active in the preservation, restoration, and conversion of historic buildings and has written several books on São Paulo architecture and urbanism.

However analyzed, the rise of opera houses in Brazilian cities—where they are known simply as "theaters"—has exceptional significance. Buildings that evoke the sights of Paris, they manifest the civic pride of those who sought to attain lofty cultural standards.

Although other aims should not be discounted, the fact that such buildings ennobled a city could have justified the related investment. Moreover, it was not enough that they serve their functional purpose. They had to look the part, have the *physique du rôle*. The importance of that image is evidenced by the new Opera of the Bastille in Paris (1983), which critics promptly excoriated, though not because of inadequate operating conditions; quite the contrary, the problem was merely iconic—it lacked the image of an "opera house."

According to Argan's convincing explanation, "A 'culture of images' actually exists and is of fundamental importance to the history of civilization; the history of art is the history of culture organized not conceptually but through images."[1]

Perhaps that is why some Brazilian cities built theaters right in the middle of squares, lending them the appearance of lone monuments, a trend more noticeable in northern towns, such as Belém, Manaus, Recife, and Fortaleza. The location of those buildings apparently indicate that Camillo Sitte had no followers there.[2]

In São Paulo, Rio de Janeiro, and certain other cities, opera houses built by local authorities became the most representative mark of majestic city planning, of which the Rio de Janeiro Municipal Theater is an eloquent instance.

Early in the republican era, President Rodrigues Alves (1902–1906) promoted the modernization of the city of Rio de Janeiro, then the federal capital. Sanitation was the first priority, to put an end to endemic diseases, which was achieved with the brilliant help of scientist Oswaldo Cruz. The renovation of Rio de Janeiro harbor facilities must also be mentioned among many vital works then undertaken. An extensive list of projects executed under Mayor Francisco Pereira Passos (1902–1906) included the opening of several spacious boulevards, which the city had lacked; the most notable was Central Avenue, later renamed Rio Branco Avenue (fig. 1), as it is known today.

Central Avenue left a deep imprint on Rio de Janeiro. In 1904 an international competition was held to define the facades of its buildings. Bidders were free

1. Giulio C. Argan and Maurizio Fagiolo, *Guia de história da arte* (Lisbon: Estampa, 1992), 39.
2. [Camillo Sitte (1843–1903), a pioneer of modern urban design, wrote on city planning related to artistic principles. Ed.]

Fig. 2. Rio de Janeiro

Municipal Theater. Photograph

from *Álbum Rio de Janeiro*

(Rio de Janeiro: Vigiani, 1910).

to let their creative imaginations soar, restricted only by lot size and height standards. Interior planning was of secondary importance, a procedure no present-day architect would even begin to understand or condone. At that time, however, one hundred and seven professionals—civil engineers and architects—submitted tenders.

Well-preserved plans, drawings, and a memorable set of photographs by Marc Ferrez document the undertaking and show an impressive display of architectural leanings, so diverse and complex that it would be difficult to find their equal among any other city planning efforts.

Within that context, also in 1904, a contest was held to choose plans for a theater on a par with the best Europe could offer. The winner was Francisco de Oliveira Passos, whose name is remembered together with that of his father, the aforementioned mayor of Rio. Architect Victor Dubugras, a Frenchman educated in Buenos Aires who became a tenured professor at the State of São Paulo Polytechnic School, placed second. The originality of the *art-nouveau* plans submitted by Dubugras diverged from the academic recipe of the then prevailing eclecticism. As he was responsible for the most expressive *art-nouveau* buildings erected in São Paulo, his entry would certainly have resulted in an outstandingly original building of that style in Brazil.

The winning entry (figs. 2 and 3), in turn, was clearly inspired by the Paris Opera. The building committee was chaired by Francisco de Oliveira Passos himself; other committee members were René Barba, Antoine Raffin, Charles Peirroton, Émile Bion, and J. Personnene. Work began in 1905 and was completed in 1909. Paulo Santos points out the exceptional quality of the building— "details, such as the great marble staircase in the foyer, display so perfect an execution that they still have no equal in the city" (fig. 4).[3]

3. Paulo Santos, "Arquitetura e urbanismo na Avenida Central," in Marc Ferrez, *Álbum da Avenida Central* (São Paulo: João Fortes Engenharia/Ex Libris, 1982), 34.

Fig. 3. Rio de Janeiro

Municipal Theater. Photograph

from *Álbum da Avenida Central*

(São Paulo: João Fortes

Engenharia/Ex Libris, 1982).

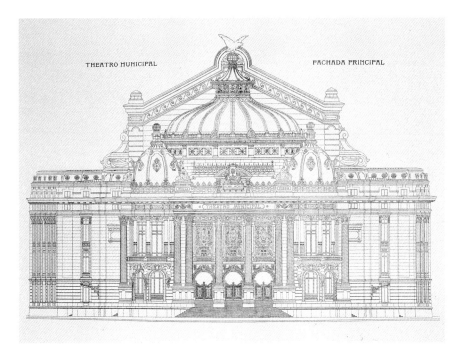

Fig. 3. Rio de Janeiro Municipal Theater. Photograph from *Álbum da Avenida Central* (São Paulo: João Fortes Engenharia/Ex Libris, 1982).

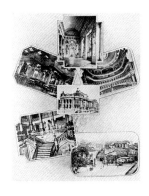

Fig. 4. Rio de Janeiro Municipal Theater, interior views. Photomontage from *Impressões do Brasil no século vinte* (London: Loyd's Greater Britain Publishing, 1913).

The same author mentions other striking features, such as "stained glass designed by Stuttgart Professors Fennerstein and Fugel, mounted in the Munich atelier of Meyer and Company; statues by Rodolpho Bernardelli representing Music, Poetry, Dance, Song, Comedy, and Tragedy; [and] bronze chandeliers by French sculptor Verlet, also symbolizing Poetry and Dance.

"Dumont made the decor of the staircase ceiling; in front of the stairs, a statue by famous sculptor Ingelbert represents Truth; the ceiling paintings are by painter Enrico Bernardelli; and the foyer ceiling, the stage curtain [fig. 5], the upper frame of the proscenium, and the dome were painted by Ângelo Visconti."[4]

The architectural significance of the building was admirably summed up by Mário Barata: "Clearly inspired by the Paris Opera built by Charles Garnier (1825–1898), which was opened in 1875, the Rio de Janeiro Municipal Theater is a superb academic palace, endowed with magnificent, varicolored marbles in the lobby and stairs; [and] mosaics, enameled ceramic panels, and colored tiles on the walls and floors of service areas. It may easily be defined as the symbol of our country's full-fledged eclecticism."[5] From this standpoint, the theater is the most illustrative architectural work to grace Central Avenue.

A few other comments must also be mentioned, for instance, those of Paulo Santos on the paintings by Eliseu d'Ângelo Visconti. "The proscenium and dome paintings, done in the pointillist manner that branched out of the European impressionism of the last quarter of the nineteenth century, became in Brazil the expression of accredited art, the forerunner of the modern age that would only come into its own twenty-five years later."[6]

4. Ibid., 37.

5. Mário Barata, "Século XIX. Transição e início do século XX," in Walter Zanini, *História geral da arte no Brasil* (São Paulo: Walther Moreira Salles, 1983), 435.

6. Santos, "Arquitetura e urbanismo," 37.

Even today all of the above features—added to a well-planned interior; an ample stage vault; and generous spaces surrounding the orchestra seats, the stalls, and the box seats—place this theater of great societal significance among the best in Brazil.

Likewise, the São Paulo Municipal Theater was a major point of departure in that city's growth. For three centuries the town of São Paulo persisted in clinging to the hill where it was founded, an acropolis surrounded by two rivers. From that central core roads departed to all points of the compass, a fact that led a city planner to say São Paulo had grown with the shape defined by Eugène Alfred Hénard, whose progressive city plans are described in all books on urbanism.

Surrounding that nucleus were a number of small farms placed along beaten earth trails, one of which led to the tea plantation of General Arouche de Toledo Rendon, who pioneered tea farming in São Paulo. When tea plantations gave way to streets and plots of land, the so-called New City emerged on the other side of the Anhangabaú Valley, hungrily swallowing yet another tract of farm land owned by the baron of Itapetininga.

Jules Martin, a French lithographer who lived in São Paulo, proposed the building of a viaduct to span the valley and brook, linking two opposite hills, one of which was the site of the old historic downtown and the other that of the New City. After numerous problems were overcome, the viaduct was finally built; completed in 1892, it was given the suggestive name of Tea Viaduct and opened a further area for the city's growth.

Fig. 5. Eliseu d'Ângelo Visconti, stage curtain, Rio de Janeiro Municipal Theater. Photograph from *Impressões do Brasil no século vinte* (London: Loyd's Greater Britain Publishing, 1913).

When the idea of building an opera house compatible with the city's development came to the fore, the chosen site was in the New City, on top of Tea Hill, a privileged, highly visible location. The plan was drafted by the office of Ramos de Azevedo; in addition to Azevedo himself, two other architects, Claudio Rossi and Domiziano Rossi (who, notwithstanding their family names, were not related), are said to have coauthored the plan. Begun on 5 June 1903, the work was completed on 30 August 1911.

How can we define the style of that building, also inspired by the Paris Opera? We might start by asking what the style of the Paris Opera is. The classic work of Sir Banister Fletcher, *A History of Architecture on the Comparative Method*, places that theater in the French Renaissance chapter under the subtitle "Modern Architecture." "The Opera House, Paris (A.D. 1861–74), by Charles Garnier, is probably the most important of all modern buildings in France. The magnificent façade well conforms to the idea of the sumptuous treatment suitable for a national opera house."[7]

While Fletcher is rather imprecise about the style, Nikolaus Pevsner gives a different interpretation. "Thus, about 1850–60, italianate forms became also more and more exuberant, until a Neo-Baroque was reached. Charles Garnier's Opera in Paris (1861–74) is one of the earliest and best examples."[8]

After pointing out how functional the building is, how compatible with the prevailing spirit, and how rationally its external mass balanced its interior, Pierre Lavedan mentions its profuse décor, which for modern eyes is in rather

7. Sir Banister Fletcher, K.N.T., *A History of Architecture on the Comparative Method* (London: Batsford, 1954), 713.
8. Nikolaus Pevsner, *An Outline of European Architecture* (Middlesex: Penguin Books, 1957), 274.

Serie B No. 24.   Viaducto do Chá.

bad taste, a rich display bordering on vulgarity, "a confusion of ornaments borrowed from every period (antefixes, palmettes, antique caryatids) but above all the Venetian Renaissance, that is, eclecticism."[9]

If European authors have failed to define the Paris Opera, Ricardo Severo—a partner of the Ramos de Azevedo office—had this to say about the São Paulo Municipal Theater (fig. 6). "The exterior architecture was fashioned in the Baroque Renaissance style that Italian artists have named *Seicento*. It is a classical style, with modules pertaining to the Greco-Roman Renaissance, perhaps more varied, appropriating and ornamenting such recurrences with more imaginative freedom when making use of curves, motifs, and ornamental details."[10]

Considering all these approaches, we might well conclude that we are dealing with eclecticism, both architectural and literary.

Although contemporaneous and arising from the same source, approaches to municipal opera houses differed. In Rio de Janeiro, architecture was taught at the School of Fine Arts. In that city fine arts professionals considered a public competition to define facades as natural as breathing. Conversely, in São Paulo architecture was taught in the Polytechnic School, founded in 1893 and modeled after the Polytechnic School of Gand, Belgium. At that time its dean was alumnus Francisco de Paula Ramos de Azevedo, principal of the office in charge of the planning and building of the theater.

9. Pierre Lavedan, *French Architecture* (Middlesex: Penguin Books, 1956), 226.

10. Ricardo Severo, *Theatro Municipal de São Paulo* (São Paulo: n.p., 1911), 13.

Fig. 7. São Paulo Municipal Theater, main floor, ca 1911. Photograph from Benedito Lima de Toledo, *Anhangabahú* (São Paulo: Federação das Indústrias do Estado de São Paulo, 1989).

Fig. 8. São Paulo Municipal Theater, grand staircase, ca. 1911. From a postcard (H. Rosenhain, São Paulo). Benedito Lima de Toledo collection.

SÃO PAULO   THEATRO MUNICIPAL-ESCADARIA

"MONTBLANC"
A CANETA TINTEIRO
DE QUALIDADE

Fig. 9. São Paulo Municipal
Theater, foyer, ca. 1911.
From a postcard (H. Rosenhain,
São Paulo). Benedito Lima
de Toledo collection.

Fig. 10. São Paulo Municipal
Theater, foyer bar, ca. 1911.
From a postcard (H. Rosenhain,
São Paulo). Benedito Lima
de Toledo collection.

Ramos de Azevedo, who organized the architecture courses, also participated in founding a school dedicated to the training of specialized craftsmen—the Lyceum of Arts and Crafts. Master craftsmen of several nationalities were called to teach. The institution's artistic production improved until it matched the best, which had previously been imported. A monograph by Ricardo Severo, published when the theater was dedicated, includes in its final pages a list of "suppliers and contractors," with credits to craftsmen and manufacturers from various countries—stained glass from Stuttgart, mosaics from Venice, plasterwork from Milan, metal framework from Dusseldorf, wrought iron from Frankfurt, statuary from Paris—and, repeatedly among them, the Lyceum of Arts and Crafts.

It cannot be said often enough that an undertaking as important and exquisite as the finishing and decoration of the theater was not only a major influence but also set a standard of quality against which all São Paulo buildings were to be measured (figs. 7, 8, 9, and 10). In its sumptuously ornamented interior, in the vestibule, are two lovely Venetian mosaics, "Rheingold" and "The Cavalcade of the Valkyries." These decorative panels were crafted by Pusello Moselli; Pangella Giuseppe; Sparapani Sebastiano; and Oscar Pereira da Silva, one of the outstanding artists of São Paulo, who painted the foyer's ceiling as well as many portraits and allegories that graced private mansions and official buildings.

When it was constructed, the theater stood practically alone in its grandeur among a scant number of small buildings. However, according to a city alderman and professor of the Polytechnic School, the view from the theater toward the historic downtown area was not at all grand but rather shabby— just the backyards of homes.

At that time the valley between the two sections of the city was half-wild, occupied only by modest farms with a creek running past. Such a situation could not be tolerated by city notables, who decided to do something about it. Three groups, comprised of professionals and entrepreneurs, submitted to the Town Hall their particular plans to remodel the valley. Spurred to act, but hoping to escape a decision that could only be politically adverse through favoring one over another, the mayor decided to seek an opinion on the

Fig. 11. Peace Theater, Belém, Pará, ca. 1900. From a postcard (União Postal Universal, E. U. do Brasil). Maria Cecília Monteiro da Silva collection.

Fig. 12. Peace Theater, Belém, Pará, main floor, ca. 1900. From a postcard (Widow Eduardo Fernandes). Maria Cecília Monteiro da Silva collection.

proposals from Joseph Antoine Bouvard, holder of the prestigious office of Honorary Director for Architectural Services, Boulevards, and City Planning of Paris, then visiting Buenos Aires.

More than a city planner, Bouvard proved to be a diplomat who tactfully conciliated all factions. The Bouvard plan (1911) gave the downtown area one of its most notable parks, which included both slopes of the valley. Alongside the Municipal Theater, a half circle of majestic imperial palms made a background for a group of sculpture. When the park was dedicated, the theater, surrounded by beauty, became a high point of the urban landscape. Local inhabitants showed their appreciation, fondly dubbing the park the "calling card of our city." One thing cannot be denied: the theater was the moving force behind the urban renovation of the valley.

Analyzing what happened in Rio de Janeiro and São Paulo, it is easy to conclude that early in the republican era, and in addition to the prevailing ambition to achieve higher cultural standards, opera houses were associated with extensive city renovation plans which, to a certain extent, they came to symbolize.

The importance of opera houses in the northern region of Brazil is very aptly defined by the words of Augusto Carlos da Silva Telles. "The nineteenth century opened new vistas. The most imposing buildings were possibly the theaters. In the region now being studied, mention must be made of the Peace Theater in Belém, Pará; of the Amazon Theater in Manaus, Amazonas; and of the José de Alencar Theater in Fortaleza, Ceará;..." [11]

The first two, in Belém and Manaus, are the central focus of large squares, proudly positioned within the urban context. Also highly visible, the Fortaleza opera house is of the "garden theater" genre, exported to the tropics by the English.

Belém's Peace Theater (figs. 11 and 12) was planned in 1869 by First Lieutenant José Tibúrcio Pereira de Magalhães. Portuguese contractor

11. Augusto Carlos da Silva Telles, *Atlas dos monumentos históricos e artísticos do Brasil* (Rio de Janeiro: Fundação Nacional de Material Escolar/Divisão de Apoio à Cultura, 1975), 213.

118   *PERNAMBUCO · Teatro S. Isabella*

João Francisco Fernandes was in charge of construction, following the recommendations of engineer Antônio Augusto Calandrini de Chermont who, despite his name, was a native of Pará. He somewhat altered the original plans. Although finished in 1874, the theater did not officially open until 1878.

The interior décor was by Italian painter Domenico de Angelis; the stage curtain, displaying an allegory of the republic (proclaimed in the preceding year), was the work of French set designer Carpezat who came to Belém in 1890. The Peace Theater is eloquent proof of the wealth then enjoyed by that region, a product of the rubber boom.

Little is known about Magalhães, who planned a symmetric frontispiece endowed with neoclassic elements such as the triangular pediment. The svelte columns that grace its frontage and lateral elevations escaped the proportions usually adopted in buildings of that style. The edifice, however, lacks the allure, the elegant composition, of others of the pre-neoclassic style that Bolognese architect Antonio Giuseppe Landi (1713–1791) left in the city, whose vistas are among the richest and most varied in Brazil.

The name of Magalhães also appears in connection with the 1870 restoration of the Santa Isabel Theater in Recife after a fire in 1869. Built between 1840 and 1846, the theater was then the city's most important building, planned by Frenchman Louis Léger Vauthier who held the office of public works engineer for Pernambuco Province. A former student of the Polytechnic School of Paris, he lived in Recife for a period of six years during which he built the graceful mansions adorning the city, examples of the neoclassic style then prevailing in Brazil. As a matter of course he planned the opera house in that style, endowing it with all the refinement of lines and language characteristic of the time (fig. 13). The décor of the lobby includes large mirrors and stylish period furniture. In addition to the orchestra seats, the main floor contains five tiers of boxes. The theater's sober, refined furnishings avoid the excesses typical of the post-Garnier period.

Manáos   *Theatro com Monumento*

Fig. 14. Amazon Theater,

Manaus, Amazonas,

ca. 1906. From a postcard

(G. Huebner and Amaral,

Photographia Allemã,

Manáos). Maria Cecília

Monteiro da Silva collection.

MANÁOS   Salão de Honra do Theatro Amazonas

Fig. 15. Amazon Theater, Manaus, Amazonas, lobby, ca. 1907. From a postcard (Agência Freitas,

Manáos). Benedito Lima de Toledo collection.

Fig. 16. José de Alencar

Theater, Fortaleza, Ceará.

Photograph by Benedito Lima

de Toledo, 1981.

Sharing a number of similar features, the Amazon Theater in Manaus (figs. 14 and 15) opened in 1896, also a direct consequence of rubber-boom riches. Many foreign artists were engaged to assist in its construction, based on a plan designed by Italian architect Enrico Mazzolani. Its many paintings were created by Crispim dos Santos, a Brazilian, and Domenico de Angelis, an Italian. Placed in a privileged location within the context of the city, the opera house can be defined in its entirety as one more instance of eclecticism in Brazil.

Undoubtedly the most singular of Brazilian opera houses is the José de Alencar Theater in Fortaleza (fig. 16). Architect José Liberal de Castro, an outstanding scholar and expert on that theater, has rightfully said, "It is certain that the José de Alencar Theater is the most significant instance of Ceará's architecture, undeniably the most prized by its people."[12]

Initial plans were drafted by Lieutenant Bernardo José de Mello, but the extent of his participation remains a mystery. Its original architectural concept was comprised of three different sections, namely, a two-story block, an inner courtyard, and the main floor, whose metal framework is fully opened to the patio, making the best possible use of sea breezes that are one of the most agreeable features of northern seaside towns.

The street level floor of the block holds offices and rooms for the administration of the theater and, above it, the lobby. From the patio one may gaze at the veranda and have the best view of the unusual pediment, with its modulated

12. José Liberal de Castro, "Arquitetura eclética no Ceará," in *Ecletismo na arquitetura brasileira* (São Paulo: Nobel, 1987), 229.

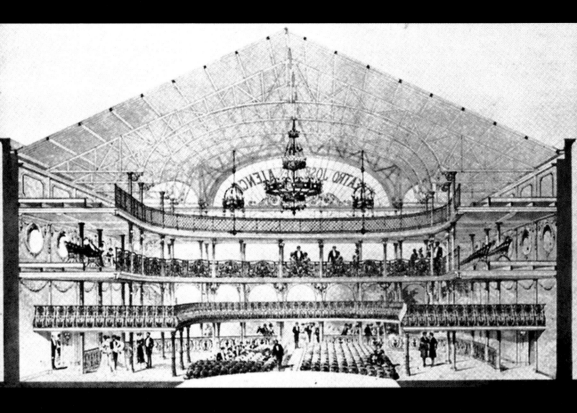

Fig. 17. José de Alencar Theater, Fortaleza, Ceará, designs. Photograph from *Suplemento con illustraciones*, a catalogue of Walter MacFarlane and Company, Glasgow, ca. 1912. José Liberal de Castro collection.

metal framework lightened by the delicate lace of wrought-iron railings and crowned by baskethandle arches that surround stained-glass panels. The composition of the facades is echoed in the interior of the main floor.

The metal framework was made by Walter MacFarlane and Company. "Perhaps the largest and most significant, as well as the most influential of all iron-founders in the component industry was the Glasgow-based firm of Walter MacFarlane & Co. [It was] founded by Walter MacFarlane on the Saracen Lane, Glasgow, [hence] the name Saracen Foundry by which the firm was known for over a hundred years." [13]

Components made by MacFarlane can be seen in several regions of the country. Early in this century, the metal framework of the Luz Railroad Station in São Paulo came from the Glasgow company. Their markets and bandstands still exist in several states. In Belém, in addition to the city's markets, there is a unique shop, Paris na América, whose remarkable staircase by MacFarlane immediately reminds one of the stairs of the Belo Horizonte Liberty Palace [see page 105].

One of MacFarlane's catalogues, published in Spanish (ca. 1912), displays the pediment and interior design of the main floor of the Fortaleza opera house (fig. 17) with the legend "este teatro fué ideado y construido recientemente por nuestra casa" (Our firm recently conceived and built this theater). [14]

Architect José Liberal de Castro, who gave us the above information, also wrote that "foundries usually resorted to other industrial sectors in order to supplement their works ([with] steel girders, zinc roofing, and so on). As regards the José de Alencar Theater...Walter MacFarlane & Co. were helped by the Glengarnock Iron Works and by Cargo Fleet." [15]

A remarkable event for Brazilian culture occurred in 1970. The theater was in extremely bad repair, its framework corroded by rust, at risk of toppling down. The people were mobilized and voiced their opinions, and the government, although lacking the resources required by the restoration budget, had to respond.

Restoration plans and supervision of the projects were entrusted to José Liberal de Castro, who offered to work without remuneration. Federal Railway boilermakers recovered the framework; engineers of the State of Ceará Superintendency of Works were charged with masonry and fixtures. The National Assets Protection Service offered the assistance of restorer Francisco dos Santos Brito to take charge of the paintings. The chairs, originally by Thonet, of Austria, were replaced by perfect copies made by the Gerdau group of Rio Grande do Sul. In addition to the above, many other professionals contributed to the success of the endeavor. Thus civic spirit rescued the theater from dereliction (figs. 18, 19, 20, and 21).

A later renovation of the José de Alencar Theater (1990) eliminated some of its essential features, for instance, adding a glass curtain to separate the main room from the patio and installing air conditioning and lighting equipment that adversely affect the unusual and elegant solutions originally found. Fortunately, such additions are not irreversible.

13. Gilbert Herbert, *Pioneers of Pre-fabrication: The British Contribution in the Nineteenth Century* (Baltimore and London: The Johns Hopkins University Press, 1978), 173.

14. José Liberal de Castro, *Arquitetura do ferro no Ceará*, offprint of the *Revista do Instituto do Ceará*, vol. 106 (1922): 78.

15. Ibid., 79.

Fig. 18. José de Alencar

Theater, Fortaleza, Ceará,

detail. Photograph by Benedito

Lima de Toledo, 1981.

Recently a number of theaters in Brazil have been restored to their former splendor. Among them are the municipal theaters of São Paulo (1988) and Rio de Janeiro (still in progress). Many other Brazilian opera houses are of interest, such as the Arthur Azevedo Theater in São Luís do Maranhão, built early in this century and recently restored; the São Pedro Theater (1858) in Porto Alegre (fig. 22); and the Djalma Maranhão Theater (originally the Carlos Gomes Theater) in Natal (fig. 23) by Herculano Ramos, a renowned architect born in Minas Gerais. An alumnus of the School of Fine Arts in Rio de Janeiro, Ramos worked in Recife and finally settled in Natal. He was invited to paint the stage curtain and sets of the José de Alencar Theater in Fortaleza. Back in Natal, he contracted to renovate the Carlos Gomes Theater where, influenced by the Fortaleza opera house, he made a small-scale reproduction of it, a sort of "Brazilian garden theater."

Naturally theaters have always stood out among other city buildings because of their privileged locations and the special attention dedicated to their planning. However, a glance at the rise of opera houses in Brazil over the analyzed period evidences their social importance as the fruit of the people's legitimate ambition to achieve higher cultural standards. Given the elaborate construction and finishing that required the use of noble materials and, initially, the assistance of foreign artists and craftsmen, these buildings established an enduring standard of quality for our cities, a testimonial that will always be a part of our national heritage. □

Fig. 19. José de Alencar
Theater, Fortaleza, Ceará,
detail. Photograph by Benedito
Lima de Toledo, 1981.

Fig. 20. José de Alencar
Theater, Fortaleza, Ceará,
detail. Photograph by Benedito
Lima de Toledo, 1981.

Fig. 21. José de Alencar
Theater, Fortaleza, Ceará,
detail. Photograph by Benedito
Lima de Toledo, 1981.

Fig. 22. São Pedro Theater,
Porto Alegre, Rio Grande
do Sul, ca. 1911. From a
postcard (A Miscelanea,
Porto Alegre, Pelotas).
Jamil Nassif Abib collection.

Fig. 23. Djalma Maranhão

Theater (originally the

Carlos Gomes Theater),

Natal, Rio Grande do Norte.

Photograph by Benedito

Lima de Toledo, 1991.

PREÇOS DAS ASSIGNATURAS PARA A CORTE.	ANNO XV.	PREÇOS DAS ASSIGNATURAS PARA AS PROVINCIAS
Trimestre...............5$000	N. 729	Trimestre 6$000
Semestre...............9$000		Semestre 8 91.2 11$000
Anno..................16$000		Anno 18$000
Avulso 500 RS.	Publica-se todos os domingos	Avulso 500 RS.

COM ESTE NUMERO PRINCIPIA A «SEMANA ILLUSTRADA» O SEU DECIMO QUINTO ANNO

Dr. Semana... graças ao *sol* (que são os meus assignantes) á minha boa *estrella* (que podiam ser os meus collaboradores) e á *lua* (de mel em que vivo,) cheguei a este ponto.

Moleque.—Agora não se esqueça de regar o seu jardim com vinho do Rheno e adubal-o com aquillo com que se compra os melões e os donos dos melões.

Illustrated Books and Periodicals in Brazil, 1875–1945

By José E. Mindlin

José E. Mindlin is a book collector who started his library of approximately thirty thousand volumes at the age of thirteen. A former secretary of culture, science, and technology of the state of São Paulo, he is a board member of many cultural institutions, and an honorary member of the International Council of the Museum of Modern Art in New York. He is also on the Board of Governors of the John Carter Brown Library in Providence, Rhode Island. Besides being a booklover, he is a law graduate and a businessman.

It is no easy task to present an overview of seventy years of books and periodicals. Here I am in my library, facing a pile of volumes selected from the bookshelves, realizing at once that I have much more information than can possibly be included in the limited space of this article. Therefore I must give up seeking other sources of information, though I do not have, by far, all possible references on the subject. Still, my books and magazines hold an amazing variety of information: dozens of artists in whose work one finds romanticism and realism, reverence and irony, imitation and originality, academy and innovation, formality and creativity. The greatest difficulty lies in choosing what to show the reader, especially one who is not familiar with Brazilian culture.

The last decades of the nineteenth century were poor in book illustration, and the little that was done generally made use of European rather than original productions. On the other hand, there were many illustrated periodicals of excellent quality, where caricature flourished. These magazines continued into the twentieth century. The golden age of illustrated books began just before the 1920s, when the modernist movement was forthcoming. (Incidentally, Brazilian modernism should not be confused with so-called Spanish-American modernism, which was much more formal and more influenced by the classical, romantic, and symbolist tradition.)

Books and magazines with new graphic features, illustrated covers, and texts by young artists who were later to become famous names in Brazilian art gave great impetus to publishing and broke many taboos. It is not possible in a single article to introduce all the fine illustrators, but I will try to pinpoint those who seem to me to be most significant. It is an arbitrary choice, influenced by personal preferences. It can therefore be easily disputed, but I see no alternative. If the works mentioned or reproduced arouse the reader's desire for deeper research, this article will have fulfilled its purpose. I would then be delighted to send the reader additional information.

The art production covered here is concentrated in Rio de Janeiro and São Paulo. Although there were good illustrators in other states—and a few will be mentioned—limited space does not allow more lengthy references. In the specific case of magazines Rio prevailed, since it was the seat of the imperial court up to 1889 and the political and cultural capital of the country until the fifties.

One of the best illustrated magazines, which appeared in December 1860, was still being published in 1876, thus allowing its inclusion here. I refer to *Semana Illustrada* (Illustrated week) (fig. 1) edited by Henrique Fleiuss, a German draftsman, cartoonist, and lithographer, who came to Rio in 1859.

Fig. 2. Angelo Agostini, *Revista Illustrada*, front page of the first issue, 1 January 1876.

Fig. 3. *Revista Illustrada*, political cartoon, 6 January 1889.

Fig. 4. Julião Machado,

illustration in *A Bruxa*, 1896.

The main events in Brazilian life, such as the war with Paraguay from 1865 to 1870, are registered there in caricature. The genius of the period, however, was the Italian cartoonist Ângelo Agostini, who also arrived in Rio in 1859, coming from Paris where he had studied painting. He stayed three months, then moved to São Paulo; a surprising decision as, at that time, São Paulo was a small town of twenty thousand inhabitants. Remaining there for some years, he published two magazines with lithographic illustrations: *Diabo Coxo* (Lame devil) in 1864, and *Cabrião* (The annoyer) in 1866–1867. Agostini returned to Rio in the sixties and published cartoons in several magazines, for instance *O Mosquito* (The mosquito), which began to circulate in 1869; but his greatest feat was to launch *Revista Illustrada* (Illustrated magazine) (figs. 2 and 3) on 1 January 1876. In the nineteenth century this was the most important Brazilian illustrated periodical after *Semana Illustrada*, and it lasted until 1898. Other important magazines are *O Mequetrefe* (The scoundrel), published from 1875 to 1893, to which Agostini also contributed; *O Besouro* (The beetle) in 1878, with cartoons by the great Portuguese cartoonist Raphael Bordallo Pinhciro, who lived several years in Brazil and appeared in many other magazines; *A Bruxa* (The witch) (fig. 4) from 1896 to 1897 and *O Mercúrio* (Mercury) in 1898, in which the great illustrator was Julião Machado; *Dom Quixote* by Ângelo Agostini, from 1895 to 1903; *A Cigarra* (The cricket) in 1895; and *A Estação* (The season), a magazine with fashion illustrations, similar to the French *La Saison* but with texts of greater literary interest, published from 1879 to 1904—all in Rio de Janeiro. In these periodicals we find the main illustrators of the period.

At first *Semana Illustrada* was drawn and lithographed by Henrique Fleiuss himself, but later he had the help of H. Aranha, Aristides Seelinger, Ernesto de Souza e Silva (known as Flumen Jr.), and Aurélio Figueiredo (who went on to illustrate the magazine *O Diabo-a-Quatro* [Millions of things] in the state of Pernambuco). Other artists from this period who should be included are Cândido Faria, Luigi Borgomainerio, Belmiro de Almeida and, at the end of the century, Raul Pederneiras, K.Lixto (Calixto Cordeiro), and J. Carlos (José Carlos de Brito e Cunha).

Besides the magazines from Rio, there were, in the nineteenth century, worthy illustrated publications in other states. Because of space limitations I will mention only three: *O Polichinelo* (The puppet), a weekly published in São Paulo in 1876 reaching thirty-eight issues, with contributions from Ângelo Agostini; *O Diabo-a-Quatro*, published in Recife, Pernambuco, from 1875 to 1879, with cartoons by Raphael Bordallo Pinheiro and Aurélio de Figueiredo; and *Galeria Illustrada* (Illustrated gallery) published in Curitiba, Paraná, from 1888 to 1889, with beautiful illustrations by local artists such as Júlio Bellini, M. Leschaud, and Narciso Figueras. Magazines of such good quality are surprising, especially in Curitiba, which at the time was still a village. Although São Paulo and Recife were small provincial towns too, an explanation can be found in the existence of their two law schools, which had served as poles of attraction for the country's intelligentsia since 1827.

What must be pointed out is the importance that all these periodicals—and many others that were born and died in the same period—had on Brazilian cultural development and in forming a public political conscience. Up to 1889 Brazil was a monarchy with a parliamentary regime, the emperor acting as moderator, similar to the English monarchy. There was a considerable gap between the people, mostly illiterate, and the governing elite. Political satire played a key role by revealing the regime's failings, denouncing abuses, and backing measures of public interest. The two political parties alternating in power controlled each other in large measure with the help of the illustrated magazines.

Before leaving periodicals of the last decades of the nineteenth century, it seems important to mention three Brazilian magazines published abroad, one in New York, *O Novo Mundo* (The new world); one in London, *Echo Americano* (American echo); and one in France, *Revista Moderna* (Modern review).

From October 1871 to December 1879, *O Novo Mundo* was edited in New York by José Carlos Rodrigues, who later, in Rio, was editor of the newspaper *Jornal do Comércio*, the oldest and for more than a century one of the most prestigious Brazilian newspapers. The literary content of *O Novo Mundo* was of a very high level. Printed in Portuguese, it was sent to Brazil but was also addressed to Brazilians living in the United States, most of whom were students and professionals. The illustrations came partly from Brazil and partly from American newspapers and periodicals, with a very curious result: the editors sought texts to match the illustrations they bought!

Echo Americano was published in London from May 1871 to December 1872, one of the editors being Alexandre Mello Moraes (an ancestor of Vinícius de Moraes, well-known poet, songwriter, and originator of Bossa Nova). It circulated in Brazil and Portugal as well. Each issue contained portraits of personalities of the day. A curiosity to be mentioned is that in this portrait gallery, along with Emperor Pedro II and Queen Victoria, one finds "Dr. Carlos Marx" (fig. 5)! The illustrations in both magazines are reproductions of etchings and have the characteristics of many European and North American periodicals of that time.

Revista Moderna was edited by Martinho Arruda Botelho (a millionaire's son residing in Paris, who generously gave Patek Philippe watches to his subscribers). It was an attractive fortnightly that began in 1897, boasting pretty *art-nouveau* covers, photographs as well as black-and-white and color illustrations, and a section on fashion. Carlos Schwabe was among its illustrators.

As mentioned earlier, illustrated books at the end of the nineteenth century were not impressive. Books were usually printed without illustrations. There were some outstanding illustrated paper covers (fig. 8); and children's books

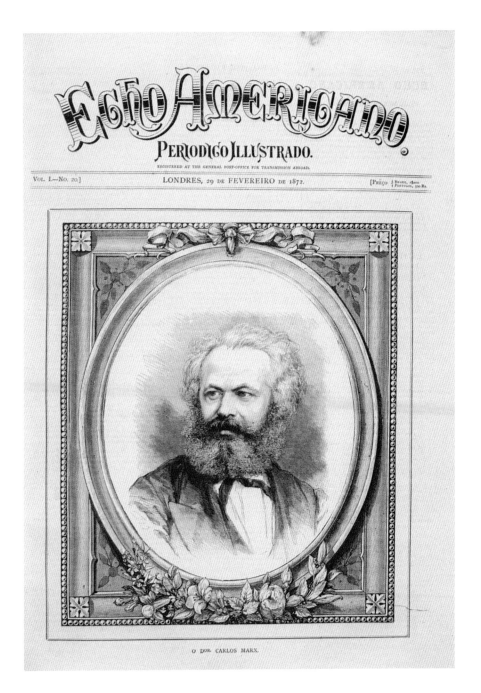

Masthead reading:

Echo Americano

PERIODICO ILLUSTRADO.

REGISTERED AT THE GENERAL POST-OFFICE FOR TRANSMISSION ABROAD.

Vol. I.—No. 20.]   LONDRES, 29 DE FEVEREIRO DE 1872.   [Preço { Brasil, 18oo0 / Portugal, 300 Rs.

O DOR. CARLOS MARX.

Fig. 5. "Dr. Carlos Marx"

depicted in *Echo Americano*,

29 February 1872.

such as *A Thousand and One Nights* and *Robinson Crusoe*, illustrated with so-called "splendid chromes," but with no exceptional artistic expression. In fact, it is not known whether these pictures were European or Brazilian. There were also many editions of popular booklets (fig. 6) with picturesque color prints and black-and-white illustrations—all of them anonymous.

An illustrated edition of a literary work of good quality—and an exception—is the second edition of the classical novel *O Atheneu* by Raul Pompéia (fig. 7), illustrated by the author himself at the end of the century. By the way, the beautiful cover of *Vergastas* (Whips) (fig. 8) is also by Pompéia.

Fig. 6. Popular booklet

published in 1876.

UM FACTO

DA

INQUISIÇÃO NO BRASIL.

E

HEROISMO DE UMA CAPIXABA

TRADIÇÃO POPULAR

DA

PROVINCIA DO ESPIRITO-SANTO

Com duas estampas

Rio de Janeiro

PUBLICADO E Á VENDA EM CASA DOS EDITORES

EDUARDO & HENRIQUE LAEMMERT

66,   Rua do Ouvidor,   66

1876.

A filha de Braz foi vendida a uns cunuens que a comprárão para o harem do Imperador.

Fig. 7. Raul Pompéia,

illustration from *O Atheneu*,

second edition, 1902.

114   O ATHENEU

manto da candura, refugiando-se na indifferença hieratica das vestaes. Depois, uma pontinha de ingenuo sorrir, olhos fechados ainda; gradação de infantilidade que substituia á vestal uma criança esquiva e timida, rindo, voltando a cara. Os olhos, por fim, aventuravam-se de relance, uma temeridade de noiva possivel, nada mais, volvendo ao retrahimento scismador. Depois, a contemplação confiada; romance inteiro, linha por linha, de uma virgindade Até que subito, meu castissimo Barreto! aquella virtude, aquella meiguice, aquella esquiva candura, aquella nubilidade melancolica, aquella physionomia honesta, pesarosa talvez de ser amavel, fendia-se em dous batentes de porta magica e rodava em explosão o sabbath das lascivias.

Os olhos riam, distillando uma lagrima de desejo; as narinas offegavam, adejavam tremulas por intervallos, com a vivacidade espasmodica do amor das aves; os labios, animados de convulsões tetanicas, balbuciavam desafios, promettendo submissão de cadella e a doçura dos sonhos orientaes. Dominava então pela offerta abusiva, de repente: abatia-se á derradeira humilhação, para attrahir de baixo, como as vertigens. Alli estava, por terra, a prostituição da vestal, o hymeneu da donzella, a deturpação da innocente, tres servilismos reclamando um dono; appetite, appetite para esta orgia rara sem convivas!

Fig. 8. Raul Pompéia, cover of

Vergastas, 1889.

In the twentieth century the picture changes substantially, although during the first two decades illustrated periodicals were still more plentiful than books. In 1900 *Revista da Semana* (Magazine of the week) and in 1902 *O Malho* (The mallet) began and continued until 1959. In these periodicals, besides Julião Machado already mentioned, other excellent cartoonists emerged: Raul (Raul Pederneiras), Bambino (Arthur Lucas), Yantok (Max Cesarino Yantok), J. Carlos, Luis Sá, Álvarus (Álvaro Cotrim), and Fortuna (Reginaldo José Fortuna), among others. In 1904 *Kosmos*, possibly the most beautiful magazine published in Brazil, first appeared, lasting until 1909. Besides having excellent literary content, *Kosmos* was memorable for its *art-nouveau* covers. Only one is reproduced here (fig. 9), although many others deserve to be known, due to their variety and typographic refinement. On a similar line to *Kosmos*, also in 1904, *Renascença* (Renaissance) appeared in Rio, a magazine "about literature, science, and art."

In 1905 a children's magazine began, *O Tico-Tico* (Crown sparrow) (fig. 10), that for several generations filled the dreams and stimulated the imaginations of Brazilian children (myself included). Among the active contributors were Ângelo Agostini and J. Carlos. It continued until 1959. Also in 1905 we have *Íris*, a literary magazine published in São Paulo, which lasted until 1907. It had a charming format and covers. The author of the illustrations is not mentioned—presumedly it was the editor himself, Álvaro Guerra.

Fig. 9. Cover of *Kosmos*,

April 1904.

In 1911 a weekly magazine appeared in Rio, *O Riso* (The laugh), that seems to have been one of the first publications to present the so-called "artistic nude," probably causing scandal but apparently well received since it reached eighty issues. Two new versions of *A Cigarra* were published, one in São Paulo and the other in Rio, the former from 1914 to 1917 and the latter from 1917 to 1919. A contest was held for the cover of the first São Paulo edition, and the winner was Franta Richter who, during the following year, illustrated *The Ugly Duckling* by Hans Christian Andersen, the first of a famous series of children's books published by Companhia de Melhoramentos de São Paulo. *A Maçã* (The apple), edited by a very popular author, Humberto de Campos, was published from 1922 to 1929. These magazines were appealing at the time but did not reach the level of *O Malho* or *Fon-Fon!*, which appeared in 1907, or above all *A Careta* (The grimace) that started in 1908. All these were published for more than fifty years. Also worthy of mention, among many others that began before the twenties, are *Eu Sei Tudo* (I know everything); *Leitura para Todos* (Reading for all); *O Cruzeiro* (The cross, meaning the Southern Cross), where cartoonist Péricles Albuquerque Maranhão became famous in the thirties with the cartoons "O Amigo da Onça" (The wildcat's friend), something that was popularly said of one who, calling himself a friend, brought only bad news or created difficult situations; and *Illustração Brasileira* (Brazilian illustration) and *Dom Quixote* in 1917. Perhaps the best of all was *A Careta*, with decades of cartoons by J. Carlos. There were many fine cartoonists at the time, but I venture to say he surpassed them all.

Fig. 10. Cover of *O Tico-Tico*, 11 October 1905.

Good magazines appeared during the twenties—among which I can pinpoint *A Garoa* (The drizzle) in 1921, *Ariel* in 1926, and *Arlequim* (Harlequin) in 1927—but most of them were not basically different from previous periodicals. The sensational innovation of the decade was *Klaxon* (fig. 11), published from May 1922 to January 1923 by the group of the Week of Modern Art, which was held in São Paulo in February 1922 and started a renewal process in Brazilian culture. Several other avant-garde magazines deserve to be mentioned: *Festa* (Party) (fig. 12), published in Rio from 1927 to 1929, and again from 1934 to 1935, with an original format and illustrations but lacking the irreverance of *Klaxon*; *Verde* (Green) (fig. 13), published by youngsters in the small town of Cataguazes, Minas Gerais, also from 1927 to 1929 (the editor in chief of *Verde*, Rosário Fusco, was seventeen, and the oldest editor was twenty-two years old); and, most importantly, the *Revista de Antropofagia* (Cannibal review) (fig. 14), published in São Paulo from 1928 to 1929 in two phases (called teethings). The first phase, in smaller format, from May 1928 to February 1929, was under direction of Antônio de Alcântara Machado; and the second phase, from 17 March to 1 August 1929, was under the direction of Oswald de Andrade as a supplement to the newspaper *O Diário de S. Paulo* (The São Paulo daily), in the same format as the newspaper.

Illustrations from these four magazines will, I hope, convey a sense of how innovative they were in the academic atmosphere of the times. Although French influence was strong in Brazilian life, the cultural revolution in France during

KLAXON

mens[A]rio de [A]rte mo dern[A]

S[A]O P[A]ULO

N.º 1

Fig. 11. Cover of *Klaxon*, no. 1, 1922.

Fig. 12. Page from *Festa*, vol. 1, no. 7, March 1935.

f e s t a 7

heitor alves

palavras ao vento

Vento peralta,
que andas, na noite,
de rua em rua,
assobiando, à toa,
todas as portas se fecham com estrondo,
quando tu passas.

E ha boccas que te esconjuram nos interiores...

Vento vadio,
abro-te a porta, entra!
e enche a minha sala do teu ruido
e dança em torno de mim
a dança doida que dançavas
lá fóra,
na orgia da selva,
com as arvores bebedas de somno.

Quero me divertir,
vento estroina da noite:
meu coração andou correndo,
em busca de amor,
toda a cidade,
e toda a cidade lhe bateu as portas.

Eugenio Gomes

Desenho de Cecilia Meirelles

Fig. 13. Cover of *Verde*, vol. 1, no. 5, 1927.

DIREÇÃO de HENRIQUE DE RESENDE MARTINS MENDES e ROSARIO FUSCO

VERDE

REVISTA MENSAL DE ARTE E CULTURA

NUMERO . 5
ANNO . . . 1
REDAÇÃO e ADMINISTRAÇÃO
RUA CEL. VIEIRA, 33
CATAGUAZES – MINAS

SUMARIO

NICOLÁS FUSCO SANSONE	EL NOCTURNO DE LOS CUERPOS
ASCENSO FERREIRA	MULA-DE-PADRE
RIBEIRO COUTO	A DESCOBERTA DE CATAGUAZES
GUILHERMINO CESAR	BALÁDA DO ARCO-IRIS DA GENTE
MARIO DE ANDRADE	PRÉSENTATION DE LA JEUNE FILLE (DOLOUR)
ASCANIO LOPES	PAPEL DO INSTINTO NO MUNDO ATUAL
A. FONSECA LOBO	AUTORIA DA ARTE DE FURTAR (CONC.)
JÃO DORNAS FILHO	MEUS OITO ANNOS
PEREGRINO JUNIOR	EL VANGUARDISMO EM EL BRASIL
ILDEFONSO FALCÃO	SINGERMAN, STOLEK, ETC. (CONCLUSÃO)
JORGE FERNANDES	CANÇÃO AO SOL
FRANCISCO INACIO PEIXOTO	MARIA LAVADEIRA

MARIA CLEMENCIA: FIGURA

APONTAMENTOS DE

UBYRATAN VALMONT, FRANCISCO INACIO PEIXOTO, AFFONSO ARINOS SOBRINHO, F., GUILHERMINO CESAR, PEIXOTO e R. F.

Numero especial: com um suplemento relativo aos mezes de Fev., Março, Abril e Maio

ESTE NUMERO — 1$500 ASSINATURA — 11$000

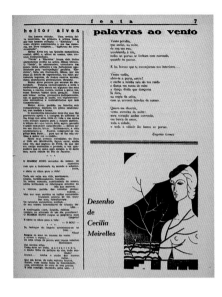

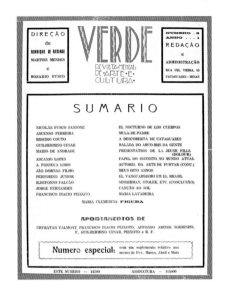

Fig. 14. Tarsila do Amaral, page from *Revista de Antropofagia*, no. 1, May 1928.

Revista de Antropofagia 3

MANIFESTO ANTROPOFAGO

Só a antropofagia nos une. Socialmente. Economicamente. Philosophicamente.

Unica lei do mundo. Expressão mascarada de todos os individualismos, de todos os collectivismo. De todas as religiões. De todos os tratados de paz.

Tupy, or not tupy that is the question.

Contra toda as cathecheses. E contra a mãe dos Gracchos.

Só me interessa o que não é meu. Lei do homem. Lei do antropofago.

Estamos fatigados de todos os maridos catholicos suspeitosos postos em drama. Freud acabou com o enigma mulher e com outros sustos da psychologia impressa.

O que atropelava a verdade era a roupa, o impermeavel entre o mundo interior e o mundo exterior. A reacção contra o homem vestido. O cinema americano informará.

Filhos do sol, mãe dos viventes. Encontrados e amados ferozmente, com toda a hypocrisia da saudade, pelos immigrados, pelos traficados e pelos touristes. No paiz da cobra grande.

Foi porque nunca tivemos grammaticas, nem collecções de velhos vegetaes. E nunca soubemos o que era urbano, suburbano, fronteiriço e continental. Preguiçosos no mappa mundi do Brasil.

Uma consciencia participante, uma rythmica religiosa.

Contra todos os importadores de consciencia enlatada. A existencia palpavel da vida. E a mentalidade prelogica para o Sr. Levy Bruhl estudar.

Queremos a revolução Carahiba. Maior que a revolução Francesa. A unificação de todas as revoltas efficazes na direcção do homem. Sem nós a Europa não teria siquer a sua pobre declaração dos direitos do homem.

A edade de ouro annunciada pela America. A edade de ouro. E todas as girls.

Filiação. O contacto com o Brasil Carahiba. **Oú Villeganhon print terre.** Montaigne. O homem natural. Rousseau. Da Revolução Francesa ao Romantismo, á Revolução Bolchevista, á Revolução surrealista e ao barbaro technizado de Keyserling. Caminhamos.

Nunca fomos cathechisados. Vivemos atravez de um direito sonambulo. Fizemos Christo nascer na Bahia. Ou em Belem do Pará.

Mas nunca admittimos o nascimento da logica entre nós.

Contra o Padre Vieira. Autor do nosso primeiro emprestimo, para ganhar commissão. O rei analphabeto dissera-lhe: ponha isso no papel mas sem muita labia. Fez-se o emprestimo. Gravou-se o assucar brasileiro. Vieira deixou o dinheiro em Portugal e nos trouxe a labia.

O espirito recusa-se a conceber o espirito sem corpo. O antropomorfismo. Necessidade da vaccina antropofagica. Para o equilibrio contra as religiões de meridiano. E as inquisições exteriores.

Só podemos attender ao mundo orecular.

Tinhamos a justiça codificação da vingança A sciencia codificação da Magia. Antropofagia. A transformação permanente do Tabú em totem.

Contra o mundo reversivel e as idéas objectivadas. Cadaverizadas. O stop do pensamento que é dynamico. O individuo victima do systema. Fonte das injustiças classicas. Das injustiças romanticas. E o esquecimento das conquistas interiores.

Roteiros. Roteiros. Roteiros. Roteiros. Roteiros. Roteiros. Roteiros.

O instincto Carahiba.

Morte e vida das hypotheses. Da equação **eu** parte do **Kosmos** ao axioma **Kosmos** parte do **eu.** Subsistencia. Conhecimento. Antropofagia.

Contra as elites vegetaes. Em communicação com o sólo.

Nunca fomos cathechisados. Fizemos foi Carnaval. O indio vestido de senador do Imperio. Fingindo de Pitt. Ou figurando nas operas de Alencar cheio de bons sentimentos portuguezes.

Já tinhamos o communismo. Já tinhamos a lingua surrealista. A edade de ouro.
Catiti Catiti
Imara Notiá
Notiá Imara
Ipejú

Desenho de Tarsila 1928 — De um quadro que figurará na sua proxima exposição de Junho na galeria Percier, em Paris.

A magia e a vida. Tinhamos a relação e a distribuição dos bens physicos, dos bens moraes, dos bens dignarios. E sabiamos transpor o mysterio e a morte com o auxilio de algumas formas grammaticaes.

Perguntei a um homem o que era o Direito. Elle me respondeu que era a garantia do exercicio da possibilidade. Esse homem chamava-se Galli Mathias. Comi-o

Só não ha determinismo - onde ha misterio. Mas que temos nós com isso?

Continua na Pagina 7

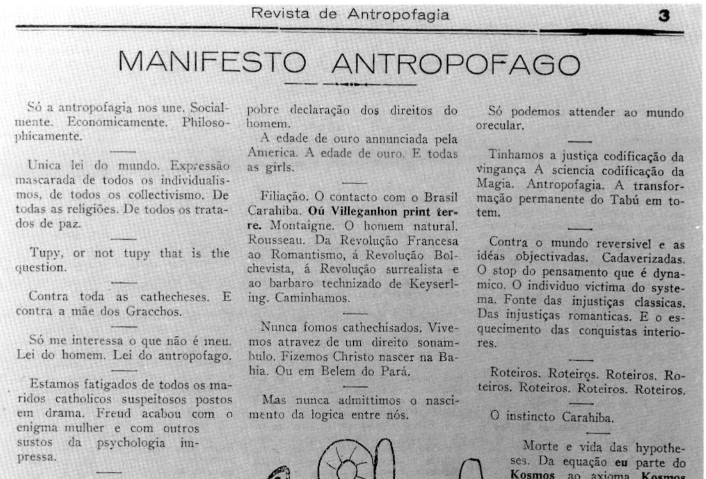

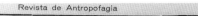

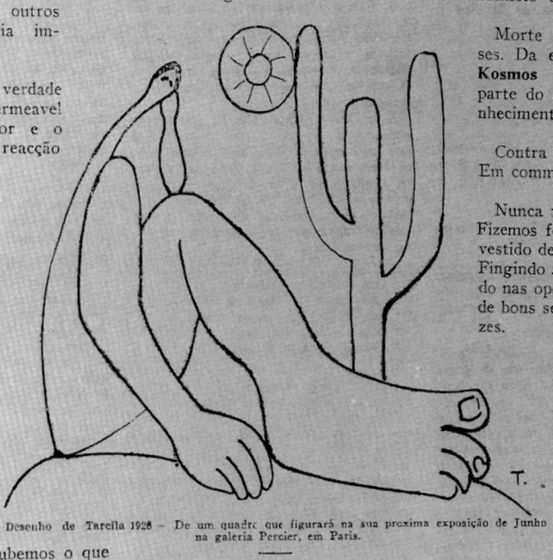

the first decades of this century did not reach Brazil until it was brought in the twenties by young Brazilian intellectuals, painters, musicians, and writers, mostly from wealthy families, who after long stays in Europe absorbed the new ideas. When bringing them to Brazil, however, they did not present them literally. They "Brazilianized" them. This was the genesis of Antropofagia (the anthropophagic movement), of which Oswald de Andrade and Tarsila do Amaral were advocates. The curious thing was that these young people took avant-garde positions, introducing new concepts in art, but this did not result in revolutionary change. They continued enjoying the privilege of high social position and, even when they did not have their own means, managed to obtain support from wealthy and condescending patrons. Their ideas were challenging, but their actions were limited to inoffensive provocations. What is important to note is that this movement did more than merely copy what was being done in Europe.

To represent this period in the field of book illustration, I have selected a number of illustrators who seemed to me the most expressive. It was not an easy choice, but I would risk naming the following: Di Cavalcanti, Correia Dias, Victor Brecheret, Voltolino, Monteiro Lobato, Paim, Cícero Dias, Mick Carnicelli, Nicola de Garo, Belmonte, Oswaldo Goeldi, Axl Leskoschek, Lívio Abramo, J. Prado, Santa Rosa, Aldemir Martins, Carlos Scliar, Vicente do Rego Monteiro, Tarsila do Amaral, Paulo Werneck, Lasar Segall, and Cândido Portinari. (I do not include J. Carlos or John Graz only because there are articles about them elsewhere in this issue.) Some of these artists had a major presence in books, magazines, and newspapers; others illustrated very few books; but all produced vigorous and vibrant work.

Let us begin with Di Cavalcanti (Emiliano Augusto Cavalcanti de Albuquerque e Mello, 1897–1976), illustrator, painter, draftsman, writer, and an extremely popular character who moved in all sorts of circles: social, political, intellectual, artistic, and bohemian. He was born in Rio but spent most of his youth in São Paulo, where he studied law but did not complete the course. Thus began his career as an illustrator living alternately in Rio and São Paulo, with several sojourns in Europe. Among many outstanding examples, he illustrated two books by Oscar Wilde: the first Brazilian edition of *The Ballad of Reading Gaol* (fig. 15) and *A Florentine Tragedy* (fig. 16).

Correia Dias (Fernando Correia Dias de Araújo, 1896–1935) was born in Portugal but came to Brazil in 1914, bringing caricatures for an exhibition in Rio. He stayed in Brazil, abandoning caricature to dedicate himself to drawing and book and magazine illustration. Typically *art nouveau*, with a decidedly decorative bent, he made extremely refined illustrations, which can be seen in the reproduction of the cover of *Nós* (Us) (fig. 17), a book by poet Guilherme de Almeida; and in the decoration of *Pergaminhos* (Parchments) (fig. 18) by writer Gustavo Barroso, where Correia Dias shows a marked concern for decoration. By the way, the woman on the cover of *Nós* is Cecília Meirelles, a great Brazilian poet to whom Correia Dias was married.

Victor Brecheret (1894–1955), born in Italy, is more widely known as a sculptor, with many notable works such as *Monumento às bandeiras* (Monument to the pioneers) in São Paulo. He took part in the modernist movement, contributed drawings to magazines such as *A Garoa* and *Klaxon*, and made a very beautiful cover for the book *A estrella de absyntho* (The absinthe star) (fig. 20) by Oswald de Andrade. On the artistic plane he seems closely related to Vicente do Rego Monteiro, mentioned below.

Fig. 15. Emiliano Di Cavalcanti, title page of *The Ballad of Reading Gaol*, 1919.

BALLADA DO ENFORCADO

POEMA ORIGINAL INGLEZ DE OSCAR
WILDE – TRADUCÇÃO DE ELYSIO DE
CARVALHO – PREFACIO DE CELSO
VIEIRA – ILLUSTRAÇÕES DE DI
GAVALCANTI

EDIÇÃO DA "REVISTA NACIONAL"
RIO DE JANEIRO. 1919.

Fig. 16. Emiliano Di Cavalcanti, illustration from *A Florentine Tragedy*, 1924.

Fig. 17. Fernando Correia Dias,
cover of *Nós*, 1917.

Fig. 18. Fernando Correia Dias,
title page of *Pergaminhos*, 1922.

Fig. 19. Voltolino, cover of *A menina do narizinho arrebitado*, 1920.

Fig. 20. Victor Brecheret, cover of *A estrella de absyntho*, 1927.

Voltolino (Lemmo Lemmi, 1884–1926) was born in São Paulo, the son of Italian immigrants. He personified the Italian-Brazilian of the first decades of this century, the *italianinho* (little Italian) that Antônio de Alcântara Machado immortalized in his literary work, especially in the book *Braz, Bexiga e Barra Funda* (names of three neighborhoods in São Paulo with the most Italian immigrants. It was said at the time that there were more Italians in São Paulo than in Rome!). One of Voltolino's most famous works was the illustration of *A menina do narizinho arrebitado* (The girl with the turned-up nose) (fig. 19) by Monteiro Lobato, which is one of the most famous children's books in Brazilian literature. Characters from *Narizinho*, like those from *O Tico-Tico*, are part of the life of several generations of Brazilians.

Monteiro Lobato (José Bento Monteiro Lobato, 1882–1948), born in São Paulo, was a great and versatile Brazilian writer. A famous author of children's books, he was also a caricaturist and draftsman who illustrated his own collection of short stories, *Urupês* (White agaric). This book is considered a Brazilian classic. Besides being a writer himself, he made many other authors known through his publishing house, Monteiro Lobato and Company. Some of his editions reached one hundred thousand copies, which at the time (and even now) was an incredible achievement. Unfavorable economic circumstances caused the company to go bankrupt, but he continued to defend his political ideas and to try to correct social injustices in Brazil by publishing polemic articles and creating the characters Jeca Tatu and Zé Brazil, a rural laborer and an urban worker continuously exploited by an unfair social system.

Paim (Antônio Paim Vieira, 1895–1988), born in São Paulo, was a versatile artist, caricaturist, draftsman, printmaker, and founder of the wonderful magazine *A Garoa* in 1921. He took part in several movements during Brazil's cultural revival, and his versatility is seen when we compare the title page of *Yara* (fig. 21), a book by romantic poet Paulo Gonçalves, to the illustration for *Pathé-Baby*, a book by modernist writer Antônio de Alcântara Machado, mentioned above. In *Pathé-Baby* Paim created a cinematographic sequence typical of silent movies, when live music accompanied the projection of films. This sequence (fig. 22), where the musical group has four participants, then three, and finally only one, was probably inspired by Haydn's *Farewell* Symphony.

Cícero Dias (born 1908), from Recife, Pernambuco, is one of Brazil's great painters. He lived many years in Paris and became a friend of painters and writers such as Picasso, Chagall, and Eluard. He illustrated several books including *A ilha dos amores* (The island of love), published in Lisbon in 1944, an episode of Luís Vaz de Camões's *Os Lusíadas* (The Lusiad). Other books were illustrated, but only after 1945.

Mick Carnicelli (1893–1967) was born in Italy but lived in São Paulo during the first half of the century. He was a sophisticated painter and illustrator, as is shown in the illustration of *A angústia de Don João* (Don Juan's anguish) (fig. 23).

Nicola de Garo (dates unknown), an Italian painter in Brazil in the twenties, exhibited his work in Belém and Recife in 1924 and in Rio in 1926, where he met modernist intellectuals and illustrated two books by Ronald de Carvalho— *Toda a América* (All America) and *Jogos pueris* (Children's games) (figs. 24 and 25). The latter's illustration is of rare beauty. Later de Garo went to the United States and never returned to Brazil.

Belmonte (Benedito Carneiro Bastos Barreto, 1896–1947), born in São Paulo, was one of its best draftsmen. He was also a writer and historian, but mainly a cartoonist. His political and social satire brought him well-deserved celebrity in Brazil. He created the famous character Juca Pato, who appears in his cartoons as a bystander and critic. The cartoons reproduced here give a glimpse at least of his talent and sense of humor (fig. 26).

Oswaldo Goeldi (1895–1947), born in Rio, was a top draftsman and printmaker, who with Lívio Abramo and Axl Leskoschek formed a group of teachers considered the pioneers of printmaking in Brazil. Some of their students are today's foremost artists in this field, such as Renina Katz, Fayga Ostrower, Darel Valença Lins (who studied with Goeldi), Maria Bonomi, and Edith Behring. Goeldi illustrated many books, among them *Cobra Norato* (The snake Norato) (fig. 27), a modernist poem by Raul Bopp; and works of Dostoevsky published in Brazil after 1940.

Axl Leskoschek (1889–1976) was born in Austria. He was a painter, draftsman, printmaker, and teacher. Coming to Brazil in 1938 as a refugee from Nazi persecution, he stayed for ten years and, working with Goeldi and Lívio Abramo, taught today's great printmakers. He illustrated Dostoevsky's works (notably *Crime and Punishment*) (fig. 28) published by Livraria José Olympio, and works by Brazilian authors such as Graciliano Ramos and Carlos Lacerda. Renina Katz, Fayga Ostrower, Misabel Pedrosa, and Ivan Serpa were among his students.

Lívio Abramo (1903–1992), born in Araraquara, São Paulo, was a printmaker, draughtsman, and journalist, completing with Goeldi and Leskoschek the trio of teachers who educated some of today's most important Brazilian printmakers. Self-taught, he faced many financial difficulties in his youth, and all

Fig. 21. Antônio Paim Vieira,
title page of *Yara*, 1922.

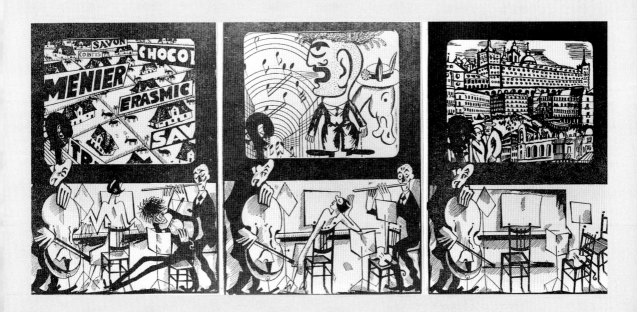

Fig. 22. Antônio Paim Vieira,
sequence from *Pathé-Baby*, 1926.

MENOTTI DEL PICCHIA

1922

A ANGUSTIA DE DON JOÃO
POEMA

MICK CARNICELLI

Fig. 23. Mick Carnicelli, illustration from *A angústia de Don João*, 1922.

Fig. 24. Nicola de Garo, title
page of *Jogos pueris*, 1926.

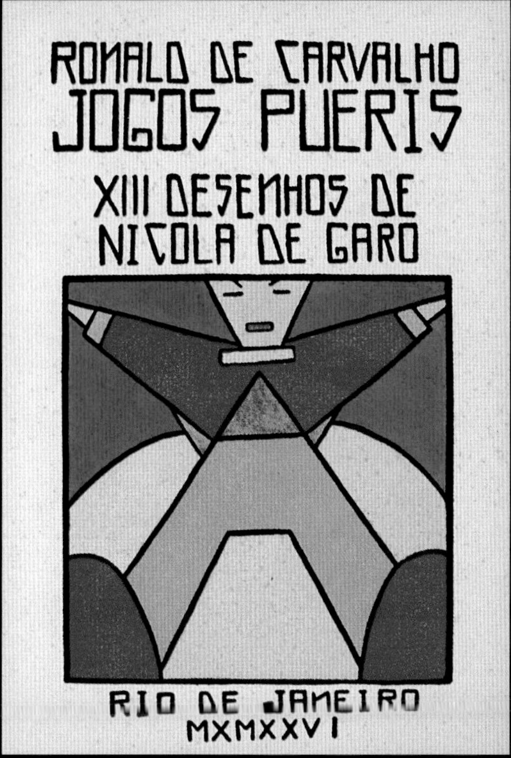

RONALO DE CARVALHO
JOGOS PUERIS
XIII DESENHOS DE
NICOLA DE GARO

RIO DE JANEIRO
MXMXXVI

Fig. 25. Nicola de Garo,
illustration from
Jogos pueris, 1926.

GEOMETRIAS, imaginações destes cami-
nhos da minha terra!
Curvas de trilhas,

Fig. 26. Belmonte cartoons
from Ernest Hamblock,
*His Majesty the President:
A Study of Constitutional
Brazil* (London: Methuen
and Co., 1935).

THE "ELECTION" OF THE OFFICIAL CANDIDATE

THE OFFICIAL CANDIDATE TAKES A STROLL

THE FRANCHISE UNDER THE PRESIDENTIALIST RÉGIME

Cartoons by Belmonte

Fig. 27. Oswaldo Goeldi,
illustration from
Cobra Norato, 1937.

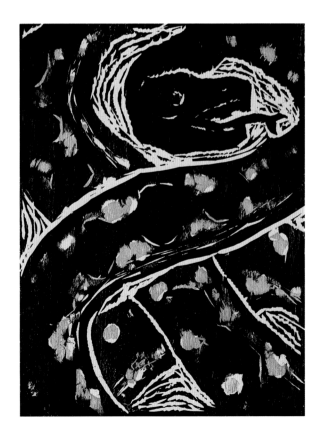

574   DOSTOIEVSKI

lhe enterrou uma faca no coração — sem lhe arrancar
sequer um grito.

Depois, com astucia criminosa e verdadeiramente
infernal, manobrou para atirar as suspeitas aos criados.
Cometeu a indignidade de apanhar a carteira de dinheiro
da morta, abriu a cômoda com as chaves encontradas
debaixo do travesseiro, e apoderou-se de alguns objetos,

Fig. 29. Lívio Abramo,

illustration from

Pelo sertão, 1948.

through his life he showed marked concern for social problems, which is evident in his works. He did mostly woodcuts and, with Goeldi and Leskoschek, illustrated a number of books published by Livraria José Olympio. His masterpiece was *Pelo sertão* (Through the backlands) (fig. 29) by Brazilian writer Afonso Arinos, published by the Sociedade dos Cem Bibliófilos do Brasil (Society of one hundred bibliophiles of Brazil).

J. Prado (Juvenal Prado, 1895–1980), born in Mogi-Mirim, São Paulo, was a painter, draftsman, and decorator. He became well known in 1921 as art editor of the magazine *A Garoa*, and was a distinguished illustrator of Monteiro Lobato's editions. Part of a group that sought an alternative form of modernism to the Week of Modern Art in 1922, he organized the First Plastic Arts Salon.

Santa Rosa (Tomás Santa Rosa Júnior, 1909–1946) was born in João Pessoa, Paraíba, in the Northeast. In 1932 he moved to Rio, where he illustrated many books. As a painter, printmaker, stage designer, playwright, and decorator, he was very popular in Rio's artistic world of the thirties and forties. He died in New Delhi.

Aldemir Martins (born 1922), from the state of Ceará in the Northeast, has lived in São Paulo since 1940. A painter, draftsman, teacher, and illustrator, he is considered one of Brazil's outstanding artists. Before 1945 he had already contributed illustrations to several magazines and newspapers. He illustrated books, but only after 1945.

Fig. 30. Vicente do Rego Monteiro, illustration from *Légendes, croyances, et talismans des indiens de l'Amazone*, 1923.

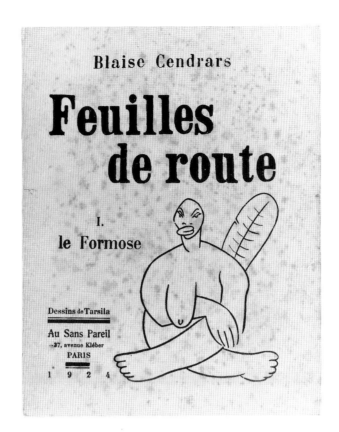

Fig. 31. Tarsila do Amaral,

cover of *Feuilles*

de route, 1924.

Carlos Scliar (born 1920) from the state of Rio Grande do Sul, is a famous painter, draftsman, printmaker, and illustrator, with various sideline art activities such as stage-sets and films. Since 1938 he has contributed to numerous periodicals and newspapers not only as an artist but also in charge of layout. Before 1945 he had illustrated six books, and up to today more than twenty.

Vicente do Rego Monteiro (1899–1970) was born in Pernambuco, in the Northeast. He was well educated, and lived in France from 1911 to 1914. Returning to Brazil because of World War One, he exhibited watercolors in São Paulo in 1920 and worked closely with the modernists, especially Anita Malfatti, Victor Brecheret, and Di Cavalcanti. Back in France in 1921, he studied painting and was in touch with Matisse, Picasso, and Lhote, eventually becoming one of Brazil's preeminent painters. Although living in France, where he illustrated the book *Légendes, croyances, et talismans des indiens de l'Amazone* (Legends, beliefs, and talismans of the Amazonian Indians) (fig. 30), he could not be left out of a list of Brazilian illustrators. Later, in Pernambuco, he started several publishing enterprises, producing the periodical *Renovação* (Renewal) from 1939 to 1946, with several issues in French. His paintings have an impressive affinity with Brecheret's sculptures but are far from being a copy.

Tarsila do Amaral, (1890–1973), born in São Paulo, was a painter, sculptor, printmaker, and leading figure of Brazilian modernism. In 1928, with her painting *Abaporu* (Cannibal, in an Indian language), she inspired the revolutionary cultural movement known as Antropofagia, led by Oswald de Andrade and the group that organized the Week of Modern Art in 1922. She illustrated, among others, the book *Feuilles de route* (Travel notes) (fig. 31) by the famous French-Swiss writer Blaise Cendrars, and the *Revista de Antropofagia*. She is considered the greatest Brazilian woman painter of our time.

Fig. 32. Paulo Werneck, cover

of *Lenda da carnaubeira*, 1939.

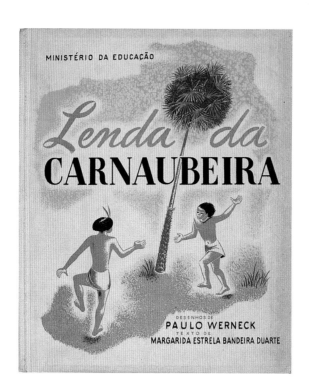

Paulo Werneck (1929–1987), born in Rio, was a self-taught draftsman, painter, and illustrator, who did excellent work in mosaic together with renowned modernist architects such as the three brothers, Marcelo, Milton, and Maurício Roberto. He was awarded a prize for his illustration of the book *Lenda da carnaubeira* (figs. 32 and 33), which was published in the United States as *The Legend of the Palm Tree*. Among other books, he illustrated *O negrinho do pastoreio* (The little black boy).

Lasar Segall (1891–1957), born in Lithuania, was mainly a painter, printmaker, draftsman, and sculptor. His first exhibition in São Paulo was in 1913, and he settled there in 1923. He took part in all the Brazilian movements of cultural revival and left a huge production that placed him among the best Brazilian artists. His illustrations are very significant. Besides those he published in Europe, a highlight in Brazil is *O mangue* (The swamp) (fig. 34).

Cândido Portinari (1903–1962), born in Brodósqui, São Paulo, the son of Italian immigrants, became one of Brazil's foremost painters. He began his studies with great academic painters, thus mastering traditional techniques, but afterward followed new paths that made him internationally famous. He illustrated many books including the classic of Brazilian literature *As memórias póstumas de Braz Cubas* (The posthumous memoirs of Braz Cubas) (fig. 35) by Machado de Assis, published in 1943 by the Sociedade dos Cem Bibliófilos do Brasil.

When I began planning this article, my assumption was that its subject matter was quite familiar to me. On the contrary, in my research I kept meeting with surprising information. There was more to say than I anticipated, and there were far more illustrators than could be covered in a brief overview. However, unveiling the tip of the iceberg was an essential first step in realizing the vitality of Brazilian illustration during this period. I fear I am doomed to extensive research, but I hope that at least some readers will have their interest awakened and be prompted to share this challenging task with me. □

Fig. 34. Lasar Segall, illustration from *O mangue*, 1944.

Fig. 35. Cândido Portinari, illustration from *As memórias póstumas de Braz Cubas*, 1943.

MACHADO DE ASSIS

Vir   Virgilio

     Virgilio   Virgilio

        Virgilio

           Virgilio

    Meu pae, um pouco despeitado com aquella indifferença, ergueu-se, veio a mim, lançou os olhos ao papel...

— Virgilio! exclamou. Es tu, meu rapaz; a tua noiva chama-se justamente Virgilia.

76

Fig. 1. Clock tower in Belém, Pará. Made by Walter MacFarlane and Company, Saracen Foundry of Glasgow, ca. 1905. Restored, 1994.

Artistic Intentions in Iron Architecture

By Geraldo Gomes

Geraldo Gomes is an architect and a professor in the Department of Architecture at the Federal University of Pernambuco. An architectural historian, he has collaborated in the restoration of many historic buildings. His publications on iron architecture include *Arquitetura do ferro no Brasil* (1986, 1988) and "L' architecture métallique belge en Amérique Latine," in *Flandre et Amérique Latine* (1993).

The utilization of iron in building is very ancient, but its production on an industrial scale intensified from the end of the eighteenth century so that it became a new element in the esthetic transformation occurring in the nineteenth century. In general, when iron is the main protagonist of architectural space, that is, when it is not covered by another material, its acceptance or rejection hinges on the mastery of esthetics.

Iron architecture developed in Europe in the second half of the nineteenth century, responding to the requirements of new building programs, to the reality of fabrication on a large scale, and to the consequent commercialization of industrial products. Competition among industrialized countries led to disputes over raw materials and consumer markets. Meanwhile, the increased production of iron brought about its utilization in the most varied forms. The great pavilions of industrial fairs, among them the remarkable Crystal Palace in London in 1851, were made of iron, as were the majority of products on exhibition. The young nations of Latin America, along with the older non-industrialized countries of Africa and Asia, became eager consumers of European industrialized products, including iron buildings. Division of the African continent among the European colonial powers was an important step in the diffusion of iron architecture, largely due to the mobility of prefabricated buildings and the short time needed to assemble them to house European colonists.

Brazil, which acquired its political independence in 1822, consolidated its position both as a supplier of raw materials and as a substantial consumer of manufactured products (fig. 1). Consequently it came under the influence of European culture, specifically that of France and England. European investments in Brazil were directed essentially to regions where there was considerable agricultural production of interest to the international market. The construction of railroads and of river- and seaports, under the supervision of British companies, was warranted by this economy geared to exports—coffee in the Southeast (Rio de Janeiro and São Paulo), cotton and sugar in the Northeast (Recife and Fortaleza), and rubber in the Amazon (Manaus and Belém).

Thus the Brazilian cities favored by this model of exportation developed and became hubs for consumption of European products, the main goal of European economic policy whose interests were shared by Brazil's ruling class. Along with British railroad stations prefabricated in iron, public markets (figs. 2, 3, 4, 5, and 6), theaters (figs. 8 and 9), water reservoirs (fig. 7), bandstands, and houses were also imported. Some of these buildings were fabricated in Europe specifically to be exported and were generally planned to provide comfort to the user in differing weather conditions. The admiration that Brazilians had for these

All photographs by Geraldo Gomes except where noted.

Fig. 2. Public market in Belém, Pará. Made in France, 1901. The gothic towers are purely decorative.

Fig. 3. Decorative cast-iron panels of the public market in Belém, Pará. Made in England, 1908.

Fig. 4. Public market in São José, Recife, Pernambuco. Made in France, 1875. Panels and gargoyles are cast iron.

Fig. 5. One of four pavilions of the public market in Manaus, Amazonas. Made by Walter MacFarlane and Company, Saracen Foundry of Glasgow, 1883–1910. The arched gable is filled with a decorative cast-iron panel.

Fig. 6. Clock tower in the public market of Pelotas, Rio Grande do Sul, ca. 1895. Origin unknown.

Fig. 7. Water reservoir in Rio Grande, Rio Grande do Sul. Made in England, ca. 1876.

◀

Fig. 8. José de Alencar Theater, Fortaleza, Ceará. Facade seen from the inner court. Made by Walter MacFarlane and Company, Saracen Foundry of Glasgow, 1910.

buildings, possibly from the simple fact of their European origin, was almost unanimous, as one can deduce from this announcement of the opening of the Fortaleza Public Market, made in France:

> In the presence of ladies and gentlemen, a great ceremony was held at the inauguration of the magnificent public market, which is the most beautiful, and perhaps the most comfortable, in South America. ...Situated on one of the loveliest squares in Fortaleza, this is the best finished work among all the buildings, public or private, in this city; and, of its kind, none in South America and very few in Europe and in the United States of America will surpass it.[1]

Comparisons with buildings on other continents can be faulted as provincial, but they express the understandable pride of the population. Ten years later a stately market would be inaugurated in Rio de Janeiro, produced in England and Belgium in a rare collaboration between companies of different nationalities (figs. 10 and 11). It was the largest public market in Brazil, but it was not welcomed by the Rio press with the same enthusiasm as that of the press in Fortaleza:

> While it is not a work...to surpass its counterparts in Europe, the new market, recently built on the...old "Largo do Moura," is however an improvement of real value, which substantially satisfies the end for which it was created and evidences the extraordinary transformation that has occurred in the nation's capital.... The market was built with great care and follows a modern and elegant style, where no easily inflammable material was used. All of the vast market is constructed with iron, stonework, and tile.[2]

In Europe, iron architecture did not distinguish itself by the novelty of the material alone but rather when iron became part of the working rationale of engineers. In the nineteenth century architects were required to give the structures of engineers architectural values, that is, decorative values. An esthetics inherent to the new material and the new architecture had not yet been defined. Prefabrication of the buildings and their assembly (rather than construction) were very advanced practices, considered exotic to architecture itself. New forms and processes for the use of iron were developed so frequently that some authors of iron architectural history only discuss techniques and not esthetics.

Fig. 9. José de Alencar Theater, Fortaleza, Ceará. Made by Walter MacFarlane and Company, Saracen Foundry of Glasgow, 1910. The decoration of the box railings reflects the social status of their users.

In the first half of the nineteenth century, corrugated iron sheets were propagated for the construction of walls and roofs. These sheets, with no ornament but their own undulation, were used on a large scale for the most diverse purposes. There was no commitment to forms of the past, which may explain their rejection by the eclectic taste existing then. However, "[p]arallel with the development of the corrugated iron prefab...was the evolution of its heavier, more substantial, and architecturally more pretentious counterpart, cast iron."[3] Producers of cast iron for building were tireless in their efforts to guarantee the novel material as important a role as traditional materials. The ability of cast iron to take any form greatly aided its acceptance by consumers with a taste for decorative elements. Thus iron borrowed the esthetics of traditional materials of construction, for instance, time-honored stone.

1. Article in the newspaper *A República* (Fortaleza), 19 April 1897. My translation.
2. Article in the newspaper *A Notícia* (Rio de Janeiro), 13 December 1907. My translation.
3. Gilbert Herbert, *Pioneers of Pre-fabrication: The British Contribution in the Nineteenth Century* (Baltimore and London: The Johns Hopkins University Press, 1978), 149.

▲

Fig. 10. Public market in
Rio de Janeiro, demolished in
the 1950s. Made by Hoppins
Causer and Hoppins,
Birmingham, and Atelier de
Willebrock, Brussels, 1907.
Photograph courtesy of the Rio
de Janeiro municipal archive.

Fig. 11. A corner tower of the
public market in Rio de Janeiro,
the only remaining part
of the building.

**Fig. 12. Recife Law School.
Made in France, 1910. Columns
are of cast iron. Arched beams
are iron sheets riveted with
structural iron sections.**

As has been already mentioned, iron is capable of all forms of architectural beauty. It must be evident that whatever forms can be carved or wrought in wood or stone, or other materials, can also be faithfully reproduced in iron. Besides, iron is capable of finer sharpness of outline, and more elaborate ornamentation and finish; and it may be added that it is not so liable to disintegration, by exposure to the elements, as other substances. To this capability of beauty we may add that of economy or cheapness.[4]

The structural element that adapted itself most to this possibility was the cast iron column (fig. 12). The production of columns drew from the decorative aspects of known architectural orders but, for economy's sake, did not reproduce the proportions of those orders. The slenderness and elegance of iron columns had very little to do with their models in stone. Although the producers of these structural elements unconsciously changed the way we read and understand architectural spaces, actual changes to the traditional formal vocabulary were few. Even when the columns were made of steel, using the juxtaposition of profiles, the structurally unnecessary capitals had forms suggesting pre-existing architectural orders or their variants.

4.   Daniel D. Badger, *Badger's Illustrated Catalogue of Cast Iron* (New York: Dover Publications, Inc., 1981), 5. Reprint of a work first published by Baker and Godwin, Printers, New York, in 1865, under the title *Illustrations of Iron Architecture Made by The Architectural Iron Works of the City of New York*.

Fig. 13. The Crystal Palace,

Petrópolis, Rio de Janeiro.

Made in France, 1884.

Fig. 14. The Crystal Palace, Petrópolis, Rio de Janeiro. Made in France, 1884.

The aspiration of the producers of structural elements in cast iron was to make them even more decorative than the motifs that had inspired them. This objective was achieved not only with columns but with railings of balconies and gardens, staircases, and structural elements subject to compression.

> [T]he chief use for cast iron was now for pavilions, conservatories, palmhouses, shelters, bandstands, and arcades and these were often for the export market. It was a new and considerable development of the architectural use of the material. The simplicity of the work of Paxton and Decimus Burton was unfortunately forgotten, and engineers and architects frequently produced designs that were really conceived for carved marble or terracotta, although they were carried out in cast iron. Ornament, as Wornum had recorded in his "Analysis," was becoming an end in itself, except in some outstanding engineering works.[5]

This desertion of simplicity occurred in the second half of the nineteenth century, exactly when the importation of the great majority of iron buildings in Brazil occurred.

But the chief contribution of iron to the creation of new architectural spaces took place when it was matched with glass (figs. 13 and 14). Small sections of iron elements and great quantities of transparent colorless glass sheets allowed a visual continuity between inner and outer space, inconceivable in traditional systems of brick and stone masonry.

> With stone, [the artist] creates openings to please the sight, without jeopardizing stability; with iron, solids are constructed to please the sight.... If we admit that, by definition, solids are the essential parts of architecture, we must recognize that iron does more than modify architecture; it eliminates it entirely. It leaves only voids.... [A]nd this is something considerable in esthetics.[6]

Following the development of structural calculations that could predict with precision the behavior of steel, it was possible to talk in a formal language proper to the new material, even though the production of cast iron continued for decorative purposes. Outstanding monuments like the Pavilion of Machines at the Exhibition of Paris in 1889 astonished the world, but they were singular buildings, conceived and constructed for very specific ends. Their formal language, a consequence of the rational use of the structural possibilities of steel, can be said to have delineated the incipient theory of early-twentieth-century modernism.

While these advances took place, the fabrication of buildings for exportation continued and was well received by non-industrialized countries. This was not an attitude of cultural servility, as it might appear at first glance; the great and nonprofessional European public was also delighted by the myth of technology this architecture represented.

One of the most important iron buildings constructed in Paris was the central market, Les Halles (1854–1866, demolished 1973). Under the administration of Haussmann, the architect Victor Baltard signed this project, but in fact it would be defined by Napoleon III. Baltard's first plan for the market had stonework walls and an iron roof. His project was begun but was soon interrupted by Napoleon III, who ordered the demolition of the first pavilion in

5. John Gloag and Derek Bridgwater, *A History of Cast Iron in Architecture* (London: George Allen and Unwin, n.d.), 250.

6. Robert de la Sizeranne, *Les questions esthétiques contemporaines* (Paris: Librairie Hachette, 1904), 37. Translation by David J. Jacobson.

stonework, nicknamed by the people "the Market Fort." It was the Emperor himself, according to Haussmann in his memoirs, who defined the general disposition of the pavilions connected by covered streets and the use of iron in both structures and street roofs. Probably the Emperor was seeking to interpret popular taste, and it seems he succeeded.

This same taste was catered to by the manufacturers of buildings for export. They produced catalogues illustrated with images of architectural components and buildings of various models. This diversity, of course, aimed to win customers around the globe. Walter MacFarlane and Company of Glasgow, in their catalogue of 1882, clearly manifested their commercial purposes and those of others:

> We are willing at all times to make up entirely new designs and patterns to suit the particular requirements of our clients, and in these cases we place unreservedly the entire resources of our establishment at their disposal.

> Whilst we are primarily Iron Founders, a large section of our business is devoted to the production of the finest Wrought Ironwork.[7]

These catalogues contained numerous architectural components as well as smaller buildings, such as bandstands, verandas, public bathrooms, and so on. The catalogues were often illustrated with pictures of larger buildings that had been sent to customers in different and distant countries. Transportation costs were not high because iron was the kind of load shipping companies preferred—it made excellent ballast! (Ships headed for non-industrialized countries were less heavily loaded than those going to industrialized countries, thus the need for added weight.) Consequently the majority of iron buildings in Brazil, in fact in Latin America, are situated in sea- or riverport cities or cities served by railroads.

7. From the preface of the sixth edition of the catalogue of Walter MacFarlane and Company of Glasgow, sent to Fontes and Company Limited of Belém in 1882.

Fig. 16. Bandstand in Belém,

Pará. Made in Germany, 1904.

As manufacturers sold not only standardized buildings, in many cases customers gave opinions about plans and even defined a building's major characteristics. Every care was taken to ensure the success of building assembly in countries lacking qualified—much less specialized—labor. Some producers, as a normal procedure, assembled export buildings at their factories in Europe (fig. 15), identified all the parts by codes, disassembled the buildings, packed the parts, and dispatched them to their destination.

It was not always customer preference that oriented the production of iron architecture, however.

> [An] issue that worried architects was one of the slimness of metallic structures. To correct it they looked first to painting, a solution that seemed to be the most rational, as in any event it is necessary to paint the iron to protect it from rust. These color researches were started by Owen Jones in the Crystal Palace…. After several tests, which roused great public debate, the exterior was painted white and blue and the interior the three primary colors, prepared according to the latest color theories: five parts of red to three parts of yellow and eight of blue, proportions recommended by G. Fields for a perfect balance (*Chromotography*, London, 1825), separated by white to avoid the effects of simultaneous contrast studied by E. Chevreul (*De la loi du contraste des couleurs*, Paris, 1839).[8]

The fact that these color experiences originated in a building considered one of the wonders of the world, the Crystal Palace, led to the diffusion of the ideas applied in it. Examples still exist worldwide. But, to have survived, they had to have been preserved, repaired, and repainted. Painting almost always followed the taste of the times and in only a few cases preserved the original polychrome.

Of all nineteenth-century iron buildings, the one that sold the most throughout the world was the bandstand (fig. 16). Situated in the midst of an important square, the bandstand was an element of decoration of urban space that,

8. Claude Mignot, *L'architecture au XIX siècle* (Fribourg: Office du Livre, 1983), 186, 207. Translation by David J. Jacobson.

Fig. 17. Detail of railing in wrought iron and steel on a bandstand in Belém, Pará. Made in Germany, 1904. Restored, 1994.

in the last century, served as a center of social life. But, more than the diversity of forms, liberal use of colors on these gracious buildings gave value to each decorative detail.

> Like the markets, the bandstands yield treasures of decorative intent due to their immense variety. [Their basic] design is unchanging—yet more than any other building they allow the exercise of style. With eight columns of cast iron, eight filigreed arcades, an iron railing [fig. 17], a brick base, a zinc roof, and a thin board ceiling, one can do everything.[9]

A few bandstands still preserve their original use in Brazil, that is, to house musicians playing for people on surrounding squares and boulevards. In Caxambu, a city famed for its fountains of healthful spring water, there is a singular utilization of the roofs of imported bandstands—each fountain in the park being covered by a different structure (fig. 18). The most notable, of Moorish inspiration, still preserves the original polychrome (fig. 19).

On the other hand, reference to a church prefabricated with corrugated iron sheets and sent to Australia at the end of the nineteenth century illustrates how that kind of building continued to be received.

> [C]olonists had ample reason for disliking these buildings. They are hot, ugly and perishable. The scorching sun draws the nails, curls the iron-plates, and makes the interior as hot as a baker's oven. The style of architecture is hopelessly unpleasing, and such as suggests the factory or the warehouse. It cannot therefore excite surprise that one parish after another declined these corrugated makeshifts.[10]

9. François Loyer, *Le siècle de l'industrie* (Paris: Skira, 1983), 170. My translation.

10. George Goodman, *The Church in Victoria during the Episcopate of The Right Reverend Charles Perry* (Melbourne, 1892), quoted by Graeme E. Robertson and Joan Robertson in *Cast Iron Decoration* (London: Thames and Hudson, 1977), 58.

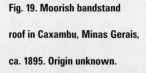

Fig. 18. Bandstand in Caxambu, Minas Gerais, ca. 1895. Original polychrome. Origin unknown.

Fig. 19. Moorish bandstand roof in Caxambu, Minas Gerais, ca. 1895. Origin unknown.

Fig. 21. Chalet, now a public building at the University of Pará, Belém. Danly system of pressed-iron sheets. Made by Forges d'Aiseau, Belgium, 1894.

Fig. 22. First floor of chalet at the University of Pará, Belém. Danly system of pressed-iron sheets. Made by Forges d'Aiseau, Belgium, 1894.

Fig. 23. Veranda of chalet, now a public building in a botanical park in Belém, Pará. Danly system of pressed-iron sheets. Made by Forges d'Aiseau, Belgium, 1893.

Although the British were pioneers in the fabrication of iron buildings for export, by the late nineteenth century French, Belgian, German, and American companies were competing for international customers and often offered products of better quality. British industrial practices made it difficult to introduce innovations, which was not the case, for instance, with the neophyte Belgians. It was a Belgian citizen by the name of Joseph Danly who, in 1885, patented a process for fabrication with pressed iron sheets. According to the inventor, this process, in which there was also a clever device for thermal insulation, would overcome the well-known rejection of buildings made of corrugated iron sheets.

> [T]he rooms are entirely freed from outside temperature variations, and the iron sheets are given appropriate decorative and architectural forms. ...The pressing, designed to stiffen the iron sheets, also gives them decorative and architectural forms similar to elements used in freestone constructions. These forms have the added advantage of counteracting the effects of the metal's expansion.[11]

Buildings prefabricated according to this system were first exported to the Congo, then a Belgian colony, and later to several countries of the Americas, including Brazil (fig. 20). The system showed itself to be efficient in regions subject to earthquakes, such as Central America. On the other hand, it is difficult to analyze the results of Danly's esthetic efforts. Contemporary opinions of owners and users are rare as he made very few buildings compared to those made of corrugated iron sheets.

In Belém, three houses were assembled according to Danly's system (figs. 21, 22, and 23), and there is no record of rejection by the owners or society as a whole

11. André Vauthier, "Les habitations métalliques, système Danly," *Le Génie Civil* (Paris) (October 1893): 409–411. Translation by David J. Jacobson.

Fig. 24. Railroad station in Bananal, São Paulo. Danly system of pressed-iron sheets. Made by Forges d'Aiseau, Belgium, 1889.

on the basis of esthetics. But here the rarity of this kind of building contributed to its value, as we can conclude from this newspaper advertisement of 1893:

> For sale—important and comfortable iron chalet, located at Bragança Road, close to "Largo de São Brás," which has the following accommodations: three [rooms] downstairs, two bedrooms behind the chalet and three upstairs. The chalet style is something rare in this city, near to transportation and all that one could desire, and a rural life.[12]

A railroad station assembled according to the same system in the city of Bananal in the state of São Paulo also received praise from the local newspaper:

> The railroad station to be assembled is very elegant and is already at the Rialto Station. Truly, we must say that we know of no other building such as this. It is entirely metallic, including the roof of paneled double sheets, of Belgian construction, with a floor of authentic Riga pine [fig. 24].[13]

Very often simple frameworks were given decorative supplements that bore no relation to their main structural elements, which, as mentioned before, foreshadowed twentieth-century modernism. This was the case with the circles, flowers, and stars over the arched roof of the Luz Railroad Station in the city of São Paulo (fig. 25), and with the leaves close to the capitals of the columns of the Recife Railroad Station (fig. 26). Cast-iron structures frequently utilized consoles and other elements which, working by compression, shortened the length of the free spans and were molded with evident decorative appeal, as in the São José Public Market in Recife (fig. 27).

In some cases the very special disposition of a structure in itself shows an artistic intention, as in Recife's Teatro do Parque (fig. 29). This building, with a rectangular ground plan, did not need a roof where the half trusses followed the horseshoe form of the boxes. Certainly no other material than iron could have produced the graceful and elegant artistic/structural solution we find there.

12. Advertisement in the newspaper *O Democrata* (Belém), 7 July 1893. My translation.

13. Article in the newspaper *A Nova Fase* (Bananal), 1 January 1889. My translation.

Fig. 25. Trellis of the arched roof of the Luz Railroad Station in São Paulo. Made in England, 1901.

Fig. 26. Cast-iron columns with decorative supplements at the railroad station in Recife, Pernambuco. Made in England, 1888.

Fig. 27. Roof spandrils in cast iron at the public market in São José, Recife, Pernambuco. Made in France, 1875.

Fig. 28. Veranda in the inner court of the Law School, Recife, Pernambuco. Made in France, 1910.

Fig. 29. Teatro do Parque, Recife, Pernambuco. Made in France, 1913. Roof half-trusses accompany the horseshoe shape of the boxes.

In Brazil, the utilization of iron in architecture also had the connotation of high social status, since these structures were almost all imported from Europe. Buildings constructed with traditional materials and techniques could increase their value by adding secondary structures of iron. Among these were verandas surrounding rural houses and, more frequently, the inner courts of urban buildings, like the one at the Recife Law School (fig. 28). Brazil imported architectural components in iron on a considerable scale—such as columns, roof trusses, and railings for balconies and stairways. The most valued was the interior stairway (figs. 30 and 31). Its mere existence in a building constructed according to a traditional system is not enough to make it an example of iron architecture. Still, the stairways are spectacular and deserve mention.

Finally, attention should be called to the use of iron as an overlay for other material. This is purely decorative and limited almost always to interior spaces.

Fig. 30. Cast-iron stairway in a public library in Manaus, Amazonas. Made in England, ca. 1895.

Fig. 31. Cast-iron stairway in the Liberty Palace, Belo Horizonte, Minas Gerais.

Made in Belgium, ca. 1895.

Fig. 32. Pressed-iron sheets in the ceiling of the Antonio Lemos Palace, Belém, Pará, 1897–1911. Origin unknown.

Fig. 33. Pressed-iron sheets covering the walls and ceiling of the Antonio Lemos Palace, Belém, Pará, 1897–1911. Origin unknown.

Fig. 34. Pressed-iron sheets covering the wall of a house in Belém, Pará, ca. 1895. Origin unknown. The picture is also made of pressed iron.

The industrial production of galvanized iron or zinc sheets allowed the covering of great expanses of walls and ceilings, where the most common formal design was a repeating figure (figs. 32, 33, and 34). In only one case, at the Brennand Mansion in Recife, does external overlay appear (fig. 35). The volume of the roof of the second story, in the interval corresponding to the main entrance of the building, has three walls covered by iron sheets, whose intent was obviously to add to the artistic value of the house.

The development of iron architecture was interrupted when reinforced concrete became the construction system most coherent to the language of modernist architecture. With rare exceptions, its history has always been written from an analysis of its monumental examples. That is why it is a pleasant surprise to discover, dispersed all over the world, modest buildings that are eloquent witnesses to creativity, talent, and beauty in iron architecture. □

Fig. 35. The Cornélio Brennand mansion in Recife, Pernambuco. Made in Belgium, ca. 1895.

Fig. 1. J. Carlos, cover of *O Malho*, special issue, 1928.

The Art of J. Carlos

By Isabel Lustosa

Translated by Paulo Henriques Britto

In memory of Luiz Carlos de Brito e Cunha

Isabel Lustosa is a researcher at the Rui Barbosa House Foundation in Rio de Janeiro. Among other publications, her *Histórias de presidentes: a república no catete* (1989) and *Brasil pelo método confuso: humor e boêmia em Mendes Fradigne* (1993) are books on humor and caricature as a form of Brazilian expression.

In 1902, when J. Carlos began to publish his cartoons in Rio de Janeiro, the Brazilian capital looked much as it had in the old days of the empire. In many ways it remained a colonial city that had expanded in an unplanned way; its downtown area was a labyrinth of ancient streets and narrow alleys, lined with slum tenements and shanties, where the poorer section of the population lived.

The entire cultural life of the city was concentrated within the narrow confines of Ouvidor Street. Here were the major newspapers,[1] the best shops, the trendiest cafés. And it was here that famous poets, writers, and cartoonists held court—they were the great men of the times, whose bohemian lifestyles fired the imagination of the young. They set the tone of the newspapers, for right next to lengthy and sober articles there was always a lighthearted quatrain, a political anecdote, or a caricature.

The first caricatures published in Brazil date from 1837 and are presumed to have been the work of journalist Manuel de Araújo Porto Alegre. They satirized Imperial Minister Bernardo Pereira de Vasconcellos and were sold as lithographs at Victor Larré's print shop. By the 1840s publications of the genre began to multiply, and numerous talented artists surfaced, both Brazilians and foreigners. Of the Brazilians, Cândido Aragonês de Faria deserves special mention; his talent compared to that of the prominent foreign caricaturists who then prevailed in the press.

In the latter half of the nineteenth century, Brazilian caricature was dominated by a major artist, Ângelo Agostini (1843–1910). An Italian who settled in Brazil, Agostini nurtured an entire generation of cartoonists in his style, marked by rounded forms and chiaroscuro effects produced with lithographic crayon.[2] In his hands humor was a weapon in the fight against slavery and monarchy. Agostini was the author of the best caricatures of Dom Pedro II, Brazil's last emperor. In hilarious sequences that anticipated modern comic strips, he made great fun of the monarch.

Only once did his style face competition from another artist. From 1875 to 1879, Raphael Bordallo Pinheiro, a famous Portuguese caricaturist and sculptor, visited Brazil. His style—in which sharply outlined figures predominated— was highly original but never became widely influential.

Toward the end of the century, with the advent of new printing techniques such as the replacement of lithography by zincography and photogravure in

---

1. *Gazeta de Notícias, O País, O Jornal do Comércio,* and *O Jornal do Brasil.*
2. Herman Lima, *História da caricatura no Brasil* (Rio de Janeiro: José Olympio, 1963), 198.

Fig. 2. J. Carlos, cover of *Para Todos*, 16 May 1931.

the press, Agostini's influence was finally outstripped. His successful rival was another renowned Portuguese artist, Julião Machado, who had been living in France. Machado's style was more synthetic and elaborated, visibly influenced by Mucha's posters.[3] A noted bohemian, Machado became an instant celebrity and was soon active in the cultural life of Rio's intellectual elite. In collaboration with Olavo Bilac, the greatest *fin-de-siècle* Brazilian poet, he founded *A Bruxa*, a lavishly published magazine whose pages were brightened by pen-and-ink vignettes of devils and witches in silhouette. The drawings were lighter and the overall look of the pages was plainer than in Agostini's time. Then in 1898, under the influence of Machado's style, two other fine caricaturists of the turn of the century made their debut: K.Lixto (Calixto Cordeiro, 1877–1957) and Raul (Raul Pederneiras, 1874–1953).

3. Ibid., 970.

Many Rio magazines basically relied on cartoons, humor, and gossip. Soon after J. Carlos came on the scene, three magazines were started: *O Malho* (1902), *Fon-Fon!* (1907), and *A Careta* (1908). These publications were amazingly long-lived, as Brazilian magazines go: all lasted for more than fifty years. In each of them J. Carlos played an important role. He was the main illustrator of *A Careta* from 1908 to 1921, when he left the magazine to work as art director for all the publications of O Malho S.A. (fig. 1), the company that published such major illustrated magazines as *Para Todos* (fig. 2), *Illustração Brasileira,* and *O Tico-Tico* (fig. 4), the most prestigious children's magazine of the first half of our century. He left *O Malho* in 1931 and did freelance work until 1935. During this time he made some beautiful covers for *O Cruzeiro* and *Fon-Fon!* (for which he had already worked in 1907). From 1935 until his death, he was art director of *A Careta*.

José Carlos de Brito e Cunha (1884–1950) first published his work in the magazine *O Tagarela* on 23 August 1902, signing "J. Carlos." His style was still rather crude and unoriginal, imitating common caricatures printed on low-quality paper in which the figures talked to each other in profile. But by 1906 he had perfected his incomparable style, introducing different devices to the art of caricature.

> [S]pared the sfumato of the lithograph, and full of dynamic intensity, what J. Carlos brought to Brazilian caricature was something fresh and new, like the winds of change blowing into the city. His was a clean and rapid style, often moving from a subject's head to toe in one masterly serpentine stroke. His bold contours said everything, without resorting to tracing or shading.[4]

> J. Carlos used the white of a sheet of paper to his full advantage, creating a scene or situation with a minimum number of lines. He had a fine sense of graphic space and would make planes and cuts with cinematic flair. Furthermore, he was extremely economical in his use of the resources at his disposal, including color...; he preferred to be cut and dried.[5]

As early twentieth-century Brazilian caricature was largely political, the favorite target of cartoon artists was the president or the leading politician. Immortalized in J. Carlos's masterly cartoons, the figures of Brazil's not altogether glorious rulers are decidedly amiable. This is so because J. Carlos's touch is always light-hearted; even dictators—for whom the artist felt a deep-seated personal and political aversion—are turned into familiar, often smiling figures.

His true debut in the genre was his wonderful caricature of President Rodrigues Alves, "Au clair de la lune." White on a black background, its light-and-shadow effect had no precedent in Brazilian cartoon art (fig. 3). From then on, the short figure of the president became a fixture of magazine covers, popularizing the old country politician among urban readers.

But it was in President Hermes da Fonseca, a marshal of the Army whose government was marked by rebellions in various states, that J. Carlos found a worthy subject. Fonseca, nicknamed "Dudu" by the people and the press, was the butt of countless jokes that turned on his alleged attributes—incredible bad luck and utter stupidity. Before long there was another source of anecdotes

4. Ibid., 1075.
5. Irma Arestizábal, *J. Carlos—100 anos* (Rio de Janeiro: Fundação Nacional de Arte/Pontifícia Universidade Católica, 1984), 9.

Fig. 3. J. Carlos, "Au clair de la lune," caricature of President Rodrigues Alves, *O Malho*, 27 October 1906.

Fig. 4. J. Carlos, cover of *O Tico-Tico*, 16 March 1927.

about him. In the beginning of his term (1910–1914), the president became a widower, and he soon married again. His new wife was Nair de Teffé, thirty years his junior, who published caricatures under the pen name Rian. J. Carlos's best political caricatures deal with the marshal-president's courtship and wedding. In one of them, Fonseca is shown in full military uniform with a huge bridal veil on his head. Most of the cartoons allude to the president's famous stupidity. In fact, there was a special section of *A Careta* dedicated to such caricatures. One depicts Fonseca talking with his minister of foreign affairs, just back from the United States. The minister tells the president that America is an extraordinary country, and mentions as examples of its greatness the cities of New York, San Francisco, and Washington. To which Fonseca replies: "And did you visit Mr. Washington? I have a bust of him, you know."

Fig. 5. J. Carlos cartoon.

Before the presidential palace.

President Getúlio Vargas:

"Why the barbed wire fence?

All we need are the usual

banana peels." *A Careta*,

30 January 1937.

Even more of a target for J. Carlos's criticism was Getúlio Vargas, who ruled Brazil twice (1930–1945 and 1951–1954). J. Carlos's Vargas is, like Fonseca, a stubby, rounded figure, always smoking a cigar. But he is more than a man with a winning smile; above all, he is a wily, crafty, ambiguous politico, perilously perched between left and right, always managing to outmaneuver his opponents (fig. 5). J. Carlos transposed to the medium of caricature some of Vargas's famous maxims, such as "Not so friendly that they can't turn into enemies; not so unfriendly that they can't turn into friends." The cartoonist also exploited with much irony Vargas's *continuísmo*, his attachment to the presidency, his attempts to remain in power at all costs.

It was through J. Carlos's discerning eyes that Brazilian readers saw the century's two great wars. During World War One, caricatures of the Kaiser and his allies were superimposed on the most tragic battle scenes. These were always handled by J. Carlos in a restrained way, with a combination of taste and sensibility reminiscent of the definition of humor given by the English in the nineteenth century: wit with a touch of emotion. The cartoon that best expresses Brazilian sentiment of the time is one portraying Europe as an old woman with patches on her skirt, brushing crumbs from a table, telling a white kitten whose collar is the color of the Brazilian flag: "I can't give you the leftovers any more" (fig. 6).

Fig. 6. J. Carlos, "The Kitten

Lived on Crumbs," cover of

A Careta, 17 October 1914.

Fig. 7. J. Carlos, "Motherly
Punishment," cover of
A Careta, 12 June 1943.

Fig. 8. J. Carlos, "The
Untamable One," cover of
A Careta, 14 June 1919.

A remarkable rendering of the end of the Great War, a cartoon titled "The Untamable One"—in which the German soul, represented as a robust Teutonic matron tied to a tree trunk, intones: "In fifteen years, the revenge"—is evidence of an unsuspected prophetic gift (fig. 8). The same figure was to reappear during World War Two beside an Italian matron. They are shown dragging their spoiled brats, Hitler and Mussolini. The caption of the cartoon, titled "Motherly Punishment," is "The last battle will be fought at home" (fig. 7).

In World War Two, the mature artist was able to synthesize with masterly strokes the features of the major figures onstage: Roosevelt, Churchill, and Stalin on one side (fig. 9); Mussolini, Hitler, and Hirohito on the other (fig. 10). Hitler's sinister nature is hinted at in a cartoon showing him with a fortune teller. On being told that he will face troubled days, he orders: "Send the future to the firing squad!"

Though in both wars he sided with the Allies, J. Carlos always denounced the stupidity of war. His pity was reserved for women and children, the innocent victims. In a 1 January 1944 cartoon, a child asks his mother: "Why didn't Santa Claus come?" In another, the flags of the Allies at half-mast project their shadow on a mother with her child. In the caption the mother says, in verse: "Yes, my son, these flags will be joyful later. They will comfort us in our sorrow." A cover of *A Careta* shows how J. Carlos saw the bombing of Hiroshima.

Fig. 9. J. Carlos, cover of

A Careta, 17 March 1945.

Fig. 10. J. Carlos, cover of

A Careta, 3 June 1944.

Expressing his profound disillusionment with the stupidity of mankind, he contrasts the use of science for good—the discovery of penicillin—and for evil—the bomb (fig. 11).

All his life J. Carlos was averse to political commitments. But his work betrays a moderate liberal position. He is frankly critical of totalitarian regimes, right or left. At the end of Vargas's first term, he published a cartoon in which his conception of government is clearly stated: "Government: Men should be guided by light. The rod is for prodding cattle." After the war he gave Stalin the same treatment he had given Hitler. He dealt with events signaling the beginning of the cold war from an unabashedly pro-United States stance. But, in his cartoons of the 1910s, he had vigorously protested America's Mexican policies (fig. 12).

When J. Carlos began publishing his work, the archetypal artist, journalist, or poet was a bohemian, a man who spent his earnings in cafés, who treated his own life as a work of art. Even in dress, artists tried to distinguish themselves from common mortals. Until their dying days (in the mid 1950s) K.Lixto and Raul were flashy dressers who sported huge collars, cutaways in outrageous colors, and enormous hats. By contrast, J. Carlos was always sober and prudent (fig. 13). An exemplary family man, whose punctuality was quite uncommon in Brazil, he pioneered a new kind of professionalism in the press. He supported himself exclusively as a cartoonist and illustrator. He never worked for the government, as almost everyone of his class in Brazil did then at some time or other. Such independence required complete dedication. He worked long hours at the magazines he directed. Among the many curiosities found in

Fig. 11. J. Carlos, "Science. How Stupid Mankind Is," cover of *A Careta*, 29 September 1945.

Fig. 12. J. Carlos, "Mexico Is in for Some Punishment," cover of *A Careta*, 1 July 1916.

his personal files is a page on the bottom of which is written: "These draw-ings, 100 figures forming 50 groups, were drawn in a five-hour period on 21 May 1926 at the offices of *O Malho*. I made them with the sole intention of testing my own resistance, and I felt I could have gone on until nighttime." Then came the date, his signature, and those of two witnesses.[6]

It was in this determined spirit that in 1914, when he married Lavínia Taylor Neves, he promised her parents to give his wife and children the same standard of living expected of a man with a more conventional profession. He was as good as his word. That same year he bought a plot of land and buried a pencil in it in lieu of a foundation stone. Ten years later he finished building the house in which he was to live for the rest of his life and bring up five children. To this day his children keep, as a relic of their admirable father, a photograph album show-ing the construction and inauguration of the house. There J. Carlos wrote: "On the sharp point of a pencil this house was built."

6. Álvaro (Álvarus) Cotrim, *J. Carlos: Época, vida e obra* (Rio de Janeiro: Nova Fronteira, 1985), 69-70.

Fig. 13. J. Carlos at his

***A Careta* office, ca. 1920.**

Fig. 14. J. Carlos, cover of

***Fon-Fon!*, 22 December 1931.**

His children remember him as a companionable father, who loved taking them to the beach or to the movies to watch a Disney cartoon or a Laurel and Hardy comedy—in fact, J. Carlos made some excellent caricatures of Stan Laurel and Oliver Hardy (fig. 14). He was a simple man, without grand passions. His philosophy was based on elementary principles of honesty, determination, and love for his work, his family, and his country. Above all he loved Rio de Janeiro, the city in which he was born, in the pleasant Gávea district, and which he left rarely throughout his life.

He traveled abroad once, for a few days, on a courtesy trip to Argentina with other journalists. Otherwise he left Rio only twice, to go to São Paulo. The first time was during Hermes da Fonseca's administration, when he published his caricature of the president wearing a bridal veil. Fearing reprisals, J. Carlos fled. He took a room in a São Paulo boarding house, where he sat writing melancholy letters to the woman he had just married. His second trip to São Paulo was in 1914, to open an extremely successful exhibition of his work.[7]

It was perhaps his attachment to Rio, his unaffected lifestyle, and the fact that the world around him was his major source of inspiration that led J. Carlos to refuse Walt Disney's invitation to work with him in Hollywood. Disney came to Brazil in 1941 for the premiere of his feature-length animated cartoon *Fantasia*. Honors were showered on him. One event held for the occasion was an exhibition of works by the nation's best caricaturists, at the Brazilian Press Association. Caricaturist Antonio Gabriel Nássara, one of the show's organizers, recalled: "On the day of the exhibition, two of Disney's photographers began taking pictures of the caricatures. [W]hen they got to J. Carlos's work, I noticed they took their time, particularly with the parrot drawings."[8] The Ministry of Foreign Affairs gave a luncheon for the Americans and the Brazilian exhibitors, and Disney deliberately sat next to J. Carlos. It was then that the job offer was made and J. Carlos declined. Later he sent Disney a beautiful drawing of a stylized parrot, in the uniform worn by Brazilian soldiers in World War Two, hugging Donald Duck dressed as a U.S. Marine. J. Carlos's parrot inspired Disney to create Joe Carioca, a character that appeared for the first time in *Saludos Amigos* and became a comic-book Disney character in Brazil (fig. 15).

For nearly half a century, J. Carlos illustrated various aspects of Brazilian reality. It is endearing that this simple, honest, family man, who headed straight home after work, captured better than anyone else the delightful sensuality of *carioca* women. His female figures, which attained their most elaborate form in the 1920s and 1930s, are marked by a delicate, naive, but frank seductiveness. They dress lightly for Rio's hot summer days, displaying their shapely figures. And the joyous drawings by this sober-minded paterfamilias also comprise a visual history of women's fashion, including all sorts of details such as handkerchiefs, hats, gloves, a narrow waist, a Chanel suit, eye makeup, lipstick. We see girls on the beach (fig. 16), loving couples kissing, groups of beauties strolling together, or, brightening the bottom of a page, a charming flibbertigibbet reminiscent of Disney's Tinker Bell—a figure that haunted male fantasies at the time.

7. "The press—the *Diário Popular*, *O Estado de S. Paulo*, *Correio Paulistano*, *A Gazeta*, *Platéia*, and *Fanfulla*, among others—provided full coverage of the much awaited exhibition, including glimpses into the artist's personal life. The day of the opening, the weekly *A Cigarra* printed a snapshot of J. Carlos. As the show came to a close, editorials focused on the unusual fact that all of the works had been sold." Cotrim, *J. Carlos*, 63.

8. Arestizábal, *J. Carlos*, 53.

Fig. 15. J. Carlos, sketch for parrot drawing sent to Walt Disney. Luiz Carlos de Brito e Cunha collection.

Fig. 16. J. Carlos, vignette of bathing beauty.

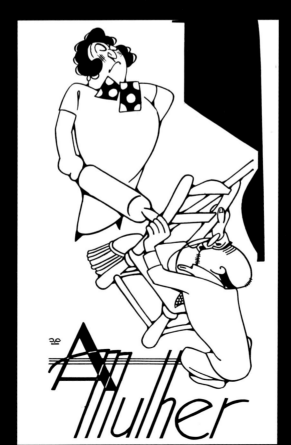

Fig. 17. J. Carlos, "The Woman" vignette.

Fig. 18. J. Carlos, vignette of

the Portuguese shopkeeper.

But ugly women—fat matrons and wiry old maids—are here too. There is the choosy lady trying to select fabric, driving the salesman mad (one of J. Carlos's favorite scenes), or quarreling with her wisp of a husband (fig. 17). There is the snobbish socialite in a bold party outfit; the grumpy maiden aunt; the brave suffragette. There are the three homely sisters spinning, each dreaming of a suitor who will never come.

J. Carlos was the ultimate portrayer of Brazilian "types." Of these, none was more frequent or captured with more mastery than the Portuguese shopkeeper (fig. 18). J. Carlos's Portuguese sports a huge, jet-black moustache, could use a shave, wears a sleeveless undershirt showing a hairy chest and back, speaks with a characteristic accent, and ogles certain female patrons. He also manifests the thickheadedness that Brazilians attribute to him—an instance of the universal ethnic stereotyping common among rival peoples. The Portuguese shopkeeper is often present in J. Carlos street scenes, in altercations in dry-goods stores, even in carnival merrymaking.

With the paternalism typical of the Brazilian elite, J. Carlos drew the black girl and the mulatto girl, the typical Brazilian house servant, sometimes with a roguish mulatto boyfriend who steals a kiss from her on a street corner (fig. 19). We see a drunkard hugging a lamppost or being carted off

O Cruzeiro
Revista Semanal Ilustrada

Fig. 19. J. Carlos, cover of

O Cruzeiro, 28 April 1934.

Fig. 20. J. Carlos, "The

Streetcar," cover of *A Careta*,

21 November 1942.

by a policeman; we see the bore, the speechmaker, the dandy. These types can be spotted in the great street scenes, on a streetcar (fig. 20), standing in an interminable line, at a political rally or a carnival ball.

Reviewing his work, one can observe not only changes in fashion but also changes—and resistance to change—in national customs. Among the street characters drawn by J. Carlos are the campaign hooligans common in the First Republic (1889–1930) (fig. 21). These were petty criminals who, in election years, were employed as canvassers. They belong in the same group as the evil-faced mugger and the stealthy burglar. Other associated types are street bums with their filthy rags and dirty beards, who panhandle or shoplift, often in groups of twos or threes. Though such characters are not usually seen as typical of J. Carlos's work, they are surely representative of part of the Brazilian

ANNO XXI

NUM. 1.034

o Malho

RIO DE JANEIRO, 8 DE JULHO DE 1922

FALSARIO

POLITICA

ALMAS GEMEAS

ELLA — *Quem é bom já nasce feito, não é, meu velho? Nós agora mandamos nessa joça.*

PREÇOS:

No Rio . . . $400
Nos Estados . $500

Fig. 21. J. Carlos, "Two of a Kind." She: "Great 'uns are born not made, eh? Now we're the bosses here."

Fig. 22. J. Carlos, "The Same

Theory," cover of *A Careta*,

27 September 1919.

Fig. 23. J. Carlos cartoon,

"The Hairdo," *A Careta*,

22 November 1941.

population. A cartoon example titled "The Same Theory" shows two thieves robbing a maximalist.[9] One of them justifies himself to his victim: "Hey, man, dontcha see? This is maximalism: everything belongs to everybody" (fig. 22).

Also representative of Brazilian popular culture are cartoons alluding to *jogo do bicho*, a numbers game where animals stand for numbers.[10] One published during World War Two is titled "Our Interests." A crowd mills around a lamppost. An onlooker asks: "What's all this crowd about? Bad news from Europe?" A man answers: "Europe, Schmeurope. I bet all I had on the pig, and the winner was the blasted cow." (The results of *jogo do bicho* are usually pasted on lampposts at busy streetcorners.)

Another archetypal Brazilian scene favored by J. Carlos is a citizen getting short shrift at a government agency. Witness the taxpayer patiently waiting at a counter where a sign says "Time Is Money," while inside the office functionaries listen, enraptured, to a young man singing and tapping his straw hat in accompaniment. The caption reads: "The office boy wrote a samba, and he's going to sing it tonight at the talent show."

9. Bolsheviks were known as maximalists in Brazil early in the century.

10. Favored by the poorer strata of the population, this illegal game has generally been tolerated by the authorities.

Fig. 24. J. Carlos, cover of

A Careta, 29 September 1917.

His domestic scenes are also charming. A fat housewife comes home with an extravagant new hairdo; her husband, her maid, even her dog are flabbergasted (fig. 23). A number of cartoons depict a family gathered around the radio or phonograph (fig. 24); others are humorous dialogues between an elderly husband and a wife much too young for him. There are adulterous couples in beautifully detailed interiors. The variety is immense, and the visual sophistication always unquestionable.

Flirtation is another theme favored by J. Carlos. One of his best cartoons of this kind is titled "Funeral Madrigal." A ladies' man approaches a beautiful woman who carries a bouquet pressed against her bosom and tells her: "I envy the fate of those flowers." To which she answers: "I'm taking them to Grandmother's grave."

J. Carlos is also the author of innumerable drawings of children (figs. 25 and 26): naughty kids and their mongrel dogs, groups of boys playing in the street, and good little children forming beautiful vignettes, with which he decorated his children's rooms. He wrote and illustrated a children's book, *Minha babá* (My nanny), a collection of stories with typically Brazilian themes. For the children's magazine *O Tico-Tico*, he produced texts and covers in addition to vignettes for titles and several comic strips.

On the covers of *Para Todos*, as well as in many illustrations he made for books, J. Carlos displayed a more serious side. These were extremely elaborate pictures, with delicate ornamentation around elongated female figures, reminiscent of Aubrey Beardsley's illustrations. The same perfectionism is apparent in other

Fig. 25. J. Carlos, vignette

of children.

Fig. 26. J. Carlos, vignette of children.

less ornate covers in which J. Carlos created unusual designs in the background, where a variety of patterns made up a sort of patchwork. Although he is above all a graphic artist whose work is meant to be printed, always reducible to the simplicity required by the electrotype, all his original drawings display more finish than is strictly necessary.

Brazilian cartoonists never gave much thought to their original drawings. Once cartoons were published, the drawings were discarded or hung on the wall for a while and then forgotten. Almost all of those in the possession of J. Carlos's family were made in the 1930s or later, and they were saved from destruction by chance: after the artist died, his children found nearly one thousand of them in a large suitcase at the *Careta* office. It was there that, on 29 September 1950, he collapsed onto his drawing board, struck by cerebral edema; he died three days later at the age of 66.

Christopher Finch has said that Norman Rockwell drew Americans as they liked to see themselves.[11] His delightful scenes are representations of the everyday lives of common folk, middle-class families, and occasionally the wealthy. This work makes up a vast portrait of United States society over many decades of the twentieth century. Like Rockwell, J. Carlos cast a benevolent, unsophisticated eye on the life of his own country. His perspective is generous and devoid of bitterness. He depicts Brazil with all its problems, where the poor can always bet on *jogo do bicho* and forget their troubles during carnival; the caricatures are never resentful, destructive, or unforgiving. In all his work there are marks of his honest, hard-working character, his belief in a better future for Brazil. J. Carlos was to Brazilians what Rockwell was to Americans: in his cartoons they saw themselves as happy, uncomplicated people.

During his long reign as Brazil's top cartoonist, J. Carlos had a few followers; for instance, Théo (Djalma Pires Ferreira, 1901–1980) and Oswaldo (Oswaldo Navarro, 1893–1970) were clearly influenced by him in their early careers. But none of these artists achieved the master's elaborate style nor his amazing multivalence.

In the late 1920s another powerful influence arose in Brazilian caricature: the Uruguayan artist Andrés Guevara. During the Artur Bernardes administration (1922–1926), he published the most violent caricatures of the period; at the

11. Christopher Finch, *Norman Rockwell: 322 Magazine Covers* (New York/London/Paris: Artabras Publishers, 1990).

Fig. 27. J. Carlos, cover of

Fon-Fon!, 10 October 1934.

time of World War Two, his work was intensely expressionistic. Guevara's style is clearly marked by the influence of modernist art, particularly cubism. Some of his more shocking productions are reminiscent of Picasso's *Guernica*. Younger cartoonists were much more influenced by him than by J. Carlos. Of Guevara's followers, the most notable is doubtlessly Antonio Gabriel Nássara, a talented cartoonist and songwriter. But from J. Carlos and the pre-Guevara generation, Nássara inherited a gentler brand of humor. Though his draftsmanship is stylized, full of sharp angles and broken lines, he is not as caustic as Guevara; his text, his humor, the treatment of his subjects, the use of verse in his captions, all these bring him closer to J. Carlos.

Be that as it may, since J. Carlos never started a school, and his followers made no effort to preserve the master's style, his work can never be confused with that of anyone else—as sometimes happens with Agostini's cartoons. J. Carlos is unique in Brazilian graphic arts. The graceful beauty of his women and the undeniable quality of his Brazilian scenes remain as the most perfect expression of an idyllic Brazil (fig. 27). □

Fig. 1. Raymundo Ottoni de Castro Maya at home in the Alto da Boa Vista, Rio de Janeiro, 1935.

The Legacy of Raymundo Ottoni de Castro Maya

By Carlos Martins

Translated by Elizabeth Wynn-Jones

Carlos Martins is director of the Castro Maya Museums. He also teaches exhibition design at the Catholic University of Rio de Janeiro. Recently he curated *Rio de Janeiro: The Overseas Capital*, an exhibition held in Lisbon as part of "Lisboa 94."

The Castro Maya Museums in Rio de Janeiro consist of the Chácara do Céu (Villa in the sky) in the district of Santa Teresa, and the Museu do Açude (Museum by the weir), high in the Alto da Boa Vista. Both were home to Raymundo Ottoni de Castro Maya (1894–1968) (fig. 1) and both are evocative of the commitments of their patron. Today these commitments are being honored, not only by the simple preservation of his memory but also by the continuation of his work: his dedicated conservationism and the dissemination and study, through his houses and collections, of the fruits of his cultural endeavors.

Castro Maya was born in Paris in 1894. He was the son of a well-regarded railway engineer, an educated man, personally invited by the emperor of Brazil, Dom Pedro II, to become tutor to his grandchildren (he did not accept!). Castro Maya's mother was heiress of an established, forward-thinking family, the Ottonis, from the state of Minas Gerais. At the age of eight Castro Maya came to Brazil, where he studied, eventually graduated in law, and became a successful industrialist.

In 1925 he and his brother Paulo established in Rio de Janeiro (then capital of the country) the Companhia Industrial Carioca, whose best-known product was Gordura de Côco Carioca (Carioca coconut fat). From its earliest stages, the company undertook to open new industrial areas and promote integration of diverse regions of the country. This was in keeping with the political interests of Paulo de Castro Maya who was active in the National Democratic Party, founded in 1926. At that time Brazilian industry was in its infancy and usually linked to the coffee trade, or in the case of Rio virtually restricted to the textile area. Thus a modern and dynamic industrial base initiating local production of items hitherto imported into the country, such as linseed oil (another Castro Maya product), signaled important economic and technological progress.

Castro Maya appears to have been truly interested in stimulating industrial expansion. Among his business enterprises was the Estamparia Colombo, which produced printed labels and packaging for a wide range of merchandise. Lithographic stones used by the Estamparia are some of the most curious items in the museums' archives, revealing a little of the history of Brazilian graphic design and advertising (figs. 2, 3, and 4): *art-nouveau* lines for certain ladies' beauty aids; stilted modernity for electrical appliances; whimsical and naive slogans for medicines and insecticides. The can for the now famous Gordura de Côco Carioca was produced by the Estamparia, and its visual appeal was strong, stressing the product's natural origins as well as the up-to-date convenience of canned goods (fig. 6).

Photographs by Hugo Leal.

Historical material courtesy of the Castro Maya Museums.

Figs. 2, 3, and 4. Lithographic stones used by Estamparia Colombo, Castro Maya's label and packaging business. Modern urban living brought into Brazilian homes a variety of new industrialized products, packaged to reflect their simplicity or their sophistication.

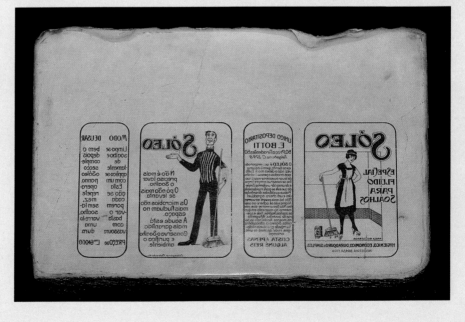

6. Lithographic stone for the label of Gordura de Côco Carioca, best-known product of the Companhia Industrial Carioca, founded by Castro Maya and his brother Paulo in 1925.

Castro Maya, the modern industrialist, was a hybrid of elements influencing the Brazilian elite: the European cross-pollinated with the North American. On one hand, he cultivated the refinement and a certain dandyism typical of the elegant figures of *fin-de-siècle* France; on the other, he subscribed to the new American ideal of businessman and sportsman. A founding member of several sports clubs, he was particularly keen on fishing, horseback riding, and water-skiing, all of which he practiced with a passion. He sponsored the first riding competitions and instituted a much-prized fisherman's trophy in Cachoeira Dourada in the faraway state of Goiás. Regattas and soccer matches at Rio's Fluminense Football Club received his patronage, and he was among the first to frequent what is now a well-known resort in the state of Rio but was then a simple fishing community, Arraial do Cabo.

Castro Maya was fascinated by all facets of a modern, urban, and cosmopolitan lifestyle. He collected automobiles (fig. 5), swam at Copacabana Beach, attended dinner parties at the Copacabana Palace Hotel, and went by ship numerous times to Europe. He visited the site of the Graf Zeppelin's landings in Rio during the 1930s (fig. 7), and later traveled in it.

He found himself in the position of sole heir to his family's diverse traditions after the early deaths of his two brothers. From Cristiano, he inherited a delight in living well; from Paulo, a constant awareness of the political relevance of his professional activities. His father's bequest was a sense of refinement and erudition, coupled with an ardent desire to collect works of art and participate in cultural life. Castro Maya's father, a bibliophile and collector, had been a founding member of the club Les Amis de L'Eau Fort (1871) and a member of the Cent Bibliophiles, both in Paris; he collected Roman coins, antiques, and nineteenth-century French painting. Allied to this love of art was Castro Maya's inclination, inherited from his mother's side of the family, toward matters of public interest. He zealously campaigned against urbanization of the site created by the removal of Castelo Hill in downtown Rio; he fought for preservation of the Carmelite convent, also downtown; he became involved in controversies over the price of electricity and the stability of the currency; and he battled

against the international beef cartels. He wrote occasional columns for newspapers in Rio and Belém, demonstrating an early understanding of the close relationship between industrial activity, urban life, and culture.

His enthusiasm for public affairs was especially visible in his work as coordinator of the Tijuca Forest project. In 1913 his father had bought a country house in the Alto da Boa Vista, neighboring the rain forest. Castro Maya had long cared for the surrounding jungle. Between 1943 and 1947, at the request of his friend Henrique Dodsworth, then mayor of Rio, he directed the remodeling and urbanization of the forest park. His salary was a symbolic annual cruzeiro—the lowest coin of the republic. At that time Getúlio Vargas was president, in what is known as the Estado Novo (New state) period, and Castro Maya was in a privileged position to bypass federal bureaucracy in order to complete his task (fig. 8). He often funded work himself, for later reimbursement.

With the end of the Estado Novo and changes in the political climate, Castro Maya was widely criticized and resigned his position. His achievements, however, are unquestionable: he restored buildings, among them the Mayrinck Chapel housing Cândido Portinari's oil-on-wood panels; he dredged rivers and lakes; he opened new roads and trails and refurbished those in disrepair; he installed rest areas, bars, restaurants, and other amenities for visitors. By extending his conservation practices as a neighboring home owner, he satisfied ecological, touristic, and artistic interests.

His house in the Alto da Boa Vista had been the principal building on a coffee plantation (one of the first in the environs of Rio) at the end of the eighteenth century. On inheriting the property, Castro Maya adhered to a new concept in Brazilian architecture, the neocolonial style, transforming the building into a comfortable home and a haven for his large art collection.

The neocolonial style emerged in Brazil in the first decade of this century, attempting to rescue a cultural identity from multiple eclectic influences on local architecture. Championed in São Paulo by Portuguese architect Ricardo Severo and in Rio by the doctor and art lover José Mariano Filho, the style did not stop with its invocation of the seventeenth and eighteenth centuries but sought lines simultaneously loyal to past and present. It gained supporters, firmly establishing itself at the international exhibition commemorating the centenary of Brazilian independence in 1922 in Rio, where various buildings in this mode met with the approval of critics and public alike. Castro Maya's friendship with Lúcio Costa, then renowned as a neocolonial architect, dates from this time.

The new style found a slightly unusual expression in the Açude house due to the use of original eighteenth- and nineteenth-century Portuguese wall and roof tiles acquired by Castro Maya in Portugal and from demolitions in the state of Maranhão. These elements suited the decoration the neocolonial style demanded and are still of special interest (figs. 9 and 10).

In this setting Castro Maya earned his reputation as one of Rio's most polished hosts. His parties were legendary: the circus was the theme of a party at which society welcomed the New Year in 1937. On another occasion, to the musical accompaniment of Debussy's *L'après-midi d'un faune* played by an orchestra hidden from sight, the attention of his guests was drawn to a spotlit golden sculpture of a man that, stirring slowly, revealed itself to be Serge Lifar, the famous ballet dancer. Sometimes guests at Castro Maya parties took part in living tableaux representing well-known European paintings.

At these festivities Castro Maya disclosed his playful and genteel side, supervising every detail. Invitations and menus were custom-produced by his architect and friend Wladimir Alves de Souza as well as by Brazilian artists; Castro Maya took great interest in the dishes to be served and the fancy dress costumes to be designed. More than just dinners, these occasions were snapshots of his lifestyle and its cultural ambiance.

Fig. 8. Brazilian president Getúlio Vargas at Castro Maya's Açude house, 1935.

Dedication to the arts led him to bring to Brazil the cultural initiatives he had encountered in France. In 1943 he founded the Sociedade dos Cem Bibliófilos do Brasil (Society of one hundred bibliophiles of Brazil), for the purpose of publishing luxury editions of Brazilian literature illustrated by the country's finest artists (fig. 11). Over a period of twenty-three years, twenty-three books were produced, some of which are landmarks in Brazilian publishing history (fig. 12). *Pelo sertão*, for example, with Afonso Arinos's stories and Lívio Abramo's illustrations, is considered a turning point in the São Paulo printmaker's career. Here Abramo's refined technique; his near abstractionism; and his use of themes from popular culture, which characterized his later work, are evident (fig. 13). Members of the Cem Bibliófilos pre-bought one hundred numbered copies, printed and handbound at a printing house acquired by Castro Maya for this purpose. Portinari and Di Cavalcanti were among the featured artists who illustrated both books and menus for the book-launching banquets. Original art work and print plates were then sold at society auctions, and often the winning bid was Castro Maya's. Thus, in addition to the books, the museums' archives contain sketches, proofs, rejected illustrations, menus, and even special editions interleaved with original illustrations.

Castro Maya's prestige as a sponsor of the arts grew as he commissioned these works. The collector became the patron, committed to Brazilian culture, helping local artists. From 1953 Rio artist Darel Valenca Lins was technical director

Fig. 9. On inheriting the Açude property, Castro Maya gradually added elements of the neocolonial style, such as the arches and the tiled eaves.

▶

Fig. 10. In keeping with the neocolonial style of the Açude house, Castro Maya incorporated Portuguese roof tiles and a Brazilian bell from colonial times.

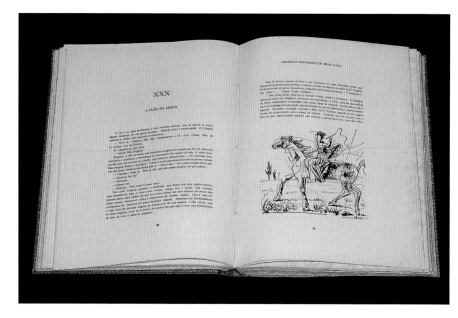

for the Cem Bibliófilos and also illustrated two of its publications. He became a favorite artist of Castro Maya's, and numerous examples of his art may be seen in the collection.

The celebrated Brazilian painter Cândido Portinari was, without a doubt, the artist who benefited most from Castro Maya's cultural largesse. He illustrated Cem Bibliófilos editions of Machado de Assis's *O alienista* and José Lins do Rego's *Menino de engenho*. He painted Castro Maya's portrait in 1943. Portinari's genius is represented in the Castro Maya collection through eleven canvases and hundreds of works on paper—noteworthy among them are twenty-one colored pencil drawings for the *Don Quixote* series, executed at a time when the artist was forbidden to use the oil paint that was slowly poisoning him. Additionally, Castro Maya sponsored several Portinari exhibitions (at the Automobile Club of Brazil and the Jockey Club, for example) and became a close friend of the painter and his family.

In 1948 Castro Maya founded the Amigos da Gravura (Friends of the print). Its objectives were to assist local artists and encourage respect for the print—whose techniques were well known but little appreciated—as an art form. For over ten years, this society produced an impressive collection of graphic works by famous as well as relatively unknown artists: Fayga Ostrower, Oswaldo Goeldi, Poty, and Darel, among them.

The same year, 1948, marked the founding of Rio's Museum of Modern Art, to which Castro Maya contributed and whose first president he became. He allied his personal desire to collect for his own enjoyment with a desire to take art to the people. In 1940 he had established the Sociedade dos Amigos do Rio de Janeiro (Society of friends of Rio de Janeiro), designed to assist the authorities in their preservation of the city's historical patrimony. Thus it can be seen that his concern with the promotion of a culturally sound environment in the city was constant.

As the capital of the country, Rio and its artistic activity were invariably linked to public institutions. In this context, where the state fulfilled the role of patron through scholarships and official commissions, it is that much more

Fig. 13. Between 1945 and 1948, Lívio Abramo worked on illustrations for *Pelo sertão*, short stories by Afonso Arinos.

remarkable that Castro Maya became such an outstanding patron of the arts and a principal figure in the life of the city. His leadership of the committee organizing celebrations for the four hundredth anniversary of the city of Rio (in 1964–1965) and his work with the Chamber of Historical and Artistic Patrimony at the Federal Council of Culture, to which he was nominated in 1967, are especially noteworthy.

Also to his credit are publications of works by Jean-Baptiste Debret (*Viagem pitoresca e histórica ao Brasil* [1954]) and by Gilberto Ferrez (*A mui leal e heróica cidade de São Sabastião do Rio de Janeiro* [1965]). His own book on the Tijuca rain forest, *A Floresta da Tijuca*, was published in 1967. However, he is remembered above all for the establishment of the Raymundo Ottoni de Castro Maya Foundation in 1963, to which he immediately donated the Açude house and which became heir to the Santa Teresa house after his death. Both properties were bequeathed complete with all the treasures they contained and were opened to the public as museums, the first in 1963 and the second in 1972.

The two residences and the collections in them form a living archive of the cultural life of their times. Decorative arts like Oporto ceramics that enhance the architecture and gardens; Luso-Brazilian wall tiles; and an outstanding group of popular ceramics from Northeast Brazil grace the Açude house. It is the first museum of its kind in Brazil, where numerous items of furniture, porcelain, silverwork, and other household furnishings are systematically exhibited (fig. 14).

The Chácara do Céu (fig. 15), built in 1957 after the designs of architect Wladimir Alves de Souza, is a physical manifestation of the essentially modern man Castro Maya was. In its spacious and airy rooms are found the collection of French paintings started by his father, ranging from eighteenth-century landscapes to abstract art; collections of paintings, prints, and watercolors by local and visiting foreign artists of the eighteenth and nineteenth centuries; works of modern Brazilian art; oriental *objets d'art;* and household furnishings and decoration. Currently all works on canvas and paper are kept and exhibited at the Chácara do Céu on a rotating basis. Castro Maya's dining room and library are maintained approximately as they were during his lifetime.

Fig. 14. Living room of Castro Maya's Açude house showing a seventeenth-century Netherlandian mantelpiece, from the period of Dutch colonization in Pernambuco.

In 1983 the Raymundo Ottoni de Castro Maya Foundation ceased, and its assets were transferred to the state. The museums came under the management of the National Foundation Pró-Memória, currently known as the Institute of Historic and Artistic National Patrimony, ensuring access by the public to the Castro Maya collection and thereby fulfilling the collector's greatest wish.

Balancing the contradictions of city and country, of erudite and popular, of public and private, Castro Maya's personality found its niche in Rio, a city marked by dichotomies of all kinds. If current world thinking condemns large cities as politically ungovernable, economically draining, and noxious to the physical and mental health of their inhabitants, it is because we have lost sight of urban living as the origin of all culture and the epitome of social interaction. Faced with the challenges of urban violence, vandalism, and neuroses, nothing could be more appropriate than to recall the example of responsible citizenship set by Castro Maya, who loved Rio for its qualities as a communally held cultural asset. □

Note
My thanks to Vera Beatriz Siqueira, curator at the Castro Maya Museums, for her assistance in compiling material for this article.

Fig. 15. View of the Chácara do Céu.

Fig. 1. Emil Bauch, panorama of Rio de Janeiro (central district), lithograph, ca. 1873. Collection of the Bank of the State of Rio de Janeiro. Photograph by Nelson Rivera. Here the city of Rio de Janeiro is seen from east to west at a moment when its limits had passed those reached by the Luso-Brazilian period. Expansion of the city began in the mid-sixteenth century, with the nucleus of Castelo Hill, soon followed by occupation of the coast between there and São Bento Hill, the latter situated before the large island in the right foreground of the etching. From this coastline an approximately symmetrical street plan extended over the plain defined by these two hills and the ones just beyond—Santo Antônio to the south and Conceição to the north—until they reached Santana Field, which appears as a large horizontal green area. The area west of the field began to be occupied in the early 1800s. The coast north of the São Bento and Conceição hills gave safe anchorage to ships. South of Castelo Hill is Glória Cove. The bordering green patch corresponds to the Passeio Público, a park dating from the end of the 1700s.

Rio de Janeiro, 1875–1945: The Shaping of a New Urban Order

By Rachel Sisson

Translated by Elizabeth A. Jackson

Rachel Sisson is an architect with her own firm in Rio de Janeiro. A lecturer and writer, she has received ten awards from the Architects' Institute of Brazil. Since 1984 she has been a member of the Historical and Geographical Institute of Rio de Janeiro.

This work discusses examples of changes affecting the urban space of Rio de Janeiro—some completed, others only suggested—all utilized, intentionally or not, to deliver different types and levels of propaganda.[1] For the ordering of urban space, historically relevant spatial landmarks, instrumental in facilitating legibility, were chosen as the unifying thread.[2]

The time frame—1875 to 1945—reflects the coincidence between the period of interest of the *Journal of Decorative and Propaganda Arts* and that which encompasses two significant and complementary periods for the theme in question: 1875 through 1900 and 1901 through 1945. In the first period, there was a growing impetus toward the achievement of clearly defined aims. In the second period, those aims materialized through successive and meaningful urban interventions.

In spatial terms the observations concentrate on the present-day center of the city, an area corresponding closely to that occupied by the Luso-Brazilian city in which, for the most part, the spatial landmarks and alterations mentioned throughout this text are located (fig. 1).[3]

At the turn of the eighteenth century, urban order in the Luso-Brazilian city was characterized by the dominance exercised simultaneously by two sets of landmarks. The first were religious, dispersed throughout the urban fabric. The second, of different types, had as its common denominator the representation of power—civil, religious, imperial, and military. Different from the spatial distribution of the first set, the second was concentrated in one location, Palace Square, which thus became the politico-administrative center, or "core," of Luso-Brazilian Rio de Janeiro.[4]

1. Propaganda here means "propagation of principles, ideas, knowledge, or theory." Aurélio Buarque de Holanda Ferreira, *Novo dicionário da língua portuguesa* (Rio de Janeiro: Editora Nova Fronteira, n.d.), 1146.

2. According to Kevin Lynch (*The Image of the City*, [Cambridge, Mass: MIT Press, 1960], 2–3), a city's "legibility" depends on the ease with which its parts can be recognized and organized into a coherent whole. A legible city would be one in which the districts, landmarks, limits, and roadways are easily identifiable and easily grouped into global structures. "Spatial landmarks" are spatial references demarcating the daily urban life of the population. The term "core," in turn, relates to strategic foci where the spectator may enter. They are formed by concentrations of landmarks and/or by intersecting roadways, irradiating their influence over spatial units of different scales for which they act as symbols.

3. "Luso-Brazilian" refers to the period of politico-administrative association with Portugal, ending with independence in 1822. Founded in 1565 in a fortified stronghold at the entrance to Guanabara Bay, the city was transferred in 1567 to Castelo Hill, farther inside the bay, where its urban life began.

4. From the de facto point of view, the colonial phase ended in 1808 with the arrival in Rio of the Portuguese court, in flight from Napoleon's troops. Legally, it ended in 1815 when Brazil became part of the United Kingdom of Portugal, Brazil, and the Algarves, with its seat in Rio, which was to be the nation's capital after independence in 1822. The imperial period begins in 1822 and ends in 1889 with the proclamation of the republic.

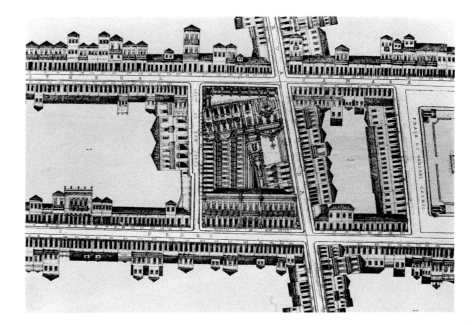

After 1808 this arrangement was affected by the implantation of diversified spatial landmarks: ministries; legislative and judicial institutions; public administration offices; foreign legations; commercial, industrial, and educational establishments; hospitals; cultural entities; and so on (fig. 2). Secular landmarks became prevalent, distinguishable from earlier ones both stylistically and structurally.

In the new landmarks the baroque style was substituted by neoclassicism, officially introduced in 1816 by the French Artistic Mission led by Grandjean de Montigny[5] and, paradoxically, consisting of exiled Bonapartists. As for spatial structure, in the case of religious buildings the longitudinal axis, leading always to the sacred, was omitted in the most imposing examples in favor of a centrally located entrance serving the distribution of wings and levels, a transition representing secularization accompanied by semantic dilution. If in the baroque certain forms always denoted the same religious function, in the neoclassical a single morphological type served a variety of functions.

The decline of religious landmarks accompanied worsening friction between church and state, the latter allied with the lay brotherhoods, while reformist bishops, opposed to nobility and supported by the Holy See, sought to substitute Roman Catholicism for traditional Luso-Brazilian Catholicism.[6] The reduced prestige of the clergy, the extinction of religious orders, and even the use of convents to quarter troops were factors in conflicts assuaged only with the coming of the republic and the separation of church and state.

Finally, spatial distribution of the newly constructed landmarks led to the formation of a new politico-administrative center in the imperial period, much as Palace Square had been in the Luso-Brazilian period. The new core appeared in Santana Field (fig. 3), eastern border of the city until the beginning of the

5. The architect Grandjean de Montigny was also well-known in Rio de Janeiro as a landscape designer and urbanist.

6. According to R. Azzi (*O episcopado no Brasil frente ao catolicismo popular* [Petrópolis: Editora Vozes, 1971], 9), traditional Catholicism, principally in the Luso-Brazilian period, was "lay, medieval, social, and family-oriented," while the Roman Catholicism that followed was "clerical, Tridentine, individual, and sacramental."

Fig. 3. Aerial view of Santana Field, 1930s. Photograph from the Oliveira Reis archive. Santana Field preserved many of the spatial characteristics of the period in which it was the center of the imperial city. In the upper left corner the main train station is visible and, continuing clockwise, the Army General Headquarters on the north side of the field. On the east side are the Rivadávia Correa School and the neoclassical City Hall. The tower of the Fire Department Headquarters is the vertical reference point on the south side. On the west the large building with a patio is the former Mint, preceded by the building that housed the imperial senate. The upper portion of the photograph shows port installations created in the early 1900s as well as the building for the newspaper *A Noite*, located at the extreme north of Central Avenue.

nineteenth century, where there was still much available space. The location of the core contributed to the westerly direction taken by the expansion of the city, starting in the area polarized by Palace Square, leading to Santana Field, and from there on to the imperial palace in the Quinta da Boa Vista still further west in São Cristóvão, which soon became an aristocratic district.

The east-west axis, strengthened by the privileged western route,[7] was tangential to Santana Field and opened access to the entities locating there—the Army General Headquarters, the Imperial Museum, City Hall, the Mint, and the Dom Pedro II Railroad Station, inaugurated in 1858. The urbanization of Santana Field was completed with the inauguration in 1880 of Anglo-Chinese-style gardens designed by the French botanist Auguste François Marie Glaziou.[8]

The introduction of improvements in urban and rail transportation, sanitary drainage, and public lighting dates from the mid-nineteenth century (fig. 4). Also, beginning in 1850, there was intensified economic progress—accompanied by the emergence of the commercial class—and debates on topics such as abolition and the republic.

7. The route was formed by successive segments of several roads. The segment in the center of the city would only materialize in the middle of the following century with the construction of a monumental road axis.

8. In the case of Santana Field, the introduction of the picturesque was one more case of the utilization of European models in the formation of locally significant spaces, since it maintained the essential unity of the site in terms of the taste for escape peculiar to romanticism, whether in time—in the direction of an architectonic classicism—or in space—in the oriental origins of the style. The picturesque had already been introduced by Glaziou in the Passeio Público, a park in the French style from the late 1700s by Mestre Valentim, a local artist. The original layout is still witnessed by the distribution of decorative elements such as pyramids and fountains, fortunately not eliminated as were various full-grown trees obstructing the new composition. Besides these notable examples one must also cite, in the landscaping of Rio de Janeiro in the 1800s, the important tradition of gardens in suburban residences, as well as the reforestation, exceptional for the period, of one hundred thousand trees planted on the hillsides denuded by coffee plantations.

Fig. 4. Glória Square and Hill. Photograph from *Kosmos*, July 1905. The church of Nossa Senhora da Glória, located on Glória Hill, dominated the cove of the same name where fishermen anchored their boats. Beginning in the mid 1800s its setting was violently altered by the construction of a sewage treatment plant, endowed with an enormous chimney, a symbol of progress for many decades. Rio was one of the first world capitals to have this type of service. The plant was inaugurated by Emperor Pedro II, who was always interested in technological conquests and innovations.

Despite this, living conditions in the city were adverse because of population growth[9] and epidemics of smallpox, cholera, and yellow fever. Added to these factors after the 1870s were political, financial, and social crises generated by the Paraguayan War (1865–1870), leading to a growing impatience with the vestiges of the Luso-Brazilian city, even more unacceptable when compared to the favorable aspects of European cities.

The question of modernization became a priority for the nation, an attitude that in 1874 led the emperor to lay the cornerstone of a school building located on Santana Field, one of several built in the 1870s under government initiative (fig. 5).[10] From this also originated, in the same year, the appointment of the Commission for City Improvements, a body designated by the imperial government to establish directives relative to sanitation, circulation, and beautification of the national capital.

Concentrating attention on less populous suburbs, including São Cristóvão where the imperial family resided in the Palace of the Quinta da Boa Vista, their first report in January 1875 was complemented by another in 1876 containing proposals for the commercial area of the city. Developed by three well-known engineers, the reports demonstrated that the government was aware of the need to attack city problems in an integrated way, based on a technically reliable plan developed in advance. If for lack of funds the initiative was not immediately acted upon, it nevertheless formed the basis for urban renewal undertaken in the early twentieth century, carried out largely by the chief engineer of the earlier Commission for City Improvements, Francisco Pereira Passos.

Already positivism reigned in the realm of ideas, given its great influence principally among engineers and the military, providing a response acceptable to an intellectual elite on questions of a religious, socio-political, and scientific nature. In 1876 the Positivist Society, whose objective was to disseminate the thought of Auguste Comte, was founded in Rio de Janeiro. It was later to be called the Positivist Apostolate of Brazil.

Positivism was the source of an extremely significant spatial landmark for the time, the Rio de Janeiro Temple of Humanity—constructed in Glória, a district south of the central area of the city—whose cornerstone was laid in 1890. It was inaugurated on 1 January 1897, a day consecrated to Humanity. The eclectic architecture of the building corresponds to the philosophical eclecticism inherent in positivism[11] and is also compatible with stylistic preferences of the end of the century (fig. 6).

Fig. 5. The São José School, 1871. Photograph from the Oliveira Reis archive. An example of Portuguese neo-Gothic style, in its main structure, above the eight doors of the ground floor, four niches sheltered statues of the evangelists, and three dials told the time, the day, and the moon phase. After 1897 the building was occupied by the municipal council. In the early 1900s Floriano Square was created directly in front of the building, which became part of the republican city center. Later demolished, in its place a new seat for the municipal council was constructed.

9. The population of the city grew from approximately 50,000 in 1808 to 112,695 in 1821; 266,466 in 1849; 552,651 in 1890; and 811,443 in 1906 (Ferreira da Rosa, *Rio de Janeiro em 1922–1924*, Prefeitura da Cidade do Rio de Janeiro, Coleção Memória do Rio, no. 3, 1979).

10. At the end of the Paraguayan War, a subscription campaign was begun to build a statue of the emperor cast out of bronze artillery taken from the enemy, just as bas-reliefs of the Vendôme column had been cast with metal from German and Austrian cannons captured by the French at Austerlitz. Emperor Pedro II preferred, however, that the funds collected be applied to public education. The desire for modernization was symbolized in the facades of several of these schools, where clock dials indicated the banishment of traditional Iberian time—magical and poetic—in favor of chronological Anglo-Saxon time, governed by activist values derived from Calvinist mysticism and the industrial revolution. See Gilberto Freyre, *O brasileiro entre outros hispanos* (Rio de Janeiro: José Olympio, 1975).

11. Eclecticism in philosophy is the "method that consists of uniting theses of different systems, whether simply juxtaposing them or organizing them into a superior, new, and creative unity." Ferreira, *Novo dicionário*, 497. In architecture, eclecticism employed the most diverse historical styles, even combined in a single building.

Fig. 6. Temple of Humanity, Rio de Janeiro. Photograph by Maurício Prochnik, 1994. One of the most important examples of eclectic architecture in Rio de Janeiro, the Temple of Humanity has inscribed on its frontal frieze the sacred formula of positivism: "Love as a principle and order as a basis; progress as the goal." In 1921 the portal was reconstructed under the architect Cipriano de Lemos. Consonant with positivism's sympathy for technical progress, the architect employed a very advanced structural solution for the period.

The architectonic plan for the Temple of Humanity is similar to the longitudinal plan of churches, differing only in the fixed number of lateral chapels—fourteen—always for the same figures, the thirteen leaders of human evolution, with the last chapel dedicated to women.[12]

From Islam Comte adopted the Mecca principle, requiring that temples of the Great Being have their longitudinal axis oriented in the direction of Paris, this city to be substituted by Constantinople if positivism should prevail. In Rio, because of the proportions of the site, it was not possible to follow this precept.

Since there were no instructions as to the principal and lateral facades, the model for the former, in the proportion one to three, was that of the Panthéon in Paris, a building Comte aspired to have as the seat of his new cult. For the laterals, a combination of stone and exposed brick recalls materials used in buildings of the period for industry or urban services.

Positivism made a fundamental contribution to the proclamation of the republic in 1889. Hence its political slogan, "Order and Progress," was inscribed on the Brazilian flag, part of a search for symbols promoting acceptance of the new regime by the populace.

Bases for the image of progress and modernization sought by the recently inaugurated republican regime were found in urban spaces created, and in large part completed, during the government of President Rodrigues Alves (1902–1906), whose reforms were extensively praised (and also criticized) in the media of the period. Made possible because of improvement in the national economy, this joint project of federal and municipal governments built on those same plans of 1875–1876 of which the recently appointed Mayor Francisco Pereira Passos had been one of the authors, other suggestions dating from the 1800s also being incorporated.

The renewal of Paris undertaken by Haussman under Napoleon III is often cited as a model for the renewal carried out in Rio. Other contributing factors would be the great influence of France on the Brazilian elite, and the fact that the Parisian renewal had been witnessed by Passos during a European tour in 1857. The objectives of sanitation, beautification, and circulation were in both cases answered by the opening of great avenues, the straightening and widening of streets, and extensive demolition of anti-hygienic residences concentrated in areas densely occupied by a low income population (although thereby creating a serious housing crisis).

The renewal in Rio fulfilled important longstanding local needs. For example, along the northern coast basic port facilities connected to warehouses and rail lines were constructed on landfills begun in the previous century. These followed the direction of Rodrigues Alves Avenue, built during the same period, also serving as an access to suburbs north of the city. In the city's southern zone—preferred by the elite—access was facilitated by the opening of Beira-Mar Avenue, more than five kilometers long, a landfill project initiated at the end of the 1800s and continued by the municipality in 1903.

12. The thirteen leaders are: Moses (initial theocracy), Homer (ancient poetry), Aristotle (ancient philosophy), Archimedes (ancient science), Caesar (military civilization), St. Paul (Catholicism), Charlemagne (feudalism), Dante (modern epic poetry), Guttenberg (modern industry), Shakespeare (modern drama), Descartes (modern philosophy), Frederick of Prussia (modern politics), and Bichat (modern science).

Since the dense occupation of the center of the city made the connection between these radial arteries difficult, and consequently the north-south connection of the city as well, it was necessary to promote a juncture by means of a diagonal: Central Avenue (now Rio Branco Avenue), whose opening contributed to the elimination of many remaining traces of the old Luso-Brazilian city.

The placement of imposing landmarks at the terminus of great avenues for effect, as in Paris, was not imitated literally on Central Avenue, still Rio's principal artery. The landmarks demarcating its extremities were much more modest, however not less significant. At the extreme north of the avenue, a statue was raised of the principal pioneer of Brazilian industrialization in the 1800s, the viscount of Mauá, standing on a Doric column facing the port—recalling the Nelson monument in Trafalgar Square. To the south an obelisk was erected, donated by the construction firm of Januzzi and Irmãos, who built the largest number of buildings on Central Avenue. These landmarks possessed, therefore, morphologic affinities in their verticalness and thematic ones in their homage to the commercial class.

The obelisk, in turn, was not an isolated element. It was part of the recently created politico-administrative center of the republic, set at the extreme south of Central Avenue where it intersected with Beira-Mar. In this republican core, as in those formed earlier, legislative, judicial, cultural, and social landmarks representative of the new regime were concentrated: the Federal Senate, the Federal Supreme Court, the Municipal Theater, the National Library, the National Museum of Fine Arts, and the Military Club, to which eventually the Naval, Jockey, and Derby Clubs were added (fig. 7).

These buildings encircled Floriano Square (fig. 8), which acquired its current rectangular shape only in 1913 with the demolition of the eighteenth-century convent Nossa Senhora da Ajuda. Notwithstanding, the republican center did not lack religious connotations. They were present in positivist mottoes and symbols embedded in the monument to Floriano Peixoto, the "iron marshal," and the second president of the republic from 1891 to 1894.[13]

Besides the French taste still dominant in the architecture of buildings lining Floriano Square, American influence on the republican center became evident in 1906, following the Third Pan-American Conference. The name of the Senate building was changed to Monroe Palace[14] in honor of James Monroe, fifth president of the United States and author of the famous doctrine "America for the Americans," to which Brazil was the first nation on the continent to adhere. This influence intensified with the wide dissemination of American customs and values through the cinema. In the twenties movie theaters were concentrated on Floriano Square, on the previous site of the Ajuda Convent, forming the district known as Cinelândia.

13. When he was thus honored, Floriano Peixoto had already adopted measures that would cause Rio to lose its position as federal capital, since in accordance with the constitution he had sent a commission to the central plateau charged with delimiting the perimeter within which a new capital would be constructed. It is precisely in this new capital, Brasília, that one can identify the influence of a positivist rationalism in the monumental axis: for its affinity on an urbanistic scale with spatial-temporal correlations on an architectonic scale in the Temple of Humanity.

14. The demolition of Monroe Palace, authorized by official order in 1979, was one of the factors contributing to the weakening of Rio's republican core, whose existence—along with those corresponding to the Luso-Brazilian and imperial periods—has not yet been recognized by any governing body.

Fig. 8. Floriano Square.

Photograph from *Revista da*

***Semana*, 9 March 1929.**

Characterized by well-planned

spatial organization, the square

was diluted by successive and

unsatisfactory alterations. The

Municipal Council Building to

the right, in Louis XVI style,

replaced the former neo-Gothic

seat. The group of buildings

between the Monroe Palace

and the council became known

as Cinelândia because of all

the cinemas located on their

ground floors.

Neoclassicism, the symbolic style of the imperial period, had gradually been abandoned after 1889 in favor of eclecticism. While eclecticism persisted until the 1930s (fig. 9), differing stylistic preferences of variable duration and depth were utilized as dressing for other spatial landmarks, among them *art nouveau*, art deco, neocolonial, architectonic modernism, and even the modern classicism favored by authoritarian regimes.

In the early 1900s, a taste for *art nouveau* appeared in the graphic arts and in decorative elements such as tiles and graceful iron railings used in the abundant vernacular architecture, generally produced by unschooled craftsmen (fig. 10). They were often censured by the erudite for their stylistic transgressions, not entirely absent, in fact, from the more pompous academic buildings.

Art deco, introduced in the 1920s, would make a notable contribution, principally in the 1930s, in the general composition and decoration of new residential buildings serving the middle class (fig. 11). Considered models, these buildings were also technically innovative for their generalized use of reinforced concrete.

Despite the intensive use of art deco in this widespread type of construction, the principal landmark of the style in Rio is the thirty-meter-high statue of Christ the Redeemer, crowning the seven hundred meters of Corcovado Peak.[15] Erected at the end of the 1920s and inaugurated in 1931, the Christ is a monument to the Sacred Heart of Jesus, a devotion then promulgated in Europe and introduced in Brazil with the aim of strengthening Roman

15. The masterly implantation and proportions of the monument are due to local architect Heitor da Silva Costa. The sculptural project was designed with great sensitivity and expertise by the Frenchman Paul Landowski.

Fig. 9. State of São Paulo pavilion, National Exposition of 1908. From *Kosmos*, July 1908. Photograph by Maurício Prochnik. Commemorating the centennial of the opening of ports to friendly naitons, the exposition highlighted the nation's progress in industry and agriculture as well as the variety of its natural resources. Each state erected a pavilion, many of which, like that of São Paulo, carried eclecticism to delirious heights.

Catholicism. Attributes of the redemption—the cross and the globe—are expressed in the monument, the former through the position of the image and the latter, symbolically, through the city at its feet.[16]

Art deco was contemporary with modernism, a movement that burst on the scene in São Paulo through the intellectual and elite promoters of the Week of Modern Art in 1922. Mixing formal innovations from European art of the period with an interest in Brazilian themes, this modernism was conservative to a certain degree because it employed only traditional means of artistic expression, such as literature, painting, and music.

At that time in Brazil there was a growing preference for neocolonial architecture, common to Latin American countries. Its academicism diverged from the reigning academicism in a search for models from the continent's past. Paradoxically, some authentic examples would be rebuilt to satisfy the taste for neocolonial patterns.

Use of the neocolonial style in school buildings was consciously part of a nationalist orientation in the education of coming generations (fig. 12). Use of the mission neocolonial style, associating Hispanic forms then in vogue with Brazilian colonial forms, was symptomatic of a politics of approximation with other countries on the continent. Another important direction of this interest in the architectonic production of the Luso-Brazilian past was in preservation, leading to the creation by the federal government in 1934 of a pioneering entity in this area, the Inspectorship of National Monuments, connected to the National History Museum.

In terms of urban development, alterations following the urban renewal plan of the first decade of the century were complementary to the expansion and growing complexity of the city, among them the demolition of Castelo Hill as well as the use of material from it for the construction of Paris Square, along Beira-Mar Avenue. Its gardens, perfectly adapted to the site with their parterres and luminous fountains, signified a momentary return to French taste and *le culte de l'axe* (fig. 13).[17]

The first master plan for the city dates from the end of the 1920s, developed by a group of specialists headed by the French urbanist Alfred Agache and published in 1930.[18] Agache thought that Rio lacked monumental attributes compatible with its position as national capital. This was due, in his opinion, to the demolition of scenic areas at the beginning of the century as well as to the city's uninteresting appearance (with the exception of two old churches) and the dispersed placement of its governmental entities and ministries.

Despite other appreciable contributions, Agache used this evaluation as a basis for two proposals fortunately not carried out, both utilizing future landfills contiguous to the center. One was to group all the ministries in a single location, and the other, nicknamed the "Entrance to Brazil," proposed the creation of a ceremonial entrance to the shore, with monumental columns demarcating access to important official landmarks (fig. 14).

16. Paul Zucker, *Town and Square: From the Agora to the Village Green* (New York: Columbia University Press, 1959), 234.

17. The French "taste for the axis" was rounded in this case to accompany the gracious curve of Glória Cove.

18. *Cidade do Rio de Janeiro: extensão-remodelação-embelezamento* (Paris: Foyer Brésilien, 1930).

Fig. 10. Vernacular architecture, Sete de Setembro Street, ca. 1915. In some parts of the center of Rio de Janeiro, as well as in other areas of the city, it is still possible to find many examples of vernacular architecture from the beginning of the century, whose forms and colors create a typically *carioca* atmosphere. The city's spatial identity in part depends on the interaction between these groups of lesser buildings and the monumentality of certain spatial landmarks.

Fig. 11. Itahy Building, Nossa Senhora de Copacabana Avenue, 1932. Photograph by Maurício Prochnik. The Itahy's main entrance, flanked by fluting in majolica, has iron doors whose composition was inspired by vegetable forms.

Fig. 12. Angelo Bruhns and José Cortez, Normal School. From *Revista da Semana*, 24 November 1928. Photograph by Maurício Prochnik. The neo-colonial style was required in an architectural competition for the Normal School, a teacher training program. Through this style the school intended to give a nationalist stamp to its training of future teachers. Its monumental appearance is due to its proportions and to the use of details inspired by some of the most imposing Luso-Brazilian architectonic examples.

Fig. 13. Paris Square, ca. 1940. Oliveira Reis archive. The gardens of Paris Square were built along Beira-Mar Avenue in the late 1920s. The flat beds, reflecting pools, and fountains have much in common with French taste of the 1700s. The photograph also shows buildings concentrated on Floriano Square, the recently opened esplanade of Castelo Hill and, in the distance, the *A Noite* building.

In its own way, Rio had already responded to these two requirements. Floriano Square—the republican core—had provided a concentration of official landmarks for the previous twenty years. Fitting naturally into daily urban reality, they were stripped of the monumentality and inaccessibility intimidating to the common man. Agache's grouping of ministries would have been disadvantageous; and, given the impossibility of keeping up with constant changes in governmental organization in terms of built spaces, its loss of validity would have been fatal. Removed from Agache's literal and conventional proposal but with deep local roots, the second requirement was already under way in the monument to Christ the Redeemer, ruling the entrance to the bay and access to the national capital (fig. 15).

Another illustrious professional, Le Corbusier, arrived in Rio in 1929, giving lectures and presenting suggestions for the city before an enthusiastic public (fig. 16). That visit was made at the dawn in 1930 of another phase in the political, economic, and cultural life of the nation—the Vargas era, whose final and most authoritarian stage was known as the Estado Novo (New state) (1937–1945) (fig. 17).

This was a period of notable vitality for architecture and urbanism (fig. 18). The demand for new types of buildings and for a new monumentality led the government to open competitions (although the winners were not always allowed to proceed with their projects!).

While ideological conflicts culminated in rebellions on the left and the right, in 1935 and 1938, professional accomplishment seemed to be the driving force of disputes between modernists and conservatives. The clearest difference between the two groups could be seen in the architectonic styles and cultural politics of the simultaneously constructed buildings of the Ministry of Education and Public Health (1936–1943) and the Ministry of Finance (1939–1943).

The former, based on suggestions of Le Corbusier and in response to his principles, had its final project designed by his followers, the architects

Lúcio Costa, Carlos Leão, Jorge Moreira, Oscar Niemeyer, Affonso Eduardo Reidy, and Ernani Vasconcellos. Freely distributed, the building spaces did not conform to the pattern of compact structures with a common central area proposed for the Castelo Esplanade. Such a disposition facilitated the use of areas at sidewalk level for the construction of gardens which, like that of the Ministry of Education's terrace, were designed by Roberto Burle Marx, a great Brazilian star of the environmental arts, known worldwide for the originality, artistry, and breadth of his work.

At the same time, the nearby Ministry of Finance harmonized perfectly with the modern classicism favored by contemporary authoritarian regimes. Its massive

Fig. 16. Le Corbusier, plan for Rio, 1929. Photograph from *Arquitetura Revista*, no. 5, 1987: 6–7. While visiting Rio, Le Corbusier showed much concern over its future development. To harmonize the city with its natural beauty, he conceived of a monumental structure combining roadways and residential units. This structure, which would have traversed the city linearly, was fortunately not executed; while intending to avoid certain problems, it would surely have created others.

Fig. 17. *Gaúchos* by the obelisk, 1930. Photograph from the Getúlio Vargas Foundation/ Center for Research and Documentation of Brazilian Contemporary History/Oswaldo Aranha archive. When Getúlio Vargas arrived in Rio, heading the victorious revolution of 1930, the *gaúcho* horsemen in his guard hitched their horses to the obelisk located in the republican center of the city. That action, along with its

Fig. 18. Aerial view of Rio, 1930s. National History Museum. Photograph by Maurício Prochnik. Rio Branco Avenue (formerly Central Avenue) and the center of the city can be seen from north to south. On the axis of the avenue is the monument to the viscount of Mauá. In the left foreground lies São Bento Hill and the towers of the São Bento monastery church. Mauá Square comes next, followed by the start of the docks and Rodrigues Alves Avenue. The *A Noite* building of 1931 was then the tallest in South America. Located on its upper floors, National Radio transmitted programs throughout the country. In the background the characteristic profile of Sugarloaf Mountain, one of the city's trademarks, is prominent.

volume, as well as that of other neighboring buildings, provided a favorable framework for the Ministry of Education, whose spatial solution did not offer—or even pretend to offer—an acceptable model of usage for the Castelo Esplanade as a whole.

In 1936 Le Corbusier returned to Rio as consultant for the Ministry of Education and the Federal University projects. For the latter, architect Marcelo Piacentini, highly regarded by Mussolini, had also been in Rio the previous year as consultant. Many projects were designed for the university city, one by Le Corbusier and another by Piacentini, sent from Italy in 1938. For several years many suggestions, some reasonable and some bizarre, were presented for these projects, which had already been discussed in the Agache plan and even earlier. Despite this discussion, final agreement was not reached until the end of the 1940s.

Marking the end of the second period under consideration—from 1901 to 1945—an extensive project in the center would be built to honor the leader of the republic. This was President Vargas Avenue, begun in 1941 and inaugurated on 7 September 1944 (figs. 19 and 20). It commemorated one hundred twenty-two years of independence, on the eve of national and international events that would exert enormous influence on the future of the nation and the city: the end of World War Two in 1945 and, in October of the same year, the ouster of the recently honored President Vargas.

Thus we see that, throughout the nineteenth century, the growth of Rio de Janeiro and the dissemination of new spatial landmarks contributed to the dilution of the urban order[19] dominant during the transition from the 1700s to the 1800s. New landmarks, like earlier ones, followed European models, though they relied on local values to unite type and distribution. Besides expressing the centrality of the city, they showed a desire for modernization

19. Order here is understood as a disposition of parts subordinated to a useful, agreeable, or harmonious principle.

through the details and functions of their construction, also evident in governmental plans for urban renewal announced in 1875 and 1876.

Only at the start of the twentieth century, under the republic, were these renewal plans enacted. Based on earlier plans, drawn up during the imperial period, they transformed the seat of city government into an efficient symbol of modernity and progress, serving the propaganda of the new regime. With this renewal landmarks and spaces arose, articulated with preexisting ones, reinforcing the urban order of the beginning of the century to which many other landmarks and urbanistic and landscape alterations contributed into the 1940s.

Through all these changes, the constant European influence raises a question about the degree to which local production should be considered culturally dependent. The answer to this question is mixed. Given that the use of European patterns and models is undeniable, it is also evident that their introduction into the city's space responded to a specific and original scheme, favored by frequent and masterly incorporation of elements present in the city's natural setting.

The result was an urban space of notable legibility and environmental quality. This was later affected by the removal and demolition of spatial landmarks as well as by structures interfering with their field of vision, utilized—intentionally or not—to deliver other types and levels of propaganda whose analysis transcends the scope of this work. □

Figs. 19 and 20. The opening of President Vargas Avenue, 1944. Oliveira Reis archive. Creating this avenue caused the demolition of a large number of buildings, mostly corresponding to a very early urban tract. The photographs show a stretch between Santana Field and the monumental Church of Nossa Senhora da Candelária, spared by a bifurcation at the extreme eastern end of the avenue. The tallest buildings are those then constructed along Rio Branco Avenue (formerly Central Avenue) or nearby, a tendency that would spread.

Roberto Burle Marx: The Last Interview

By Conrad Hamerman

Conrad Hamerman practices landscape architecture in Philadelphia, Pennsylvania. He has taught at the University of Delaware and lectured extensively at other institutions. For the past thirty years he has represented Roberto Burle Marx in the United States.

"O Senhor de Guaratiba," as Lúcio Costa aptly named him, died peacefully at his country place outside of Rio, at half past midnight on 4 June 1994.

César, his loyal housekeeper, alerted friends and relatives who had attended him during the last months of his illness, as well as gardeners and household help living in the nearby village of Ilha. Together they dressed the body and laid it out in the lofty space of the recently constructed atelier on the hill above his residence. The gardener Ataíde and his helpers cut all the orchid flowers blooming that morning and mounted a decoration worthy of the master. When the work was finished candles were lit, and friends and workmen formed a circle to pray an Ave Maria and a Pater Noster.

During the day other friends, relatives, and coworkers began to arrive. Late that afternoon, the casket was taken to the nearby cemetery. Roberto's body was laid to rest under a magnificent mango tree and next to the grave of his beloved nurse, Ana Piasceck (fig. 2), who had first taught him how to put seeds into the ground.

Roberto was born on 4 August 1909 at the Vila Fortunata on fashionable Paulista Avenue in São Paulo. He was the fourth of six children from the marriage of Cecília Burle and Wilhelm Marx (fig. 3). The Vila Fortunata stood in a formal and somewhat eclectic garden, typical of the period. Roberto retained vivid memories of this early environment. He spoke fondly of seeing his mother pruning roses on clear, crisp winter mornings or tending begonias and caladiums in her small conservatory, delicate tropical plants brought from her home in Pernambuco. He remembers his nurse, Ana, showing the children how to prepare a plant bed and the excitement of watching seedlings turn into little red radishes. The property extended behind the house to include a piece of original forest and orchard, with horse stables at the boundry. From here the energetic head of the family set off every morning for an hour's ride to his tannery. In business Wilhelm Marx played for high stakes, not always without suffering reverses. A change of fortune in 1913 dictated his move to Rio, where he soon recovered his losses. He founded a new tannery, the Cortume Carioca, and eventually was able to buy the old house of a former plantation, Fazenda do Leme, at one end of Copacabana Beach. The property extended up the wooded hillside to the top of the Morro da Babilônia, a hill which much later became familiar to movie fans in the story of *Black Orpheus*.

A military edict prohibited building above the elevation of eighty meters. This did not prevent squatters from setting up picturesque huts here and there among the trees. As a result, many of the city's poor were able to enjoy

Fig. 2. Roberto Burle Marx, pencil drawing of his nurse, Ana Piasceck, ca. 1929.

Photographs by the author except where noted.

Fig. 3. Cecília Burle and Wilhelm Marx, photographic portrait, no date.

Rio's most spectacular views. A phenomenal population growth soon turned these hillsides into *favelas* with no space for greenery, just as the city below became densely packed with high-rise buildings.

In 1920 however, when the Marx family acquired the property, Leme still was a tranquil backwater of Rio. The narrow strip of land between the white sand and the foot of the hill was scattered with comfortable homes surrounded by quiet, walled gardens. On empty lots between the houses, beach grasses and wild morning glories tried to maintain their supremacy. The old plantation house consisted of a spacious bungalow, surrounded by a deep shady porch and lush tropical vegetation. It is here that Roberto grew up, in a large and rather typical Brazilian household. There were servants, tutors, and frequent guests from the extended family, both native and foreign. The children, who spoke Portuguese among themselves, became fluent in German, English, and French. Their mother instructed them in music and took them to gala performances at the Rio Opera House.

In retrospect, it seems that throughout his life Roberto went on expanding and enriching the hospitable and cosmopolitan environment of his youth. It was at the house in Leme that, at the age of seven, he began his plant collection. When the family later moved to a new home, Roberto established his first office and atelier at the old house.

In 1943 he founded the firm of Burle Marx and Company with his younger brother, Siegfried, who first helped him organize his business and supervised his landscape and maintenance crews. The firm prospered. The office moved to larger quarters, and the brothers looked for more land to accommodate the expanding plant collection and nursery.

In 1949 Siegfried brought news that he had spotted what seemed to be the ideal site. It was a neglected former coffee plantation, Sítio Santo Antônio da Bica, near the beach of Barra de Guaratiba. At that time it was over an hour's drive from Rio. The property included a good running stream descending the hillside. The land reached from the top of the hill to the flat marshes below, providing different plant environments. Halfway up the hill stood an old chapel and a modest farm house which Roberto restored and enlarged (figs. 4, 5, 6, and 7). Over the next four decades he planted here one of the most extensive plant collections of South America, gathering specimens wherever he went; on frequent excursions within Brazil, on lectures tours, and on visits to countries throughout the world. It always gave him special satisfaction when a new species was named after him. At his country place Roberto spent the weekends painting (figs. 8 and 9) and entertaining visitors (fig. 10)—colleagues, students, clients, politicians, and foreign dignitaries. And always there was his circle of old friends.

At his office in Rio, Roberto, with his staff and subsequent partners, functioned very much like a Renaissance *bottega*. In addition to landscape projects (fig. 1), they designed floral decoration for important receptions, murals and sculptures, stage sets, jewelry, and textiles. The office produced more than two thousand plans for private gardens (fig. 12), public squares (fig. 11), and parks. At first these projects were confined to Brazil and other Latin American countries, but eventually commissions came from Europe, the United States, and Asia.

Roberto received national and international honors and awards in all areas of his activities. But he is best known as the greatest innovator in landscape design of our time.

Fig. 4. Sítio, covered porch of residence. Photograph 1973.

Fig. 5. Sítio, chapel. Photograph 1973.

Facing page

Fig. 6. Sítio, new atelier behind a facade salvaged from the demolition of an old commercial building in downtown Rio, 1994. Architects A. G. Borsoi and J. da Costa.

Fig. 7. Sítio, stone wall and pond. Photograph 1985.

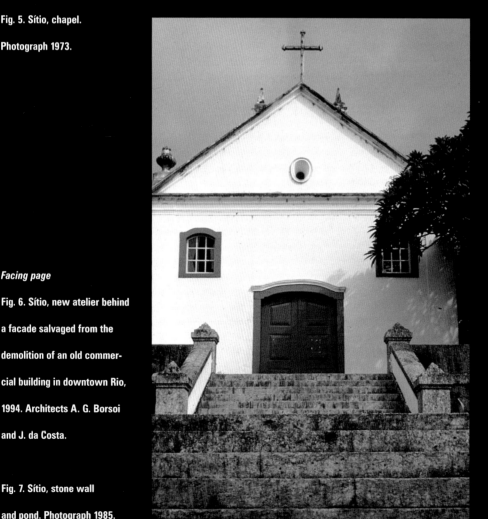

Fig. 8. Roberto Burle Marx painting at Sítio, 1991.

Fig. 9. Roberto Burle Marx consults a book on De Kooning, Sítio, 1991.

Fig. 10. Roberto Burle Marx and gardener Ataíde decorating the dinner table at Sítio, 1991.

Fig. 11. Terreiro de Jesus, a nineteenth-century square in Salvador, Bahia, redesigned by Roberto Burle Marx in 1952, retaining the traditional fountain at the center. Roberto Burle Marx office archive. Photograph by Pierre Verger, 1973.

Fig. 12. Roberto Burle Marx supervising a landscape project for Raul Martins, Petrópolis, state of Rio de Janeiro. Photograph 1991.

In February 1994 I flew down to Rio to guide a group of West Coast architects and landscape architects through Roberto's gardens and other wonders of Brazil. As always I was a guest at Roberto's country place. The *Journal of the Decorative and Propaganda Arts* had asked me to conduct an interview for their projected issue on Brazil. Roberto was ill. At times he felt better than others, and he tried to take care of some business every day.

On March 22 he sat down at the head of the long dining room table, which was spread with one of his own painted cloths, white with a sophisticated linear design in black. On a small piece of furniture across from him stood a baroque figure of Saint Lucia. I faced open French doors leading to the covered porch and sunny garden beyond. Behind me, in a large aquarium set in the wall, tropical fish moved about slowly.

I began the interview; it was the last he was to give.

CH: Roberto, I'd like to discuss the main events that led you to become a painter and landscape architect.

RBM: In the early twenties my parents took a trip to Switzerland after my father sold his tannery, the Cortume Carioca, to a Swiss firm. When they returned to Rio, my father brought back a number of issues of *Gartenschoenheit*, a German garden magazine. I read the principal articles and they strongly influenced me.

When I went to Germany in 1928, I already had a small background in ecology because I had attended a course at the Rio Botanical Garden given by the botanist Dr. Silveira. In Germany I began to see Brazilian plants carefully nurtured in the glasshouses of the Dahlem Botanical Garden.

CH: Would you say that your interest in designing gardens began with your visits to that garden?

RBM: No, you have to understand, I was uncertain then, I didn't know whether I was going to dedicate myself to music or to the plastic arts. My father took the whole family to Europe to give his children a thorough "culture bath." We rented a house in Berlin, and from there we took occasional trips to other parts of Europe. Berlin at that time had a fantastic cultural life. There were often three or four outstanding musical performances in the same week. I went with my mother, sisters, and brothers; we all went. Sometimes we attended the same performance again the next night.

CH: Today we read a lot about the colorful nightlife and cabarets in Berlin of the late twenties. Were you exposed to any of it?

RBM: Yes, I went to some cabaret—not much. Our lives revolved around the theater, the concerts, the opera, Wagner, Richard Strauss.... The whole musical panorama I knew well.

Fig. 13. Roberto Burle Marx,

Brazilian Marine in Red Tunic,

oil on canvas, 71 x 101 cm, 1938.

CH: Were you enrolled in any formal study course in Berlin?

RBM: I received singing lessons from a teacher at the Staatsoper, and I attended a drawing course at the school of Degner Klemm.

CH: How good a teacher was Klemm?

RBM: His was a second-rate school, but it was not academic in the sense of our schools in Brazil.

CH: In previous conversations you often mentioned a lady, Erna Busse, who seems to have exerted an influence on you.

RBM: Miss Busse had been hired as a German tutor for my younger brother, Siegfried. But she felt a special affinity toward me and took it upon herself to guide my steps. She was familiar with the local ambiance, and she told me what to see: what plays, museums, and art galleries. You can imagine the fabulous collections there. I was suddenly confronted with the actual works of old masters. And I saw the first major exhibit of Van Gogh's work. It filled me with enthusiasm; those paintings—that violent expression—invaded my whole being! I realized painting would have to be my medium [figs. 13 and 14].

I always thought one could, within a month, transform oneself into a Leonardo da Vinci—but time is wise and hides the difficulties. If we knew to begin with all the difficulties we had to overcome, we often would not have the courage to start or to persist. But it is time that gives us a wider perception, through comparison, through our ability to measure the time still ahead of us, and our desire to find the proper direction. For the artist all of life is an experiment...in which certain moments assume importance by the confluence of certain elements. Such moments exert an influence throughout life. But it is, how would you say, a superimposition of such elements that make the life of an artist. It is always a search, the curiosity to encounter something he has not known before. Here you can repeat that famous statement by Picasso: "I'd rather copy others than copy myself." Naturally we all have our own structure,

Fig. 14. Roberto Burle Marx

painting, ca. 1940. Roberto

Burle Marx office archive.

Photographer unknown.

and we are not from one day to the next going to be somebody else. And so the artist follows his way, as a French philosopher said: "de l'incertitude à l'incertitude." He may be understood at first by only a small number of people, because generally the artist precedes his time. He discovers and others follow. At first they resist but eventually they accept. What do you think?

CH: That's undoubtedly true. So now you felt you had found your vocation, and after returning to Rio you enrolled in the National School of Fine Arts to study painting?

RBM: Yes, the school then was under the direction of Lúcio Costa and it included the department of architecture. I began to meet some of the people with whom I was to collaborate later.

CH: Could you name any teachers who influenced you or were able to guide you.

RBM: There was Lucílio de Albuquerque. He was an academic painter but very knowledgeable and understanding. The students drew forever from the cast rather than from the figure so as not to create a scandal. But I introduced life figures into the course. I was never a conformist.

A teacher who had a considerable influence on me in the second year was the German expressionist Leo Putz. During a trip to Angra dos Reis, he pointed out a group of old mango trees. He spoke of the symphony of colors in their massive crowns, the shiny copper tufts of the newest twigs which then turned to an intense light green and stood out against the somber green masses of older foliage. But Putz never failed to stress the need of the artist to detach himself from the object: "My son," he told me, "for the artist, nature is pretext—a point of departure."

CH: Do you feel Cândido Portinari had an influence on you?

RBM: Later there were other teachers, Celso Antônio, Pedro Correia de Araújo, and Portinari as well.

CH: Since your aim was now to become a painter, how did you ever get into garden design?

RBM: I lived at my parents' house surrounded by a garden, and I continued to acquire new plants. One day I laid out a bed of caladium and purple coleus in a somewhat unconventional pattern. Lúcio Costa stopped by and saw me working on it. He looked at the layout and then made a proposal. He was designing, together with Gregori Warchavchick, the first house in the modern style in Rio. Would I accept the commission of doing the garden? He did not, of course, mean to imply that I should became a gardener but...I hastened to assure him that I had no problem with that. So in 1932, while still a student at the School of Fine Arts, I did my first project. It was a residential garden for the Schwartz family at Copacabana.

CH: Did you make drawings for this garden?

RBM: Yes, I made a drawing and showed it to Lúcio. It was probably not very professional, but he said it was just fine. Sometimes one needs to encourage beginners.

CH: How did you became director of parks in Recife, the capital of the state of Pernambuco?

RBM: In 1934 the governor of Pernambuco, Lima Cavalcanti, came to Rio on state business. Among other things he had in mind finding a competent person to redesign and restore the decaying public gardens in Recife. In Rio he lodged at the Copacabana Palace Hotel. During a walk along the beach, he saw the Schwartz residence. He liked the garden and found out who did it. He then called our house and invited me for an interview at the hotel. I went there with my brother Walter, and after a brief talk Cavalcanti offered me the position of director of parks. I was then twenty-five years old.

CH: In accepting the position did you have any misgivings about your qualifications for the job?

RBM: Yes, I was extremely apprehensive. I had, for instance, no experience in drawing up plans. But my friends encouraged me and promised to help

wherever necessary. An important friend was the architect Luís Nunes, who had worked with the botanist Aristides Leão in Rio. Nunes was a man with an ample vision and possibly one of the most cultured individuals I have met. He was employed as a city engineer in Recife and was interested in creating a strong architectural department. Working with him was the engineer and poet Joaquim Cardoso. These people were all very encouraging and said if you have any difficulty we will help you. So when I assumed my position in Pernambuco, I tried to apply the things I had learned reading the magazine *Gartenschoenheit* and visiting the Dahlem Botanical Gardens.

My first project was the Casa Forte Garden [fig. 15], inspired by a picture I had seen of the aquatic gardens at Kew Gardens in England. It was divided into three parts: a circular pond flanked by two rectangular ponds. The central pond I devoted entirely to plants of the Amazon. One of the rectangular ponds contained Brazilian plants of different regions, and the other rectangle I planted with exotics.

The second garden I projected there was based on a cactus garden I had seen in Germany. The cacti corresponded to our flora of the *caatinga*. I tried to apply here what I knew of the *caatinga*, the arid region of our Northeast, made famous by Euclides da Cunha in the book *Os sertões*.[1]

CH: This garden was then renamed Euclides da Cunha Square [fig. 16].

RBM: Yes, I gave it that name. Then I made a garden based on plants of the coastal region and so on.... If you want to know more, just ask me.

CH: Roberto, would you like to take a rest now?

RBM: No, let's go on.

1. Published in English as *Rebellion in the Backlands* (Chicago: University of Chicago Press, 1944).

CH: As a landscape architect working in the United States, I'd be interested in knowing how you started a project, how it was approved and executed by the city. Supposing it was decided that you should redesign a certain public square.

RBM: Yes, I would go there and see what was ugly and what was beautiful and eliminate what was bad.

CH: You would go back to the office and draw up a plan....

RBM: Just as we do today, except that the plans were perhaps more primitive, less developed.

CH: And based on the proposed ground plan you would draw up the perspectives in pen and ink. These are the drawings that were recently exhibited at MOMA [Museum of Modern Art, New York].

RBM: I began to make perspectives so that people could understand the proposed design.

CH: Was the design submitted to a committee for approval?

RBM: No, [in Recife] the decisions were made right in our department.

CH: When the plans were completed, who implemented them?

RBM: I did the planting myself with gardeners who worked for the city. I undertook several excursions to get plants from the *caatinga* for Euclides da Cunha Square.

CH: Did you also go to the Amazon?

RBM: No, I did not go there until 1950. The plants for the water garden came from the Botanical Garden in Rio.

CH: What was the public reaction to your innovations?

RBM: They thought it was marvelous—that is, not everyone did. There was opposition as well. Some citizens felt threatened by the native plants I brought in.

They claimed I was trying to return their city to the jungle. Others were incensed because I had removed a monument commemorating a battle won by the colonists against the Dutch. It was a sculpture of very dubious artistic value. Still, when one is young, one does certain things.... I don't know whether today I would have the courage....

CH: What was your impression of the city when you lived there?

RBM: The city was just beautiful. I knew Recife as it had come down from the colonial period, almost intact. The building boom came later. It is pitiful how much was destroyed. It is a city where the rivers were always of great importance and there were the *mucambos*, the vast shanty towns built on stilts on the muddy flats along the rivers. I was impressed by so much poverty; the incidence of tuberculosis was the highest in Brazil. These people lived on miserable earnings.

CH: Did you see in the architecture of the city any influence of *art nouveau* or art deco?

RBM: There always is in these cities. But above all there was the Dutch influence. What was typical of the old cities of northern Brazil were the colonial mansions of the cultivators of sugar cane. They retained the milieu of masters and slaves so well described by Gilberto Freyre in *Casa grande e senzala*.[2]

CH: What kind of social life did you have in Pernambuco?

RBM: I lived in the house of my cousin Laura Burle and her husband, Maurício Ferreira. They were fond of me and treated me as one of the family. After work I would usually go home for dinner and then take the streetcar to meet my friends at the Café Gambrinus or Café Leite. Joaquim Cardoso had gathered around himself a group of young intellectuals. We carried on exciting discussions, often long into the night. There I met Clarival do Prado Valladares and his brother José. Clarival was a medical student and later an art historian. We became lifelong friends. There was also Gibson Barboza, then about eighteen years old, our future ambassador to many foreign countries. I met the sociologist and writer Gilberto Freyre and Cícero Dias the painter. But the figure who held our circle together was Joaquim Cardoso. He was the *chef d'école*, as the French say; an extraordinary figure whose interests ranged from ecology to all the different art forms.

CH: What topics did you discuss?

RBM: Everything one discusses today.

CH: Poetry?

RBM: Poetry, music, the history of painting, political problems. It was a troubled time—the period of the suppression of the Communist Party. Through Clarival I was introduced to Russian literature and to contemporary French authors.

CH: Can you name the author who most influenced you?

RBM: Dostoevsky was very important in my life, and then Tolstoy and other Russian writers. But that doesn't mean the German literature of a Thomas Mann was not important, or a Gide or a Kafka. It is the conjunction of knowledge in a person that brings about a larger vision of life.

2. Published in English as *The Masters and the Slaves* (New York: Knopf, 1964).

CH: After holding the position in Recife for two years, you decided to resign and return to Rio?

RBM: Yes, I had some disagreements with the mayor over a political issue. I decided to set up my own atelier as a painter and accept private commissions as a garden designer. I resumed closer contact with my former colleagues from the School of Fine Arts.

CH: In 1937 and 1938 you also worked as a studio assistant to Cândido Portinari. How was your relationship with him?

RBM: Portinari had moments when he could be very agreeable and others where he was diabolical, a difficult character. Above all, Portinari was a man who feared competition; he tried to eliminate it. He accepted no criticism, he disliked it.

CH: In 1936 Lúcio Costa invited Le Corbusier to come to Rio to guide the design of the new building for the Ministry of Education and Public Health. The young team assembled to carry out the project included many architects who became leaders of the modern movement. How did you become part of that team?

RBM: Through Lúcio. We lived on the same street in Leme.

CH: On Rua Araújo Gondim?

RBM: Yes, it has since been renamed after a member of his family, General Ribeiro da Costa.

CH: You assisted Portinari in the execution of a series of murals representing the economic cycles of Brazil, which were painted for the minister's office.

RBM: That's when I was asked to design the plaza below the building, the terrace garden for the minister's office [figs. 17 and 18], and the roof garden.

CH: The design of these gardens shows a complete break with the classical layout of your public gardens in Pernambuco. Is it here that your individual style of clearly defined curvilinear patterns of solid color areas was created?

RBM: No, it was not here. People who don't know what went before may

think so. I used curves before, it was always a mixture. But above all at the Ministry these forms became more clear.

CH: Who are the architects with whom you worked on that project? Oscar Niemeyer...

RBM: Niemeyer...also Affonso Reidy, an important figure; Jorge Moreira; all of them, Ernesto Vasconcellos, Roberta Leite, the architect Modesto.

CH: During the building boom in Brazil over the next three decades, most of the architects you mention became leaders in the modern movement. You collaborated on different projects with them [figs. 19, 20, 21, and 22]. How close was your actual design collaboration?

RBM: With some architects, like Reidy, I worked closely on such projects as Glória Park. In São Paulo there was a strong collaboration with Rino Levi, especially on the residence of Olivo Gomes [fig. 23], where the architect incorporated some of my tile and mosaic panels into the building. But in most cases the architects would simply leave the areas assigned to the gardens to my judgement. There was no interference.

CH: You were all part of the same movement and spoke the same language. There was no need for you to sit together to create a unity between building and garden.

RBM: That was true in many of the modern buildings.

CH: Which was the first residential project you did after your return to Rio?

RBM: I did a garden for the Brennand residence in Recife. The first garden I did in Rio was for Castro Maya at the Tijuca Forest. Then came the garden of Heloísa Marinho, the granddaughter of Oswaldo Cruz; then the gardens of Wallerstein; Fazenda Samambaia in Petrópolis; the Monteiro garden.... And so it began [figs. 24, 25, 26, 27, 28, and 29].

CH: During the early forties you had the participation of the botanist Mello Barreto.

Fig. 19. Roberto Burle Marx, gardens at the Museum of Modern Art, Glória Park, Rio de Janeiro, designed 1961. Architect Affonso Eduardo Reidy. Photograph by Marcel Gautherot.

Fig. 20. Roberto Burle Marx, aquatic garden at the Itamarati Ministry of Foreign Affairs, Brasília, designed 1965. Architect Oscar Niemeyer. Photograph by Marcel Gautherot.

Fig. 21. Roberto Burle Marx, Santo André Civic Center, São Paulo, designed 1967. Architect Rino Levi. Photograph by Marcel Gautherot.

Fig. 22. Roberto Burle Marx,
aquatic garden at the Ministry
of the Army, Brasília, designed
1970. Architect Oscar
Niemeyer. The white concrete
sculptures were inspired by
rock crystal formations.

Fig. 23. Roberto Burle Marx, garden and pond at the Olivo Gomes residence, São José dos Campos
near São Paulo, designed 1950. Architect Rino Levi.

Fig. 24. Roberto Burle Marx, garden of Walther Moreira Salles, Rio de Janeiro, designed 1951. The tile mural shows a transition from figurative to abstract work. Photograph by Marcel Gautherot.

Fig. 25. Roberto Burle Marx, plan for the Odette Monteiro Garden, Correas, state of Rio de Janeiro, gouache on paper, 1948.

Fig. 26. Roberto Burle Marx, the Luiz Cezar Fernandes Garden (formerly the Odette Monteiro Garden), Correas, state of Rio de Janeiro. Some of these flowering trees are native to the area and bloom in the forest-covered hills, providing a link with the natural surroundings.

Fig. 27. Roberto Burle Marx, the Luiz Cezar Fernandes Garden (formerly the Odette Monteiro Garden), Correas, state of Rio de Janeiro. Bed of yellow and purple coleus shows use of curvilinear shapes and solid color.

Fig. 28. Roberto Burle Marx, the Ralf Camargo Garden (formerly the Alberto Kronsfoth Garden), Teresópolis, state of Rio de Janeiro, designed 1955. In contrast to the Fernandes Garden, where colorful beds are placed in different parts of the composition, the beds here are interlocking and continuous.

Fig. 29. Roberto Burle Marx, the Ralf Camargo Garden (formerly the Alberto Kronsfoth Garden), Teresópolis, state of Rio de Janeiro, designed 1955.

RBM: Mello Barreto was somewhat my senior and proved to be not only a friend but an enthusiastic tutor and collaborator. He felt strongly that plants should be studied in their native habitat. Together we undertook excursions to different phytogeographic regions in Brazil, and he pointed out to me the distinctive communities and explained how certain plants depend on each other for survival. We collaborated on some public parks in Rio [fig. 30] and on a large project in Minas Gerais. Here I wanted to create a series of ecological gardens in which I tried to combine the fauna and flora of specific regions together with the underlying rock formation. Unfortunately the project proved too costly and only a few of these gardens were carried out.

CH: Roberto, in Rio you frequented the salon of the baronesa de Bomfim....

RBM: I knew the family because my parents had made a trip to Europe together with the baronesa de Bomfim.

CH: Was hers a literary salon of the Parisian type?

RBM: No, it was a social salon. It was there that the flower of society met, although it included some artists as well. It was another salon, that of Laurinda dos Santos, that was frequented mostly by artists and writers.

CH: Did you learn much at these salons?

RBM: I did not experience the intellectual fervor of our circle in Pernambuco. But you can always learn something in society, you become more polished in your intercourse with people.

CH: Your parents also gave musical evenings and recitals of poetry and so on.

RBM: My father was fond of good food and good wine and intelligent discussion. We often had distinguished guests. I remember one night we had a party for the Austrian author Stefan Zweig. Portinari came there, and Le Corbusier. My brother Walter was connected with the musical world [fig. 32] and was a good friend of Villa-Lobos. The Chilean pianist Claudio Arrau would stay at our house when he performed in Rio.

CH: It seems to me that in the Brazil of your formative years there was still a strong cohesion between high society and the intellectual elite. There were more personal contacts between artists and scientists; certain people were active in both areas without detriment to either. One did not sense the specialization and detachment of each discipline so common in the United States today.

Although art and technology fairly leapt into the modern age during the thirties and forties, Brazil's cultural outlook remained anchored in the nineteenth century. This may be partly due to more emphasis on humanistic education in its secondary schools. Would you say such a background could still be beneficial?

RBM: Certainly an artist who opens up new vistas in his field cannot confine himself to the narrow problems and technical expertise of his craft. He needs a general culture and understanding. But today, above all, he cannot remain aloof from the social and economic problems of our time. Life cannot be confronted with sentimentalities. We have to have a clear perception of events; the problem of overgrowth, of overpopulation. We are witnessing the beginning of new ethnic wars and the expansion of industry in one country that kills the industry of every other country. I don't believe socialism is quite dead. There must be a more just distribution of wealth, so people can live in dignity. The pope is against birth control; in our time that is monstrous! The human

Fig. 30. Roberto Burle Marx, plan for a zoological garden in Rio de Janeiro, a collaboration with botanist Mello Barreto, gouache on paper, ca. 1946. The plan depicts animals, as seen in ancient Egyptian garden plans.

Fig. 31. Roberto Burle Marx and assistant painting on cloth in the pavilion at Sítio, 1991. Compare similarities in form and composition with Copacabana mosaic paving.

Fig. 32. Roberto Burle Marx and his brother, pianist-composer Walter Burle Marx, in the music room at Sítio, 1980. Photograph by Andrew Durham.

population has to be controlled, to live in some kind of equilibrium with the rest of nature. I have all my life spoken out against the senseless destruction of our forests. The dumping and pollution created by industrial nations is also wrong, as is the unfettered takeover by corporations. Little do they care if they kill local industries that benefit a region.

CH: I totally agree, there must be some protection of local economies, local languages, local traditions; just as we need to protect certain unique plant communities.

But before we end this interview, I'd like to ask you something about the principles that underlie your artistic composition.

RBM: Composition is always a play, a struggle between light and dark, between dominant and dominated. The important thing is to say the most with a minimum of means. I do not believe only in the impulse. The impulse has to be controlled. We do not always arrive at positive results. But one thing is necessary, not to be afraid of making mistakes. It is by erring that we learn. Formulas only bring us sterility. It is important that we have the right to say: I made an error and I would like to correct it.

CH: Roberto, when you paint you have a right to make mistakes and correct them, it is your canvas and your pigment, but when you construct gardens you use other people's property, other people's money, and the labor of others....

RBM: Oh, this is different. But if you work on your own property, then you have the right to modify, don't you think, until you can say this is good!

CH: In that sense the paintings you do, although they are an end in them-selves, also serve as a laboratory for your garden compositions [conversely in figs. 31 and 33]. When you paint, I can see you experimenting with new forms, new juxtapositions of colors, creating certain highlights or dramatic moments. I can see you struggle to bring about a dynamic balance between unequal ele-ments, to achieve stability within the total composition.

RBM: It is as you say. My atelier is a laboratory—has to be a laboratory. In the final analysis, all of life is an ongoing experiment. □

Fig. 33. Roberto Burle Marx, mosaic paving, Atlantic Avenue, Copacabana, Rio de Janeiro, designed 1970. Photograph by Marcel Gautherot

John Graz and the Graz-Gomide Family

By Irma Arestizábal

Translated by Edward Shaw

Irma Arestizábal is director
of the Casa Rosada Museum
in Buenos Aires. She is also
an exhibition curator and
the author of numerous
publications on Eliseu Visconti,
J. Carlos, Antonio Borsoi, and
Antonio Virzi, among others.
The Grandjean de Montigny
mansion in Rio de Janeiro was
restored under her direction.

John Graz (1891–1980) was born in Geneva, Switzerland, and studied there at the Ecole des Beaux-Arts, specializing in architecture, decoration, and drawing the human figure. From 1907 to 1911 his teachers were Gabriel Venet, Eugène Guillard, and Daniel Baud-Bovy, who had been the director of the school since 1908. Graz spent considerable time with fellow students Regina and Antônio Gomide, whose father served as Brazilian consul in Geneva. Later, in Brazil, a close relationship developed between these artists who emerged as principal figures in the art deco movement in São Paulo. The three became known as the "Graz-Gomide Family" because of similarities in their work. At times it was difficult to differentiate, especially between the work of Graz and Regina Gomide.

Graz was also a disciple of Edouard Ravel, the multifaceted artist who dominated "all the techniques and all the styles of pictorial expression then in vogue: genre painting, scenes of daily life, regional art, historical painting, fresco, and works in stained glass. It was certainly at the side of this professor of the artistic 'humanities' that John Graz acquired the multiplicity of talents (eclecticism) that would be so useful to him in executing his interior decorations later."[1] While he never studied with Ferdinand Hodler[2] as Antônio Gomide did, Graz was always aware of the work of this painter of mountains and lakes and of the achievements of Heroic Switzerland, who painted reality in an essentially abstract and formal way, endowing his scenes with a unifying interior monumentality.

To understand Graz's work, we should consider these elements of the Swiss artistic tradition that must have influenced him significantly: patriotism symbolized by the mountains, the country's people, historical events, and personalities; and the idea that design was to be utilized by industry. Since the beginning of the nineteenth century, canton governments had encouraged the creation of schools for industrial design with the aim of applying art to industry—schools such as the Technical College in Winterthur (1874), the School of Industrial Arts in Geneva (1877), and the School of Applied Arts in Zurich (1878). These preached a simplification of form, an absence of luxury, and adherence to the national slogan of quality combined with durability, all in an object that was technically impeccable.

1. Dominique-Edouard Baechler, *John Graz, reminiscências do modernismo* (Reminiscences of modernism), exhibition catalogue (São Paulo: Paço das Artes, 1980).
2. Speaking of F. Hodler, Graz told Professor Walter Zanini, "I only saw him once." Walter Zanini, *História geral da arte no Brasil* (History of Brazilian art) (São Paulo: Instituto Walther Moreira Salles, 1983).

Fig. 2. John Graz. *Peçam Lance Parfum Geyser*, lithograph 100 x 68 cm, ca. 1918. National Library Collection, Berne. This poster introducing Parfum Geyser is a tribute to Colombine, who stands before an upbeat blue background studded with stars, inviting us to dance and enjoy ourselves. The make-believe, the carpe diem, was a recurring theme in art deco iconography.

From 1911 to 1913 Graz studied decoration, poster design, and advertising with Carl Moos at the School of Fine Arts in Munich. There he developed his talent for designing posters within a tradition of top quality poster art and was, without doubt, influenced by such leading artists as Ludwig Hohiwein, Lucien Bernhard, Hans Rudi Erdt, Jules Gipkens Klinger, Frits Helmut Ehmcke, and later Peter Behrens.

Munich had been a center for avant-garde visual arts since 1896. The most important movement of the period was *Jugendstil* (publication of *Die Jugend* magazine began in 1896), which was to have painter Franz von Stuck as its greatest exponent. Architect-designer August Endell, in Munich at the turn of the century, called for a strict relationship between interior design, furniture, and decorative objects.

Certain theories developed at the German Werkbund (founded in 1907) were also absorbed by Graz. These included a desire to reformulate habitat and decoration in realistic terms, in order to forge a link between industry and artists. The Werkbund thrived at a moment when Europe was engaged in a dialogue seeking to unify Morrisonian rationalism with the naturalistic vitality of Liberty. The Germans stressed the former, a functional rationalism that was the origin of the Bauhaus; of Endell's integration of interior design, furniture, and decorative objects; of Richard Riemerschmid's Munich Schauspielhaus; and of Peter Behrens's new modernism.

A similar school in Switzerland—the Swiss Werkbund—was founded in 1913 by designer-architect Alfred Altherr, who directed it in addition to Zurich's Museum of Applied Arts. Altherr emphasized that the design of an object and the design of the space to be decorated should occur simultaneously.

Graz spent a short period in France where he visited a number of Parisian studios and became familiar with the work of Paul Cézanne, whom he had known in Switzerland through Hodler. He was also in contact with the work of the cubists, with their objective vision of form; of the fauves, who celebrated the purity of painting; of the futurists; and of the Ballets Russes, where painting, dance, and music combined in a seamless unity.

Winning the Lissignol travel grant twice, Graz chose (as Hodler had done in his time) to go to Spain. "Before that harsh landscape, such a different land from the land of placid lakes, [Graz] did a series of paintings that were dominated by a sense of grandeur."[3]

Returning to Switzerland, he won immediate success as an illustrator. His work was characterized by clear, bold graphic design, constructed with concise, sharp lines. Graz worked for more than six years doing many paintings, engravings, and vitraux, like those he prepared for the Temple des Eaux-Vives in Geneva and the Temple de l'Abbaye in the Valley of Joux, Vaud. He also did extraordinary posters (figs. 1 and 2) in which he reflected the influence of Emile Cardinaux and interpreted the teachings of his masters Guillard and Venet. With a direct graphic language, Graz managed to make the work he did in advertising coherent with the urban landscape, just as his furniture and objects would later become part of the totality of the home.

His friends Regina and Antônio Gomide returned to Brazil after the death of their father in 1918. Graz followed in March 1920, the year Antônio Gomide moved to Paris. There Gomide was crucially influenced by cubism and spent time and shared experiences with Victor Brecheret, the Italian sculptor.[4]

On 14 July 1920 Graz married Regina Gomide. With a knowledge of handcrafts from Europe, she planned to make tapestries, rugs, pillows, and textiles in Brazil. In December 1920 Graz exhibited his recent paintings alongside his wife's handcrafts in the lobby of the Cinema Central. Reviews of their work were not favorable; it was considered too far removed from academic art, too modern for São Paulo society. But it received support from poet Oswald de Andrade, and soon the couple were drawn into the city's intellectual life. "In 1921 the Modernist or Futurist group, as it was then called...had not only been formed, but was cohesive and united, already representing a new force,

3. P. M. Bardi, *John Graz*, exhibition catalogue (São Paulo: São Paulo Museum of Art, 1974).

4. In a letter dated 14 May 1924, Brecheret wrote Mário de Andrade in a postscript: "I had a big surprise recently. Antônio Gomide, Regina Graz's brother, is a great painter, very modern and very solid...." Later Brecheret was active in the modernist movement in São Paulo.

Fig. 3. Regina Gomide Graz,

patchwork, painted felt,

70 x 121 cm, 1930s. Fulvia and

Adolpho Leirner collection.

Photograph by Rômulo Fialdini.

equipped with a conscience. [It was] cohesive and united in the basic options that, as is well known, are a violent reaction to all forms that are out of fashion, against any restrictive and sterile academic attitudes, against the aftermath of an overly sweet romanticism—empty of all its earthly strength, against...against.... United finally in the will to revolutionize everything in the country in the image of the current ideas of the moment...in order to create an art and a literature that expressed the times in which they lived."[5]

Graz, who had shown his work with paintings by Emiliano Di Cavalcanti in 1921, had one of his pictures illustrated in *Klaxon*, no. 7 (November 1922) and also exhibited eight works during the Week of Modern Art, all paintings previously shown in Geneva.[6] In January 1927 Antônio Gomide, just back from France, held an exhibit of his recent work in which he showed several frescos (numbers 1–13 in the catalogue). He was to be a pioneer of this technique in Brazil. The year before, his friend and the artist with whom he shared a studio in Paris, Victor Brecheret, also returned to Brazil and exhibited his work in São Paulo.

The modernists, led by novelist, critic, and musicologist Mário de Andrade, wanted to revive what they felt was a truly Brazilian art, seeking deeper roots, a common underlying essence. Graz and his wife as well as Antônio Gomide, Vicente do Rego Monteiro, and Theodoro Braga looked for inspiration in the creative world of the Indian, which became a source enlivening their artistic expression (figs. 3, 4, and 5). At the same time these artists, influenced by art deco and cubism, began to decorate interiors in which geometric lines and abstract forms appeared within indigenous motifs, or in landscapes where curved forms became elongated, elegant female figures (figs. 6 and 7).

5. Baechler, *John Graz.*
6. *Mass in the Tomb, Saint Francis talking to the Birds, Portrait of Minister G.*, a Swiss landscape, two Spanish landscapes, and two still lifes.

Fig. 6. Regina Gomide Graz, *Diana the Huntress*, patchwork of colored felt, 80 x 150 cm, 1930s. Design by John Graz. Fulvia and Adolpho Leirner collection.

Fig. 7. Regina Gomide Graz, painted velvet, 175 x 110 cm, 1930s. Fulvia and Adolpho Leirner collection.

As Yone Soares de Lima points out,[7] the modernists participated directly and/or indirectly in the graphic presentation of their published works. The elegance of their covers and title pages sometimes carried over into the rest of the publication. For example, in his book *Você* (You), Guilherme de Almeida demanded that the designs by Anita Malfatti be printed in grey not black, so that the graphic effect would be closer to that of the originals. Oswald de Andrade and Menotti del Picchia were active participants in the production of various books, even when they did not do the illustrations themselves. Other artists belonging to the movement acted sporadically as illustrators: Victor Brecheret for *A estrella de absyntho* (The absinthe star) by Oswald de Andrade, and Anita Malfatti for *O homem e a morte* (Man and death) by Menotti del Picchia and *Os condenados* (The condemned) by Oswald de Andrade.

John Graz illustrated the cover of the first edition of *Era uma vez...* (Once upon a time...) by Guilherme de Almeida, with a rich composition in which the art deco spirit marking an entire period of his work shines through. In the thirties he served as illustrator for several covers of a magazine called *Instrução Artística do Brasil* (Brazilian artistic instruction) (1931–1938), where modernistic stylization, the use of geometric design, and rationalism were striking features.

Graz was now an integral part of the cultural life of São Paulo. He was an active participant during the visit of Le Corbusier in 1929. That November he could be found at a reception in Vila Mariana, the home of architect Gregori Warchavchik,[8] which was also attended by architects Jayme da Silva Teles, Flávio de Carvalho, Décio de Morais, and Guilherme Malfatti; by painters Tarsila do Amaral and Anita Malfatti; and by a number of journalists and other guests. Le Corbusier declared at this reception that the cultural leaders of São Paulo should organize and join forces with the International Congress of Modern Architecture (CIAM), which had held its first meeting in La Sarraz in 1928. A second Congress was held in Frankfurt, and a third was projected for Brussels. It was decided that Warchavchik would be the Brazilian representative at the Congress.

In the mid-thirties Graz, together with his wife, Antônio Gomide, Elisabeth Nobiling, Rino Levi, Victor Brecheret, and Yolanda Mohalyi, formed Grupo 7.

7. Yone Soares de Lima, *A ilustração na produção literária* (The illustration of literary production) (São Paulo: University of São Paulo, 1987).

8. Gregori Warchavchik (1896–1972), a Russian architect living in Rome, arrived in Brazil in 1923 and was responsible for the introduction of modern-rationalist architecture in Brazil.

Fig. 8. Antônio Gomide, lamp base, painted wood, 30 cm, ca. 1930. Fulvia and Adolpho Leirner collection. Photograph by Rômulo Fialdini.

Composed of foreign artists and those who had studied abroad, this group met regularly at Brecheret's home or in each others' studios to verify what they were currently producing and exchange ideas about their work. The group thought of setting up—with the help of Mário de Andrade, then director of the Department of Culture—a studio/gallery to be a meeting place for the intellectuals of São Paulo. The project never got off the ground, however, and little by little the members went their separate ways until the group finally disintegrated.

According to Oswald de Andrade, the cycle of "an attack on the antiquated," initiated by the audacious Week of Modern Art at the Municipal Theater, closed with an exhibition held in Warchavchik's modernist house.[9] This exhibition was the first representation of the contemporary art movement in Brazil since the Week of Modern Art. Held in April 1930, it showed the work of the host and his wife Mina Klabin (a designer of tropical gardens), Lasar Segall, Victor Brecheret, Anita Malfatti, Celso Antônio, Cícero Dias, Di Cavalcanti, Esther Bessel, Jenny Klabin Segall, Menotti del Picchia, Oswaldo Goeldi, and Tarsila do Amaral, together with the work of many writers. Antônio Gomide exhibited frescoes,[10] John Graz a bas relief and a project for a stained-glass window, and Regina Graz pillows and a bedspread for the master bedroom. There was also a bronze sculpture by Jacques Lipchitz, pillows by Sonia Delaunay and Dominique, two French lamps owned by Olívia Guedes Penteado, and a Bauhaus tapestry belonging to Mina Klabin.

This exhibition served as an example of the integration of many different forms of artistic expression. However Brazilian technology was not geared to respond to the demand of putting industry at the service of creativity, as had happened in Europe. Thus Le Corbusier's "machine for living in" would only be accessible to the privileged, since the architects creating them had to design and produce all the components.

With the advent of modernism, interior decoration was transformed by the discovery of the sense of unity characterized by the *Gesamtkunstwerk*. The presentation of isolated pieces of furniture gave way to ensembles where the architect was the *maitre de l'oeuvre*. The concept of object was extended to the house; a new house was considered an object in itself.

A passion for interior decoration and home furnishings was common to many modern artists of the period, such as Mário de Andrade, Lasar Segall, Gregori Warchavchik, and Antônio Gomide (figs. 8 and 9). These artists, and later

Fig. 9. Antônio Gomide, vase (unsigned), terra cotta, 1930s. Fulvia and Adolpho Leirner collection. Photograph by Rômulo Fialdini.

9. Warchavchik announced his ideas about modern architecture in a manifesto published in the *Correio da Manhã* (Rio de Janeiro) on 1 November 1925. In 1927 he began construction of his home on Santa Clara Street, for which he designed all the furnishings, hardware, and lighting. He also designed a home for the Segall family in 1930, decorated with furnishings conceived by Segall himself following a similar idea of functionalism.

10. In October 1930 Gomide took part in the exhibition titled *Brazilian Art* at the Roerich Museum in New York. Frances R. Grant wrote in the catalogue, "Antônio Gomide is represented in this exhibition by tropical works, [including] several paintings of Indians. One is captivated by the rhythm, by the beauty and interweaving of color in these pictures."

Fig. 10. John Graz, painted mural, ca. 1935. Regina Gomide Graz, pillows. Photograph Annie Graz collection.

Flávio de Carvalho, were to see their creativity express itself through this new language, when possible utilizing industrial materials or those that could be adapted to industrial processes. Gomide experimented in these areas, making frescoes, vitraux, and watercolors.

By the end of the twenties, John Graz had left easel painting almost entirely and conformed his art to interior design. He was able to take advantage of a number of techniques. From art deco he adopted rich materials (fig. 10); the use of metal; decorations featuring agile, trim animals like deer (fig. 11), greyhounds, and young horses; as well as the motifs of primitive cultures. From cubism he incorporated the geometric, which was a forerunner of rationalism (figs. 12 and 13). From the modern style, evidenced by the Bauhaus, he integrated many different artistic expressions, imposing the presence of art on all aspects of life.

Fig. 11. John Graz, relief, Jaffet residence (today the SESC Club), Campestre, São Paulo, 1934–1939.

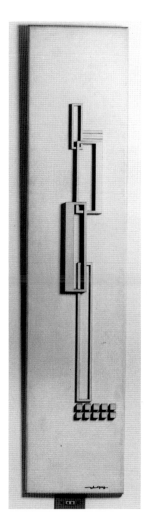

Fig. 12. John Graz, *Geometric Abstraction*, relief on painted wood, 170 x 37 cm, 1930s. Fulvia and Adolpho Leirner collection.

Fig. 13. John Graz, doorway of the Borges de Figueiredo residence, São Paulo, ca. 1935. Photograph Annie Graz collection.

Fig. 14. John Graz, living room furniture, 1930s. Fulvia and Adolpho Leirner collection. With this Graz furniture in the Leirner family apartment today, there are, *left*, two oil paintings by Lygia Clark (1959); *center*, an oil painting by Milton Dacosta (1959); *right*, a sculpture in wood by José Resende (1965); and *foreground*, a lamp base by Antônio Gomide (see fig. 8).

Fig. 15. John Graz, bedroom, Antonieta Caio Prado residence, São Paulo, ca. 1925. Photograph Annie Graz collection. The John Graz painting serves as backdrop for the sumptuous bedroom, which has pillows by Regina Gomide Graz next to the bed.

Fig. 16. John Graz, garden, Roberto Simonsen residence, São Paulo, 1930. Photograph Annie Graz collection.

Fig. 17. John Graz, bathroom, Antonieta Caio Prado residence, São Paulo, ca. 1925. Photograph Annie Graz collection. Note the profile of the chair seat repeated in the design on the door, flowing without interruption into the geometric design of the floor.

He created harmonious interiors in which he established a close relationship between painting, architecture, and the applied arts. He designed all of a house's components: furniture (fig. 14), paintings (fig. 15), reliefs in the form of wall panels, curtains, doors, objects, lighting, windows, shelves, vitraux, and frescoes; bathrooms worthy of a contemporary transatlantic liner (fig. 17); even gardens (fig. 16), giving a grand stylistic unity to his artistic accomplishments. All his creations were related to the idea of "modern," understood as the will to adjust to the reality of the moment, to the interpretation of that moment's demands, and to an adequate response to its needs through the use of unmistakably contemporary products.

There is a rupture with the past in Graz's furniture and decorations, marked by sharply accentuated geometric and functionalistic lines where all the characteristics of 1930s rationalism are evident. With the collaboration of his wife, who produced tapestries (fig. 19), pillows, and rugs (fig. 18), Graz imposed patterns of taste typical of the moment—geometric forms and an interrelation between volumes. The work can be recognized by its pure lines and the elimination of any "extras," for its rigorous symmetry and, above all, for its highly calculated sobriety.

In Brazil, Graz was the first architect to introduce the use of metals in interior design: tubes,[11] copper, steel sheeting, chrome plating, all characterized by clean-cut geometry, with the resulting negation of any hint of personalism and an outright rejection of references to the traditional. Graz continued to produce tubular furniture through 1940. Made of metallic tubing and wood

11. In 1925 Marcel Breuer, then master of the furniture workshop at the Dessau Bauhaus, created the "Wassily," the first chair made of tubular steel. The metal chair seemed to signal a new evolution, marked by the different creations of Charlotte Perriand, an associate of Le Corbusier; René Herbst; Pierre Chareau (who combined steel and wood magnificently); Louis Sognot; Charlotte Alix; and Jean and Jacques Adnet.

Fig. 18. Regina Gomide Graz,
rug, 120 x 190 cm, 1930s.
Fulvia and Adolpho Leirner
collection. Photograph by
Rômulo Fialdini.

Fig. 19. Regina Gomide Graz,
tapestry, 98 x 123.5 cm, ca.
1940. Annie Graz collection.
Photograph by Rômulo Fialdini.

Fig. 20. John Graz, entryway,

Mário de Cunha Bueno

residence, São Paulo,

ca. 1930. Photograph

Annie Graz collection.

(See page 194.)

laminates, each piece was individually designed and built.[12] With this furniture Graz contributed to the modern rationalist expression of simplifying lines, fortifying the affirmation and development of functionalistic principles, and enriching the formal repertory recognized as the hallmark of the rationalists.

Since his earliest creations, Graz received recognition and applause from those most qualified to give it. Even the public in São Paulo, unfamiliar with the 1913 Armory Show in New York or art movements in Scotland, Austria, and France, curiously enough began to accept the rules of the new geometry

12. Graz designed furniture with plans and perspectives drawn life-size to facilitate their manufacture. "[I]n the moment of execution, I will be there in order to verify that the proportions I wanted to give them are correct...." "His designs were executed in an artisanal way, commissioned, of course, by an elite." Vera Galli, *Mobiliário brasileiro: a cadeira no Brasil* (Brazilian furnishings: the chair in Brazil) (São Paulo: Empresa das Artes, 1988). Graz opened a shop for furniture in the early thirties and closed it at the beginning of the forties.

Fig. 21. John Graz, living room,

Mário de Cunha Bueno

residence, São Paulo, ca. 1930.

Photograph Annie Graz

collection. Geometrical themes

seem to leap from the vitraux

to the ceiling lamps to the

curtains (made by Beatriz

Gomide Witecy, one of Regina

Graz's sisters) to the rugs and

pillows made by Regina Graz.

enthusiastically. Graz decorated the homes of many wealthy São Paulo families during the thirties and forties, including residences of the Simonsen, Caio Prado, Noschese, Dupré, Godoy Moreira, Carvalho, Cunha Bueno (figs. 20 and 21), Jaffet, Lunardelli, Ferrabino (fig. 22), Figueroa, Borges de Figueiredo, and Celso de Figueiredo families, and also the reception rooms of the Trocadero dance hall and the Swiss Consulate.[13]

Styles changed in the fifties. The influence of the United States became more important, and Graz was given fewer commissions. In 1969 he gave up furniture making and interior design to devote himself entirely to painting. What he produced was interesting, but not as noteworthy as all he had accomplished earlier.

Graz was a modernist, concerned with contemporary language. Contemplating his *oeuvre* we find superior design, attentive to function, construction, and material, and a clear vision of what he wanted to accomplish. He left an important body of work that transformed the lifestyle of São Paulo's affluent society. □

13. Unfortunately, almost all these buildings have been destroyed.

Note
The author wishes to thank Pro Helvetia for its support, Piedade Epstein Grinberg for her collaboration, Fulvia and Adolpho Leirner for their help, and Annie Graz for all her dedication and encouragement.

PALACIO VISTO DE NOITE ILLUMINADO POR OLOFOTES

Fig. 1. Flávio de Carvalho, project design for the Governor's Palace in São Paulo, night view with floodlights, sketch, 1927, (whereabouts unknown). From a design album published by the architect, ca. 1930. Photograph by Leonardo Crescenti.

Flávio de Carvalho: Modernism and the Avant-Garde in São Paulo, 1927–1939

By Rui Moreira Leite

Translated By Izabel Murat Burbridge

Rui Moreira Leite is a São Paulo architect, art critic, and researcher. His studies of Flávio de Carvalho's work, sponsored by the Research Support Foundation of the State of São Paulo, resulted in a special room being devoted to Carvalho's production at the Seventeenth São Paulo International Biennial (1983).

Flávio de Carvalho (1899–1973) was first given special mention in the São Paulo press in January 1928, following the presentation of his preliminary building plans for the state of São Paulo Governor's Palace. At that time he was still an obscure engineer devoted to the analysis of steel and reinforced concrete structures, known only for his illustrations and reviews of dance performances. However, due to his accomplishments as an avant-garde architect, the artist achieved increasing renown to become the key figure of the São Paulo art milieu in the 1930s.

Having attained a degree in civil engineering in 1922 from the University of Durham in Newcastle-On-Tyne, England (where he also attended the school of fine arts), Carvalho showed himself to be especially sensitive to vanguard movements. He was to remain detached from trends influenced by Marxist theories, which inspired a strong tradition of social and political radicalism in modern art. Rather, he followed primitivist trends inspired by the thoughts of Nietzsche and Freud.

Perhaps the origin of his interest in German expressionism could be related to vorticism and its publication, *Blast! A Review of the Great English Vortex*. In this journal published by British avant-garde artists, Ezra Pound identified himself with Kandinsky's positions, while Wyndham Lewis stated his affinity with the primitivizing esthetic of Die Brücke painters. At an interview in the late 1930s, Carvalho also acknowledged how considerably influenced he had been by readings of the *Gilgamesh* epic and old African tales.[1]

The artist returned to Brazil in the second half of 1922. In those days modernism had not yet reached architecture. Project designs by Antônio Garcia Moya (1891–1949) and Georg Przyrembel (1885–1956) shown in São Paulo at the Municipal Theater during the Week of Modern Art did not overcome the then prevailing eclecticism and the first *art-nouveau* productions, not to mention the so-called Brazilian neocolonial style passionately advocated by Ricardo Severo (1869–1940) and José Mariano Filho (1881–1946).

Carvalho's design for the Governor's Palace was actually a manifesto. Mário de Andrade (1893–1945)—a Brazilian writer and critic and a founder of Brazilian modernism—wrote the most punctilious reviews of Carvalho's design, which according to Andrade was the only one to honor the contest.[2] Built along a symmetrical axis formed by a set of elevators, the building consisted of an arrangement of large-size cubic volumes outfitted with unprecedented weaponry.

---

1. Silveira Peixoto, *Falam os escritores,* vol. 3 (São Paulo: Conselho Estadual de Cultura, 1976), 123, 125.
2. Mário de Andrade, "Architectura moderna I," *Diário Nacional* (São Paulo), 2 February 1928.

seen from a distance of 160 m., from a height
of 2m. above the black disc level, and making
an angle of 57° with the front face of the monument

1:20

fig. 1   fig. 2   fig. 3

Design for ceramic floors: the designs were taken from the ceramics (potery) of the
Marajoara indians of Brazil, however the coloring is my own (I have only seen them in photographs)
The Marajoaras were freed from all academical restrictions and inspired themselves in
the simplicity of nature and in the virile strength of the tropical forests.
The design in fig 1 has a strong resemblance with the aztec period potery

Fig. 2. Flávio de Carvalho, Columbus Memorial Lighthouse design; and designs of ceramic flooring with Marajoara motifs, gouache, 1928, (whereabouts unknown). From an album published by competition organizers in 1931. Photograph by Leonardo Crescenti.

At that time Carvalho said during a press conference: "The Governor's Palace is a governing center. It must be fully equipped with fast airplanes and radio-telephones. In case of war, it becomes the main target for the enemy. It needs artillery for defense and airplanes for reconnaissance. The huge floodlight, set up in vertical position, is designed to guide aircraft pilots" (fig. 1).[3]

Conceived as a gigantic monument made of reinforced concrete, the project included elevated gardens planted with Brazilian trees in front of the building, and decorative panels featuring a group of dancers and a rural scene on the walls of reception halls.

Actually, Carvalho's design followed the introduction of modern ideas by an architect of Russian origin, Gregori Warchavchik (1896–1971). A graduate of the Fine Arts Institute in Rome, Italy, Warchavchik was just finishing the construction of his first modern-style house in São Paulo. During those same years, Jayme da Silva Telles (1895–1966) and Rino Levi (1901–1965) also joined

3. "O novo Palácio do Governo e o projeto modernista," *Diário da Noite* (São Paulo), 4 February 1928.

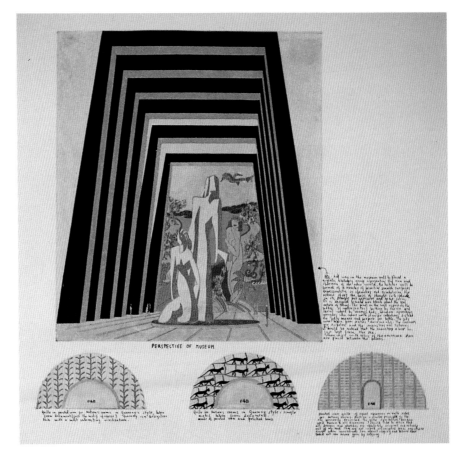

PERSPECTIVE OF MUSEUM

Fig. 3. Flávio de Carvalho, Columbus Memorial Lighthouse design, Museum Room; and iron grilles painted with Guarany motifs, gouache, 1928, (whereabouts unknown). From an album published by competition organizers in 1931. Photograph by Leonardo Crescenti.

the movement that promoted modern architecture. Among these architects, only Silva Telles, a graduate of the National School of Fine Arts in Rio de Janeiro, was to remain faithful to Le Corbusier's purism, while Warchavchik remained linked to German rationalism; Rino Levi adopted Hans Poelzig and Erich Mendelsohn as references; and Flávio de Carvalho debated between his own personal invention, expressionism, and futurism.[4] It was with a futuristic design that he entered the international competition for the Columbus Memorial Lighthouse in the Dominican Republic, also in 1928. The monumental style evident in his plan for the Governor's Palace was accentuated in the lighthouse design, comprising two immense platforms supported by arches and braced on one side by two pyramid sections, topped with buildings that surrounded a huge tower (fig. 2).

The interior design of the lighthouse combined modern wall panels, groups of sculpture, and decorative patterns from pre-Colombian pottery. In his drawings for painted cast-iron grilles for the Museum Room, Carvalho utilized Guarany (fig. 3) and Aztec motifs, and motifs of Marajoara pottery reproduced on ceramic flooring (fig. 2). For the Party Room, which he called the Feasting Hall, he wrote the following description: "The walls are decorated

4. Ricardo Forjaz Christiano de Souza, *Trajetórias da arquitetura modernista* (São Paulo: Secretaria Municipal da Cultura/Informação e Documentação Artísticas, 1982), 79.

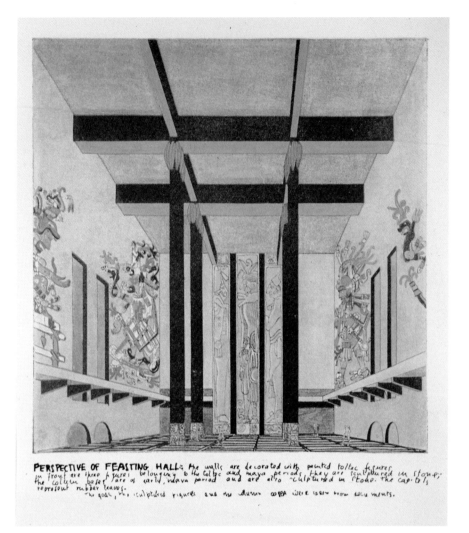

Fig. 4. Flávio de Carvalho, Columbus Memorial Lighthouse design, Feasting Hall, gouache, 1928, (whereabouts unknown). From an album published by competition organizers in 1931. Photograph by Leonardo Crescenti.

with painted Toltec figures; in front there are three figures belonging to the Toltec and Maya periods; they are sculptures in stone; the column bases are early Maya as are the sculptures. The capitals represent rubber leaves" (fig. 4).[5]

The design was officially acknowledged by the competition organizers, who reproduced it in three pages of color illustrations in an album published to advertise the second phase of the competition. Despite not being awarded any prize or honorable mention in the first phase, the design was favorably reviewed by the competition's technical adviser, Albert Kelsey, who wrote: "His skyscrapers are very interesting, his details extremely significant, and his sculpture set called *Criação* (Creation),[6] depicting the surprise and curiosity of the Earth's first inhabitants, is full of deep thoughts manifested in a sincere and genuinely spiritual form." However, at the end of his review, he questioned

5. Albert Kelsey, *Programas y reglas de la segunda etapa del concurso para la selección del arquitecto que construirá el Faro Monumental que las naciones del mundo erigirán en la República Dominicana a la memoria de Cristobal Colón* (New York: Unión Panamericana/ Stillson Press, 1931), 95–96.

6. Sculpture group positioned in front of a panel symbolizing Creation, in the Museum Room (see fig. 3).

whether this mix of modern and archaic would be "sufficiently solemn and majestic, despite all their color and splendid appearance."[7]

Carvalho also made building plans for the Argentine Embassy in Rio de Janeiro (1928), the University of Minas Gerais in Belo Horizonte (1928), and the Congressional Palace in São Paulo (1929), all of them for official competitions dominated by the reigning eclectic style. Predictably Carvalho's designs were consistently rejected, but he was definitely integrated in the Brazilian modernist group. His Columbus Memorial Lighthouse, in which modern language and the heritage of ancient American cultures and civilizations were combined, seemed to be the architectural embodiment of concepts devised by the so-called anthropophagic movement led by Oswald de Andrade (1890–1954) and Raul Bopp (1898–1984), both of whom sought to accomplish this fusion through literature. The starting point of the anthropophagic movement was the canvas *Abaporu* (1928) painted by Tarsila do Amaral (1886–1973), a Brazilian artist then married to Oswald de Andrade. In a way they represented the onset of Brazilian modernism itself, which sprang from the contact of writers (who later became movement leaders) with the work of artists such as painter Anita Malfatti (1889–1964) and sculptor Victor Brecheret (1894–1955).

It was as an anthropophagic delegate to the Fourth Pan-American Congress of Architects held in Rio de Janeiro in 1930, where the only other modernist architect was an Argentine of Russian origin, Wladimiro Acosta (1900–1967), that Carvalho read to the audience his thesis entitled *The City of Naked Man*. The thesis proposed an urban utopia, with the city transformed into an immense home, and people's needs fulfilled under the guidance of a research center that was the only chartered authority. Considering that the audience was concerned with sanctioning traditional styles, and that congress activities were entrusted to José Mariano Filho, himself a supporter of the neocolonial style, it is amazing that Carvalho's speech was publicized at all.

Concurrently with his activities as an architect, Carvalho produced artworks shown for the first time at the Modern Salon organized by Lúcio Costa (born 1902) at the National School of Fine Arts in Rio de Janeiro in September 1931. However in June 1931, and perhaps as a last anthropophagic manifestation, the artist had conducted his *Experiência no 2* (Experiment number 2). During this audacious foray into the field of social psychology, he attended a Corpus Christi procession in downtown São Paulo without uncovering his head, for which the crowd nearly lynched him.

Later he transcribed the episode in a curious book that, ironically, was dedicated to Pope Pius XI and the São Paulo cardinal.[8] The first part of the book contains a vibrant and colorful description of the incident, as prologue to an analysis based on findings of Freud (*Group Psychology and the Analysis of the Ego* and *Totem and Taboo*) and Frazer (*The Origin of Family and Clan*). According to Carvalho, his defiant attitude had transformed him before the eyes of the faithful into an extension of the Holy Father God. Therefore, only his assassination could appease the crowd's totemism, just as young men of primitive hordes, whose sexual instincts were repressed, killed their fathers.

7. Kelsey, *Programas y reglas*, 94–95.
8. Flávio de Carvalho, *Experiência no 2 realizada sobre uma procissão de Corpus Christi* (São Paulo: Irmãos Ferraz, 1931.)

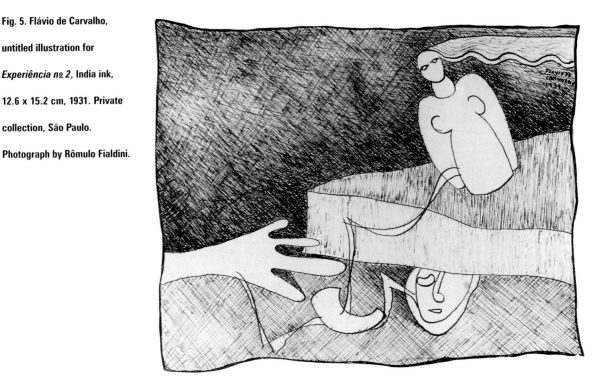

Fig. 5. Flávio de Carvalho,

untitled illustration for

Experiência nº 2, India ink,

12.6 x 15.2 cm, 1931. Private

collection, São Paulo.

Photograph by Rômulo Fialdini.

Fig. 6. Flávio de Carvalho,

untitled illustration for

Experiência nº 2, India ink,

15.2 x 21 cm, 1931. Private

collection, São Paulo.

Photograph by Rômulo Fialdini.

The book was published that same year. It contains a handsome set of India ink drawings meant to convey the author's sensations through surrealistic works characterized by their linear nature (fig. 5), and expressionist works characterized by volume and shading (figs. 6 and 7). These attributes are omitted from some of the sketchier drafts in which the artist renders his view of the faithful parading in the religious procession, just before his challenging apparition turned them into an enraged mob.

At that time he also produced a cover for the first edition of Raul Bopp's poem *Cobra Norato* (The snake Norato) (fig. 8),[9] in which we see the principle of geometrization later employed in a study for a felt panel called *Volúpia* (Voluptuousness) (fig. 9). Bopp's dramatic epic poem tells the Amazonian saga of a youth who, after killing Cobra Norato, enters the body of the monstrous beast. The cover illustration contains a reference to mythological descriptions of a barbaric world undergoing violent transformations: a long-haired female whose figure blends into the red and green graphic design, while part of her body outline suggests the reptile's winding motion in the Amazon river. In *Volúpia*, the strict geometric forms of the female body at the center of the composition were transferred from a small-scale model drawn on card paper to a felt panel six times its size. The artist's interest in

9. The second edition of the poem (1937), in a book containing original wood engravings by Oswaldo Goeldi (1895–1961), marked the introduction of color in that engraver's work which, until then, was characterized by tormented beings and the somber atmosphere of his inspiring source, Alfred Kubin. Goeldi's work was identified with that of Lasar Segall (1891–1957) and Flávio de Carvalho, all representative of an existential expressionism.

Fig. 7. Flávio de Carvalho,

untitled illustration for

***Experiência nº 2*, India ink,**

20.6 x 12.2 cm, 1931. Private

collection, São Paulo.

Photograph by Rômulo Fialdini.

geometric forms had been evident since his monument designs of the late 1920s,[10] whereas in his painting and drawing he essentially produced portraits and female figures in his own expressionist style.

Until that time Brazilian modernism had not ventured into the theater, except for a few timid attempts by Álvaro Moreyra (1888–1969) with his *Teatro de Brinquedo* (Toy theater). It was Carvalho who initiated among the activities of the Clube dos Artistas Modernos (Modern artists' club)—which he founded in late 1932 together with Emiliano Di Cavalcanti (1897–1976), Carlos Prado (1908–1993), and Antônio Gomide (1895–1967)—a first attempt by the Teatro da Experiência to renovate stage acting, following the trend launched by Gordon Craig and Adolphe Appia. The Teatro da Experiência lasted through November and December 1933.

To inaugurate the theater, Carvalho wrote *O bailado do deus morto* (Dead god's dance), a philosophical drama that presented God being born in the form of an animal, a mythological beast whose destiny is decided in the

10. *Monumento às vítimas do hidro-avião Santos Dumont* (1928) and *Monumento funerário modernista* (1930) are monuments designed with the angular planes of the cubists, like the sculpture group created for the interior of the Columbus Memorial Lighthouse. A plaster model of the second monument was later cast in bronze and shown under different titles until its exhibition at the First São Paulo Biennial (1951), when it was definitively entitled *Auto-retrato psicológico* (Psychological self-portrait).

Fig. 8. Flávio de Carvalho, book cover for *Cobra Norato* by Raul Bopp, 1931. Photograph by Leonardo Crescenti.

Fig. 9. Flávio de Carvalho, design for felt panel *Volúpia*, gouache on card paper, 12 x 24 cm, 1932. Private collection, São Paulo. Photograph by Leonardo Crescenti.

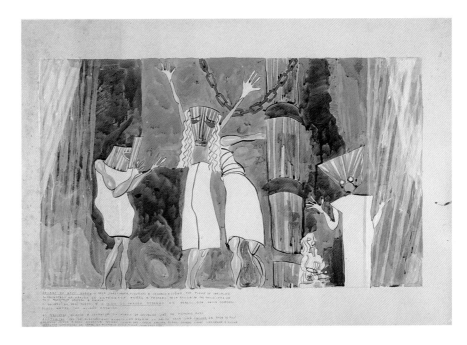

Fig. 10. Flávio de Carvalho, sketch of set design for *O bailado do deus morto* (1933), gouache on card paper, 70 x 100 cm, undated. De Carvalho family collection, Valinhos. Photograph by Leonardo Crescenti.

second act. After imploring in vain to "a silent, withdrawn God, men decide on and direct the destinies of thought, and they determine and specify God's end and the way to utilize His residue in the new world."[11]

The stage set was restricted to an aluminum column hollowed out in three symmetric sections, with a chain hanging from two points on the ceiling, enhancing the effects of stage lighting on the aluminum masks and white gowns worn by the cast (fig. 10). A small yellow ceramic statue placed next to the column was actually part of an exhibition of artworks by children and asylum inmates that was organized by Carvalho at the Clube dos Artistas Modernos.

Except for painter Hugo Adami (born 1900), whose role as Lamenter involved performing spoken parts, the entire cast was made up of black musicians and dancers directed by Henricão (1908–1984). The latter was a composer of folk music, who organized a subsequent production of dances and chants from the slavery period in Brazil. However, since the city's Catholic traditionalists apparently viewed the play written by the author of *Experiência no 2* as a new provocation, the police closed down the theater.

Thus the renovation of drama had to wait until the 1940s when, after a series of initiatives taken in the late 1930s, for example, the foundation of the Teatro de Estudante (Student's theater) by Paschoal Carlos Magno (1906–1980), the first amateur and professional theater companies were established in Brazil. In the 1950s Carvalho resumed his work as set and costume designer. His most important production was *Cangaceira*, with choreography by Aurel Miloss, based on music by Camargo Guarnieri (1907–1993), and performed by São Paulo's Ballet do IV Centenário (Ballet of the fourth centenary) (1954). Carvalho's careful costume research led to the creation of mythological beings

11. Flávio de Carvalho, "A epopéa do Teatro da Experiência e O bailado do deus morto," *RASM— Revista Anual do Salão de Maio* (São Paulo) 1 (1939): n.p.

Fig. 11. Flávio de Carvalho, leaflet advertising the travel book *Os ossos do mundo*, 1936. Photograph by Leonardo Crescenti.

Fig. 12. Flávio de Carvalho, "Mão de cabelo" (The hairy hand), costume design for the ballet *Cangaceira*, watercolor, 40 x 30 cm, 1954. De Carvalho family collection, Valinhos. Photograph by Leonardo Crescenti.

(fig. 12) that related to *O bailado do deus morto* presented in the 1930s. At that time the artist said, "through costumes, masks, makeup, lighting, and stage design, I tried to render symbols of Brazil's northeastern region."[12]

Unfortunately, Ballet do IV Centenário ended in 1955, forcing the artist to discontinue his experiments with dance sets and costume design.[13] After that, these talents were shown in only one more performance produced in São Paulo for a group of dancers directed by Yanka Rudska.[14]

It should be mentioned that the closing of the Teatro da Experiência in 1933 was not the only occasion when Flávio de Carvalho came into direct confrontation with the São Paulo police. They appeared on the scene during the artist's first solo exhibition, held in the lobby of an office building in downtown São Paulo in 1934. According to painter Raphael Galvez (born 1907), prompted by their "loathing for the nudes"[15] painted by the artist, many passersby changed their ordinary routes along the street where the exhibition was being held, taking a parallel road. This time, however, it was Carvalho who obtained a court

12. "Conversa com Flávio de Carvalho," *Jornal de Letras* (Rio de Janeiro), no. 69 (March 1955): 4. The northeastern part of Brazil is the country's poorest region, once dominated by groups of ruthless bandits known as *cangaceiros* who were a symbol of the country's social inequalities.

13. "Conversa com Flávio de Carvalho," 4.

14. A former prima ballerina of the Warsaw Theater in Poland, Yanka Rudska moved to Brazil in 1945, where she built a distinguished career as choreographer, first at the São Paulo Art Museum and later at the then recently founded School of Modern Dance at Bahia University.

15. Walter Zanini, *A arte no Brasil nas décadas de 1930–1940, O Grupo Santa Helena* (São Paulo: Nobel/Editora da Universidade de São Paulo, 1991), 24.

Fig. 13. Flávio de Carvalho, caricature of Roger Caillois, (whereabouts unknown), *Diário de S. Paulo*, 1935.

SCIENCIA E LYRISM

Os novos interesses da sciencia — O valor futuro da art

Algumas palavras com o demonologo francez Roger Caillois

(Copyright dos "Diarios Associados")

Flavio de CARVALH

RETRATO — Encontrei este homem gando pelas planicies da Moravia e Russia Subcarpatica a cata de demonios. Um homem magro e anguso vestido de preto e alto com quencia da magreza. Caillo metricamente, produzindo em co gesto e em cada phrase uma car hesitante de voluptuosidade. Elle io marchava sobre o mundo mas n pairava sobre as cousas, o corpo recia não ter peso e o contacto do u corpo com o mundo não passava uma emoção duvidosa, a sua pasgem era assignalada aqui e ali mas uitos não acreditavam na sua exisncia. Tinha olhos que brilhavam m um lustro acima do humano e dos compridos que resonavam com cadencia da phraseologia.

A sua profissão de demonologo se aptava perfeitamente ao seu physico. a um exemplar caracteristico da inlligencia franceza. Nariz aquilino, bios finos e bocca grande, como a Greta Garbo, pallido e de collarino apertado, tinha os cabellos pretos partidos de um lado e levemente bido sobre a testa. Mais tarde sou que Caillois passando certa vez pe Allemanha se submettera á mania tropometrica local... e após uma ofusão de medidas minuciosas enntraram nelle o typo perfeito do iano. Um dia ouvi a voz de Caillois

SCIENCIA E BOM SENSO

. Caillois me disse:

"Existe uma crise e sobretudo uma separação entre a sciencia e o bom senso... a sciencia torna-se lyrica. dos ultimos annos do seculo XX ella

O demonologo ROGER CAILLOIS, impressão de memoria por Flavio de Carvalho

abandona decididamente o partido do

A sciencia do seculo XIX era positivista e racionalista mas a começar semelhança e do bom senso devido ao aperfeiçoamento mesmo dos seus thodos. De maneira que a sua i pretação do mundo é tão afas quanto é possivel ser da visão co te da realidade da vespera.

OS NOVOS DOMINIOS DA SCIE

A ampliação dos dominios da s cia faz com que ella se interesse pelo sonho e por problemas m accessiveis ao pensamento racion ta, por exemplo o problema do zard objectivo, os trabalhos sobr associações de idéas não dirigid sobre a representação do mundo creança.

O VALOR DA ARTE

O resultado é que o super-real que na sua origem era um movi to literario — mas que logo rev a literatura para se consagrar á vestigação psychologica — cruz sciencia sobre diversos terrenos. super-realismo nada deseja de m que de emprehender no dominio era até hoje o dominio da esth mas com methodos rigorosos — thodos até hoje usados somente sciencia — um estudo phenome gico do problema geral da imagin

Irei mesmo até o ponto de dizer com relação a este phenomeno da imaginação empirica, a arte terá maior valor que o valor possa pretender — com relaçã theorias scientificas — as nossa plicações industriaes".

— Commentarios sobre a obra de Weininger — Não existe uma verdade a de interesse da verdade unica — Que farão os homens? — Algumas p vras com Gustavo H. Minella, o philosopho italiano

Flavio de CARVALH

O philosopho G. MINELLA

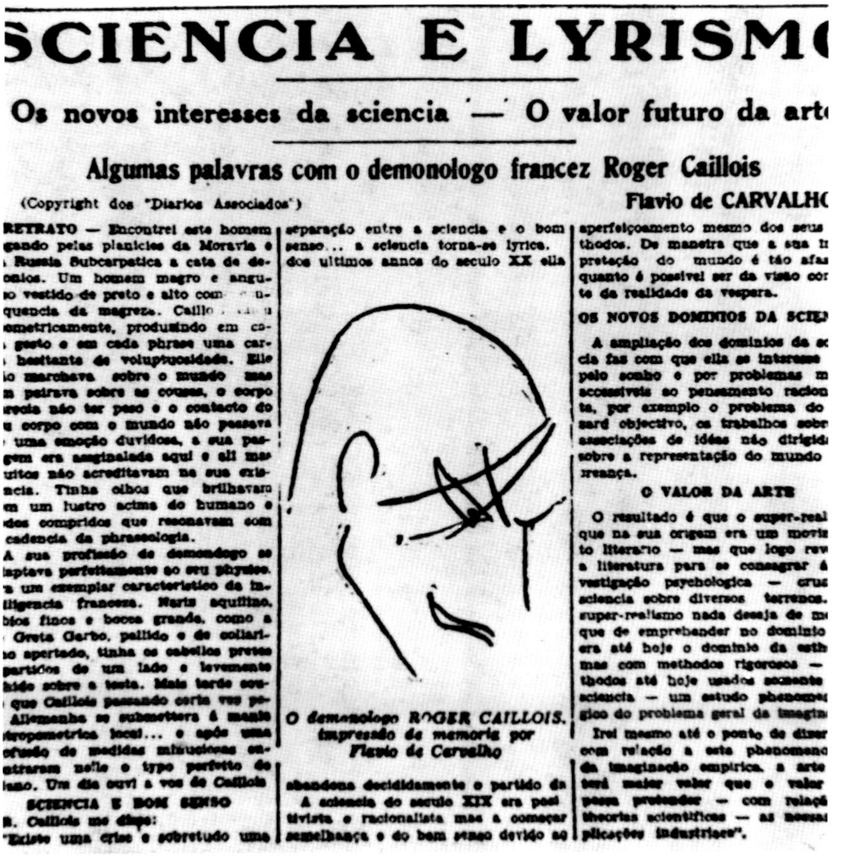

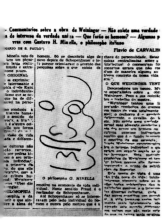

Fig. 14. Flávio de Carvalho, caricature of Gustavo Minella, (whereabouts unknown), *Diário de S. Paulo*, 1935.

order to recover the artworks taken into custody by the police and to re-open the show. Meanwhile, he was preparing to attend the International Congresses of Philosophy and Psychotechnology in Prague.

Carvalho's tour of Czechoslovakia was particularly stimulating, both for the contacts he established with artists and intellectuals and the research studies he began. The results of this trip were first published in his book of travels, *Os ossos do mundo* (The world's bones), the release of which the artist announced in a leaflet (fig. 11). In the book he combined his impressions with psychoanalytical interpretations, presenting Europe as exotic, thus inverting the European view of the Americas, particularly in romantic literature, as noted by Roger Bastide (1898–1974).[16]

Carvalho's meetings with artists, intellectuals, and other distinguished individuals were documented in newspaper interviews illustrated with a series of caricatures. In these caricatures, with only a few pencil strokes, the artist rendered the facial expressions of a French intellectual involved with surrealism, Roger Caillois (fig. 13); an Italian philosopher, Gustavo Minella (fig. 14); and the prophet Krishnamurti (fig. 15), among others. In each he captured the subject's characteristic traits: Caillois's sarcastic smile; Minella's large, rounded face without a defined expression; Krishnamurti's huge, fixed eyes that conveyed serenity. The refining synthesis and expressive details in Carvalho's caricatures were to become characteristic of his portraits.

16. Roger Bastide, *Poetas do Brasil* (Curitiba: Guaíra, 1946), 33–34. Bastide was a French sociologist who taught at the then recently opened University of São Paulo.

Krishnamurti

During the thirties Carvalho resumed architectural design and built a group of seventeen houses in São Paulo (figs. 16, 17, and 18). The unusual design of these buildings seemed to combine the architect's personal version of expressionism—the openings in some of the facades made them look like human faces (figs. 19 and 21)—and principles of interpenetration of volumes that characterized designs by the Dutch De Stijl architect Gerrit Rietveld. The high-ceilinged house interiors integrated into one environment the first floor living room and dining room and the second floor bedrooms (fig. 20).

In an article written in the 1960s, critic Luís Martins (1907–1982) mentioned that the group of houses even provoked "a certain amount of scandal, possibly not [because of] their bold style, but because the architect, who was also the owner, devised a type of...'user's manual' for distribution to his eventual tenants, in which he carefully specified 'directions for use' of the unusual buildings."[17]

17. L. M. [Luís Martins], "Ar condicionado," *O Estado de S. Paulo*, 13 April 1961.

Fig. 16. Flávio de Carvalho,
group of houses, São Paulo,
1938. Historical photograph,
private archive, São Paulo.

Fig. 17. Flávio de Carvalho, group of houses, São Paulo, 1938. Historical photograph, private
archive, São Paulo.

▲

Fig. 18. Flávio de Carvalho,
group of houses, São Paulo,
1938. Historical photograph,
private archive, São Paulo.

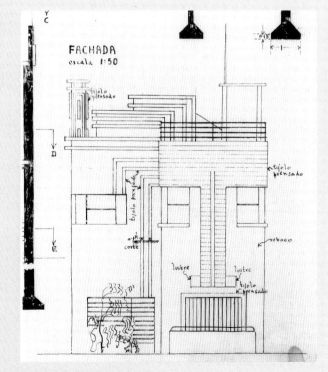

Fig. 19. Flávio de Carvalho,
house facade, original
design, 1936. De Carvalho
family collection, Valinhos.
Photograph by
Leonardo Crescenti.

Fig. 20. Flávio de Carvalho, living room and mezzanine. Historical photograph, private archive, São Paulo.

In interviews the architect preferred to address less controversial aspects of his architectural design, stressing the characteristics he considered essential for the dweller's comfort and the satisfactory solutions he believed he had found for them. For example, "[adjustable] openings are devised in such a way as to provide for greater air circulation in summer...thereby eliminating the need for air conditioning, which is considered too costly for rental homes."[18]

As shown by the neighborhood in which they were located in São Paulo, the group of houses was designed for artists and middle-class professionals, to whom they presented numerous advantages. One tenant, Georg Przyrembel, adapted the mezzanine for use as his studio,[19] while others took advantage of the integrated home environments to organize memorable parties.

Some of the house plans included a sun deck located on a semi-circular overhang on the facade and furnished with a concrete umbrella (fig. 18). According to the architect's "directions," the sun deck should be used for morning sunbathing and for evening drinks in warm weather. Journalist Sangirardi Jr. mocked this last suggestion, stating that navigating the steps to the sun deck depended on the number of cocktails consumed by the guests![20] Given unfamiliarity with such innovative design, there were ironic comments that the steps to the sun deck could very well lead to the bathroom. Brazil, unlike Argentina, lacked publications featuring the international style. Hence the impact on the São Paulo urban landscape by Carvalho's houses and the attribution of their design to Warchavchik (who had become known for his modern works in previous years).

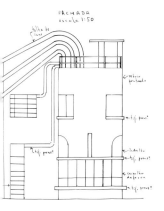

Fig. 21. Flávio de Carvalho, house facade, original design, 1936. De Carvalho family collection, Valinhos. Photograph by Leonardo Crescenti.

For his group of houses, Carvalho designed ceramic for the living room and mezzanine floors (fig. 20) as well as for the floors and walls of bathrooms and kitchens. External walls were finished with mortar applied to simulate dense circles.

18. Péricles do Amaral, "S. Paulo tem dezessete casas verdadeiramente próprias para a gente morar!" *Problemas* (São Paulo) 1, no. 8 (May 1938): 56.

19. Stella Angeli (Georg Przyrembel's daughter), conversation with author, São Paulo, 3 March 1983.

20. Sangirardi Jr., *Flávio de Carvalho, o revolucionário romântico* (Rio de Janeiro: Philobiblion, 1985), 27.

The seven houses not directly on the street did not have face-like facades and sun decks. They differed from Warchavchik's early house designs only through the treatment of external surfaces.

At a time when modern architects were building the first apartment buildings in São Paulo—the Columbus (1932) by Rino Levi and the Esther (1937) by Álvaro Vital Brazil (born 1909)—Carvalho's houses garnered only a few light comments from the press at their inauguration, when the architect hosted a cocktail party for journalists.

By this time Carvalho was building his own home at Fazenda da Capuava, his farm in Valinhos in the state of São Paulo (fig. 22). According to the artist, this design was totally poetically oriented. To him, the entire home was a product of imagination in search of an ideal way of living. As a factor for the elevation of man, he thought poetry indispensable for architectural design.[21]

The farmhouse layout was commanded by a central salon with an eight-meter-high ceiling, flanked by verandas built with reinforced concrete beams that jutted out from the main structure. The salon adjoined an open-air swimming pool equipped with underwater lighting (fig. 23). Adjacent to the back of the living room, two wings housed bedrooms, kitchen, studio, living room, bathrooms, and the ancestral room that held furniture from his family home in São Paulo, adding an old-fashioned touch to the interior of the modern building.

Actually, the unusual atmosphere of the farmhouse was created largely by its interior decoration, where Carvalho combined handicraft and feather art made by Brazilian Indians and a handicraft collection gathered during his trips through Brazil, Bolivia, and Peru. In the central salon, an aluminum fireplace hood was illuminated by a multicolor lamp set and an apparatus that continuously sprayed water on the heated hood to produce colored steam. The architect's concern for lighting extended to the swimming pool. During conversations with Hubert Herring, a friend from the United States, Carvalho

21. Dulce G. Carneiro, "A casa de Flávio de Carvalho," *Casa e Jardim* (São Paulo), no. 4 (January–February 1958): 37.

Fig. 23. Flávio de Carvalho,
front view of the Fazenda da
Capuava farmhouse, ca. 1945.
Historical photograph, private
archive, São Paulo.

expressed his desire to install red lamps in the swimming pool, to convey the idea of blood. When asked why he wanted a scarlet pool, he replied: "So that when you dive in, you feel you are entering hell!"[22]

Seen from the outside, the central salon assumes a trapezoid shape determined by facade elements—allusions to forms at the base of the Columbus Memorial Lighthouse. Despite the back part of his home being somewhat more conventional, it still features innovative details such as the fixed bed—where the bedspring rests on a brick base—and the aluminum finishing that replaces ordinary bathroom wall tiles. For his own use, Carvalho designed several pieces of furniture that were never built on an industrial scale, such as the dining-room chairs and glass-top table.

Carvalho also designed an enormous reflecting plate made of aluminum for installation on the ceiling of the central salon. It was flanked by colored lamps to provide indirect lighting that could be turned on in separate units. Its original design called for a removable aluminum plate mounted under a skylight, to admit daylight or to offer a view of star-studded skies. However, implementation of a suitable mechanism turned out to be too complicated.

22. Lídia Kliass, conversation with author, São Paulo, 18 December 1982.

If not unparalleled among the accomplishments of other modern architects, Carvalho's imposing home, springing from the dense eucalyptus forest, is perfectly integrated in his *oeuvre*, particularly among the designs of the late 1920s. Its uniqueness was widely acknowledged, for instance by critic Ruben Navarra (1917–1955) who wrote: "Although 'lightness' is one of the dogmas of modern architecture, the distinguished São Paulo architect creates building designs...[whose] volumes rise as heavy and intimidating as pagodas. The Fazenda da Capuava is an Assyrian tomb, and its monumental portal resembles a barbarian temple. His architectural style is mystical, in the primitive sense of the word."[23]

This was the period when Carvalho came of age as an artist, producing portraits that keenly revealed psychological traits, and female nudes of suppressed sensuality. His rendition of the physical features of his models at rest miraculously seemed to suggest motion. In those years his painting oscillated between oils that resemble Matisse, such as the *Portrait of Marion Konder Schteinitz* (fig. 24), and thick, palpitating oils that resemble Kokoschka, such as the *Portrait of Mário de Andrade* (1939). According to Andrade, his portrait reveals his somber side, the side he kept hidden from other people.[24] Carvalho's drawings ranged from quick, unshaded sketches to works in which he attained volume through shading, as for example in *Mulher deitada* (Woman at rest) (fig. 25).

During this period the artist strove to create in São Paulo an international art show—the May Salon—with the participation of the English surrealist group headed by Roland Penrose and E.L.T. Mesens, and of Ben Nicholson whom he had met during his travels in 1934–1935. Other exhibitors, such as Alexander Calder, Josef Albers, and a group from the American Abstract Artists including Carl Holty, Werner Drewes, and Jean Xcéron, were invited through French artist Jean Hélion,[25] who also showed at the salon. During his trip to Europe in the mid 1930s, Carvalho had the opportunity to interview Hélion and Arne Hošek (1885–1941), a Czech architect, artist, and set designer whose watercolor versions of musical compositions he found highly exciting. At the exhibition, Carvalho, who viewed surrealism and abstractionism as the basic animistic forces of the times, wanted to demonstrate the conflict between the two trends by placing them side by side. In so doing he was seeking to stimulate an artistic debate, certainly more as a propagandist than as an art critic.

His tireless activity throughout those years could be perceived as preliminary to the creation of the São Paulo Art Museum and the São Paulo Museum of Modern Art in the following decade, and to the organization of the First São Paulo Biennial by the Museum of Modern Art in 1951. From the mid 1930s Carvalho became the major promoter of São Paulo's cultural affairs. His undertakings, which involved artists and intellectuals, took place at the time of the foundation of both the Municipal Department of Culture (formed under Mário de Andrade's guidance) and the University of São Paulo, when creative movements were considerably strengthened. According to sociologist Maria Isaura Pereira de Queiroz, that era of flourishing, happy cultural activity consolidated the first Brazilian modernist generation.[26]

23. Ruben Navarra, *Jornal de Arte* (Campina Grande: Prefeitura Municipal, 1966), 348.

24. Mário de Andrade, "Um salão de feira," *Diário de S. Paulo*, 21 October 1941.

25. See Flávio de Carvalho's letters to Jean Hélion (17 November 1938 and 1 March 1939), Jean Hélion archive, Institut Mémoire et Edition Contemporaine, Paris.

26. Maria Isaura Pereira de Queiroz, ed., *Roger Bastide* (São Paulo: Ática, 1983), 11.

Fig. 24. Flávio de Carvalho,

Portrait of Marion Konder

Schteinitz, oil on canvas,

81 x 65 cm, 1938. De Carvalho

family collection, Olímpia,

São Paulo. Photograph by

Leonardo Crescenti.

The creation of museums and modernist art galleries prompted regular advertising of artistic events beginning in the 1940s. Although in that decade Carvalho no longer acted as cultural promoter within São Paulo art circles, he still entered architectural design competitions and pursued his career as an artist. He also devoted an increasing amount of time to research in which he tried to combine his interests in sociology, anthropology, and psychoanalysis. His research work was not restricted to writing essays (which were never published except as newspaper articles). His theories on the history of fashion led to his launching a line of summer men's wear (1956), on which occasion he paraded the streets of downtown São Paulo dressed in skirt and blouson! While involved in anthropological research that included an attempt to make a film in the Amazon region (1958), he challenged the expedition head to a duel with pistols. And his art production included a highly impressive series of nine charcoal drawings entitled *Série Trágica* (1947), illustrating his dying mother's facial expressions.

In the fifties and sixties the artist went back to entering consecutive architecture competitions, at which his designs were repeatedly turned down. Consequently he pressed charges against the São Paulo Legislative Assembly

(1961) on the basis of irregularities he claimed to have found in the invitation to bid. Such constant stress, which the artist referred to as "mental turbulence," was intentionally sought in his attempt to integrate art and life.

Among Brazilian artists, his multifarious activities are paralleled only by those of Vicente do Rego Monteiro, who for a while devoted himself more to poetry than to painting. Rego Monteiro also organized a remarkable exhibition dedicated to the School of Paris and held in Recife, Rio de Janeiro, and São Paulo (1930). In the early 1930s he tried to implement in Pernambuco (the state where he was born) a liquor distillery he had designed. Like Carvalho from a well-to-do family, Rego Monteiro produced works whose recognition was impaired by both his long absence from the country and his political standing during the period he lived in Brazil, in the 1930s.[27]

Carvalho's most obvious counterpart in Portuguese modernism is Almada Negreiros (1893–1970), a poet, painter, and playwright who was also known as an important set and costume designer. Just as Carvalho's writings explored the fields of sociology, anthropology, and psychoanalysis, Negreiros tried to explore the language of numbers and of geometric drawing, as shown in his last work, the mural Começar (To begin) (1969, Calouste Gulbenkian Foundation).[28]

In the 1930s the modernist movement's adoption of a nationalist esthetic resulted in Carvalho's work receiving the same treatment given to other less expressive characters—notwithstanding his active role as a cultural promoter. Trends oriented toward social and political radicalism were reaching their height. Something similar happened again in the 1950s, when abstractionist trends prevailed almost entirely. Ultimately, Carvalho's works attained recognition in the 1960s, possibly because they were remarkably identifiable with the art scene of that decade. His previous accomplishments, such as Experiência nº 2 and the launching of summer men's wear, were rehabilitated and reinterpreted as forerunners of current trends.[29] His status as member of the anthropophagic movement was recalled with the first stage performance of a play by Oswald de Andrade,[30] his late modernist colleague, who had also participated in the creation of the Teatro da Experiência.

The last years of Flávio de Carvalho's life brought successive commissions, particularly of portraits, as the result of an award from the international jury of the Ninth São Paulo Biennial (1967). Although he frequently became involved in minor demonstrations, the artist showed courage and self-respect by adequately handling both the amenities of social life and confrontations with the authorities.

27. Walter Zanini, Vicente do Rego Monteiro (1899–1970), exhibition catalogue (São Paulo: Museum of Contemporary Art of the University of São Paulo, 1971).

28. See José Augusto França, Almada Negreiros, o português sem mestre, 2nd ed. (Lisbon: Bertrand, 1983); and Lima de Freitas, Pintar o sete, ensaios sobre Almada Negreiros, o pitagorismo e a geometria sagrada (Lisbon: Imprensa Nacional/Casa da Moeda, 1990).

29. See comments by the Grupo Rex artists in their manifesto "Aviso: Rex Kaputt," in Rex Time, São Paulo, no. 5 (May 1967): 2–3.

30. O rei da vela, Oswald de Andrade's play written in 1934, was performed for the first time in 1967 under the direction of José Celso Martinez Correa (born 1937). Correa founded in São Paulo the Teatro Oficina that, with the Teatro de Arena, strove in the 1960s to surpass the acting style created by the Teatro Brasileiro de Comédia, the most important São Paulo theater company, founded in the late 1940s.

Fig. 25. Flávio de Carvalho,

Mulher deitada, pen and ink,

38.5 x 38.5 cm, 1938.

The Rodolfo Ortemblad

Filho collection, São Paulo.

Photograph by

Leonardo Crescenti.

Characteristically, some months before his death, he filed an application as a candidate for a chair at the São Paulo Academy of Letters. It was during the most repressive period of Brazil's military regime. His opponent was Minister of Justice Alfredo Buzaid.

Carvalho's activities in São Paulo represented the link between the first Brazilian modernist generation and the art movement of the sixties. His work is marked by his activities during the period 1927 to 1939, when he dominated the São Paulo art scene. □

Fig. 1. Affonso Penna Avenue, Belo Horizonte, 1930. Belo Horizonte municipal archive.

The Modernization of Brazilian Urban Space as a Political Symbol of the Republic

By Celina Borges Lemos

Translated by Elizabeth A. Jackson

Celina Borges Lemos is professor of theory and history of architecture and urbanism at the Federal University of Minas Gerais, as well as consultant on urban and cultural affairs for the city of Belo Horizonte. She is author and coauthor of publications on contemporary architecture and Brazilian urban anthropology.

This article examines the creation and planning process of two Brazilian cities, taking place during the second half of the nineteenth century and the first half of the twentieth. For this analysis we chose Belo Horizonte and Goiânia, capital cities of the states of Minas Gerais and Goiás respectively, along with the urban region of Pampulha, Belo Horizonte, developed in 1942. As the push toward modernization after the proclamation of the republic in 1889 is central to the genesis of these events, we also focus on how the state participated in this process.

The question of planned cities in Brazil is at the very least a curious one. If processes of architectonic and urbanistic preservation in Europe sought to maintain structures and urban patrimony, in Brazil these processes were frequently absent or interrupted. In this sense many cities possessed absolutely no urban infrastructure. Large cities were supplied with only partially adequate urban infrastructure. Often plans for architectonic or urbanistic renewal were not enacted completely. At other times projects and plans were not put into operation, "forgotten" by the responsible authorities.

Throughout this century, architectonic scenarios, as well as urban landscapes of Brazilian capitals, underwent a rapid evolutionary cycle. Considering the fragile conditions of these patrimonies, the absence of actions designed to preserve them led them to age prematurely. As the French anthropologist Lévi-Strauss aptly observed, while the passage of centuries represented enhancement for European cities, for those in the so-called New World, like South America, the mere passing of the years represented a decay.[1]

Not only during the provisional government (1889–1891) but also during subsequent governments, the problem of urban chaos and the inadequacy of capitals such as Rio de Janeiro (the federal capital), Ouro Preto (the Minas Gerais state capital), and Goiás Velho (the Goiás state capital) brought leaders face to face with the dilemma. Socioeconomic and political transformations after the proclamation of the republic resulted in substantial modifications in both the appearance and the makeup of the cities.[2] It fell to state governments to upgrade their capitals to meet new demands or to plan new ones compatible with the ideological and cultural values of the republican era. In the case of Belo Horizonte, and later of Goiânia, state governments opted for creating new cities rather than restoring to older capitals the capacity to grow and age

1. Claude Lévi-Strauss, *Tristes tropiques*, trans. John and Doreen Weightman (New York: Atheneum, 1975), 95.
2. Maurício de A. Abreu, *Evolução urbana do Rio de Janeiro* (Rio de Janeiro: Zahar, 1897).

Fig. 2. Aarão Reis, plan of Belo Horizonte, 1897. Belo Horizonte municipal archive.

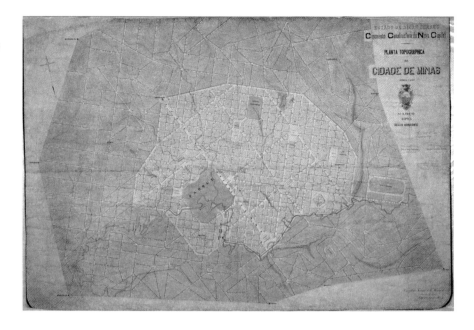

with dignity. In this context, the process of renewal of urban space and the formation of new cities during the first decades of the republic are the result of a search for modernization. Planned cities were emblematic of that search. Construction of the new came to be considered the fundamental condition that would guarantee the future.

The traditional social elite, whose fortunes were based on the export of raw materials during the empire, were learning to coexist with emerging groups. These groups were tied to financial and industrial sectors forming primarily in Rio de Janeiro, spurred by economic policies adopted during the First Republic (1889–1930).[3] Redefinition of the economic picture and changes in urban society, along with innovations inherent in European modernization, were producing a particular social mentality in the country. Progress, industrialization, and modern life became an obsession for the emerging bourgeoisie.[4]

This collective mentality, having as its principal point of reference the federal capital of Rio de Janeiro, was ruled by the idea of "regeneration," meaning not only urban regeneration but also, in the broader sense, regeneration of the country in social, economic, and political terms. The idea was widely disseminated in newspapers during the first decade of the republic. It "illuminated the spirit that presided over the movement for the destruction of the old city, complementing the dissolution of the old imperial society, in order to bring about a new urban structure."[5] Cities such as Rio de Janeiro and São Paulo could be characterized by a series of deficiencies: obsolete spatial organization, housing shortages, and the absence of urban infrastructure. The rising bourgeoisie, allied with new political leaders and positivist ideas, "cried out" for social and urban "sanitation" and "hygienization."

3. Boris Fausto, ed., *III. O Brasil republicano—1. A estrutura de poder e economia (1889–1930)* (São Paulo: Difel, 1985).

4. Nicolau Sevcenko, *A literatura como missão* (São Paulo: Brasiliense, 1985).

5. Ibid., 31

The spirit of "urban renewal" was part of the ideological climate, principally in the southeastern region, uniting under one objective the states of Rio de Janeiro, São Paulo, and Minas Gerais. Inspired by the industrialized urban spaces of Europe, these groups knew that the moment had arrived to prepare the cities for modernization. Their theoretical plans would function as "proto-cities," models for changed expectations of land use, of the economy, and of administrative and political order.[6]

The Belo Horizonte project, defined by the Constitutional Assembly of Minas Gerais in 1894, became a reference point, synthesizing the desire for change that circulated in Brazil at the end of the century. In response to the yearnings of the political and economic elite of Minas Gerais, the creation of the new capital sought to unify the state, guaranteeing its development and prosperity. Plans for transfer of the capital from Ouro Preto[7] had become a priority because its mission was political and economic innovation, besides being a stimulus for modernization. In the same way that "the Republic was born marked by the influence of the United States, the idea of regeneration had its references in the most recent urbanistic innovation in the United States as well as in Europe."[8]

Aarão Reis[9] was director of the building commission for the new capital, having been appointed in February 1894 by the president of the state of Minas Gerais, Affonso Penna. Reis was charged with completing the construction of Belo Horizonte in four years. In fact, he directed the construction until 20 May 1895; then, during the ensuing presidency of Crispim Jaques Bias Fortes, he was asked to resign and was replaced by the engineer Francisco Bicalho. Bicalho directed the project until the dissolution of the commission in 1898 after the inauguration of the new capital.

The project developed by Reis (fig. 2) effectively addressed the intentions of the political leadership of Minas Gerais. By integrating an orthogonal grid defined by the streets with a diagonal grid defined by the avenues, the author reiterated modern neoclassical urbanism. The creation of monumental axes, ordered topographically by use, relates the profile of the new capital to the urban plan of 1791 for Washington, D.C. as well as to the reconfiguration of Paris from 1853 to 1859. The French urbanist Pierre Charles l'Enfant, working in the United States, first put into practice some of the rational neoconservative principles that Haussmann later implanted in Paris. The plan for Washington adopted the concepts and perspective of the baroque, made viable by a double network of orthogonal and radial grids. Just as in the plan for Belo Horizonte,

6. C. N. Ferreira dos Santos, *A cidade como um jogo de cartas* (São Paulo: Edição da Universidade de São Paulo, 1988), 39.

7. The old colonial capital of Ouro Preto lies about one hundred kilometers from the location chosen for the new capital. Originally called Vila Rica de Albuquerque, it was the result of the integration of numerous villages that began with the mining of gold in the early eighteenth century. These villages, set out linearly, eventually grouped together spontaneously so that in 1720 Vila Rica, already consolidated, became the capital of the Capitania das Minas Gerais. See Sylvio Vasconcellos, *Vila Rica* (São Paulo: Perspectiva, 1977).

8. João Antônio de Paula, *A idéia de nação: a república e a democracia no Brasil* (Belo Horizonte: Centro de Planejamento Regional, 1990), 1–45.

9. The engineer Aarão Reis was born in the state of Pará and completed his academic studies at the Polytechnic School of Rio de Janeiro. Before assuming the task of building the new capital, he had distinguished himself as designer and executor of several federal government projects. See Celina B. Lemos, "Determinações do espaço urbano: a evolução urbanística e simbólica do centro de Belo Horizonte" (master's thesis, Universidade Federal de Minas Gerais, 1988).

Fig. 3. Liberty Square, Education Palace, Belo Horizonte, 1900. Belo Horizonte municipal archive.

by means of this concept the city gained a different character. Haussman's plan for the renewal of Paris during the empire of Napoleon III was characterized by vistas in perspective, implemented through a long series of streets. "This corresponds to the tendency repeatedly observed in the nineteenth century of ennobling technical necessities by making them artistic objectives."[10]

Searching for perfect efficiency, in a detailed study of local topography the building commission foresaw a functional organization for Belo Horizonte that was strategically distributed in space. Following the order and rationalism of that spatial and functional conception, Reis adopted positivist and sanitary innovations.[11] They shaped the living conditions, comfort, and beauty of the city through sanitation projects, lighting, and road and transport systems. Initial zoning was foreseen in the primary urban grid, a proposal containing the genesis of discrimination and segregation inherent in modern urban capitalism.

The three types of social and spatial segregation defined by Lojkine are represented at the level of housing, public services, and home/work transportation.[12] A large part of the population from the earlier village of Belo Horizonte was composed of low income groups. Since they resided in houses of poor quality, the compensation they received for moving was laughable. They were then forced to live outside the first urban zone in temporary structures. As if this were not enough, both the remaining population of the earlier village and

10. Walter Benjamin, "Paris, capital do século XIX," in F. Kothe, ed., *Walter Benjamin. Sociologia* (São Paulo: Atica, 1985), 41.

11. Positivism appeared among the guiding principles of the Belo Horizonte plan through Aarão Reis. As a spatial planner, Reis acted as an authentic "social hygienist." He conceived of the environment as being responsible for the health of the social body and of each individual. One of his primary intentions was to contribute to the formation of an industrial society in Brazil by means of urban planning. As a positivist, he considered the role of the individual and of private property relevant only when integrated with a social function, in other words, a collective representation. See Lemos, "Determinações do espaço urbano."

12. Jean Lojkine, *Le marxisme, l'état et la question urbaine* (Paris: Presses Universitaires de France, 1977), 237.

the imported workers lost their communal life based on relationships with neighbors. Additionally, entry into the urban zone —where public services were concentrated —was made difficult because of a lack of transportation between urban and suburban zones.

Nonetheless, Reis had reconciled and reinterpreted modern conceptions of urbanism, defining a new urban paradigm for the country. Belo Horizonte was inaugurated on 12 December 1897,[13] when the repertory of an eclectic architecture actually reinforced Reis's intention (fig. 3). The first public buildings, strategically situated, functioned as virtual sanctuaries. Thus values, stability, and form were brought to life in an urban image — an allegory for a political ordering (fig. 4).

The republic as idea and image of progress — a practical version of the homologous concept of civilization — preoccupied the nation's bourgeoisie.[14] The creation of the new capital may be considered the first concrete realization of the *belo horizonte* (beautiful horizon) promised by the republican future. Thus the capital of Minas Gerais became emblematic of the viability of this new world (figs. 1 and 5).

By the early 1900s the capital was showing signs of consolidation on every level. Created to symbolize present tense action and the arrival of the twentieth century, its future was becoming more assured.[15] At that moment it possessed the ability to "shape" a space for transformation, progress, and history.

13. At the time of its inauguration, Belo Horizonte was known as Cidade de Minas (City of mines). The president of the state, Crispim Jaques Bias Fortes, declared the seat of the government of Minas Gerais transferred with Decree No. 1,085. Only in 1901 did the city receive the name of Belo Horizonte. It was intended to shelter two hundred thousand inhabitants. Today the population of the capital is almost three million.

14. C. F. de C. Bandeira de Mello, "Pois tudo é assim...educação política e trabalho em Minas Gerais (1889–1907)" (master's thesis, Universidade Federal de Minas Gerais, 1990).

15. Ibid.

Fig. 5. Liberty Square,

Liberty Palace, Belo Horizonte,

1922. Belo Horizonte

municipal archive.

The 1930s represent a second phase of socioeconomic and political change in Brazil. This period was strongly marked by Getúlio Vargas who, supported by the Liberal Alliance,[16] took power during the Revolution of 1930. The nation was undergoing enormous social and political upheaval, based principally on a redefinition of the interplay of political forces and the emerging organization of urban society. The sociopolitical reality of oligarchic domination based on the hegemony of the coffee bourgeoisie was breaking up, while at the same time the urban lower classes were organizing themselves in search of political representation. Along with these factors, the formation of different parties able to express varied social interests was accompanied by a broad reconsideration of cultural issues. In this way, numerous cultural events of the 1930s are particularly tied to innovations implemented at the beginning of the Second Republic (the Vargas era). Based on changed political alliances, the Second Republic viewed construction of a modern national state as its principal goal.

Among the numerous activities of the Vargas government, the idea of creating a new capital for the state of Goiás received total support at the federal level. The option to move the capital was the result of the vision of then governor Pedro Ludovico Teixeira. The certainty for success of such an undertaking came principally from the fact that Belo Horizonte had corresponded so completely to the political and economic interests of the leaders of the First Republic.

16. The Liberal Alliance consisted of a regional front, including the vast majority of political representatives from Rio Grande do Sul and Minas Gerais, joined by the Democratic Party of São Paulo. The objective of the Liberal Alliance was to launch the candidacy of Getúlio Vargas for the presidency against the existing government in 1929. See Boris Fausto, *III. O Brasil republicano— 2. Sociedade e instituições (1889–1930)* (São Paulo: Difel, 1985).

"As the fourth largest state, even larger than Minas Gerais, Goiás was far from having the same economic vigor.... It did not possess any deep sense of unity and only the southern region had seen any development, first with gold mining in the eighteenth century and more recently with the growth of an extensive flourishing agriculture."[17]

The city of Goiás, then the state capital, was mired in decadence because of the depletion of its gold reserves. Therefore the planning of a capital was a concrete action to include the state of Goiás in the modernization process heralded nationally by the Vargas government. The modern configuration of space, together with closer proximity between the capital and the southeastern region, showed signs of guaranteeing dynamic socioeconomic interchange. Thus the primary objective for the plan of Goiânia was the representation of a new status quo, in other words, the arrival of progress in the interior.

The area selected for the capital lies about one hundred kilometers from Goiás Velho (Old Goiás — the name under which the former capital was known). Governor Teixeira invited Attílio Correia Lima from the state of Rio de Janeiro to develop the plans. An architect specializing in urbanism, Correia Lima brought from France the guiding principles of spatial conception and urban organization for the city. The plan was reshaped by the urbanist Armando Augusto Godói, who partly altered the architect's intentions.

Narcisa Abreu Cordeiro emphasizes that "initially Goiânia was planned by the architect Attílio Correia Lima, with central, north, south, west and east (university) sectors, [and] with parks and wooded areas." When Godói took over the project, he removed the east sector and redesigned the south sector. He also altered "the zoning of intra-urban uses, [and] defined the urban outlines of the planned sectors as well as the suburban ones. He also redefined the wooded areas and parks projected by Attílio Correia Lima, highlighting them as a greenbelt surrounding the planned nucleus, since Armando Godói's intention was that future settlements should occur as satellite cities at some convenient remove from the projected center."[18]

According to Correia Lima, the city's avenues and streets followed the topography, with the administrative center located on one of the highest sites. Further, the layout avoided creating spaces where water might accumulate, since the region is subject to periodic heavy rainfall. The administrative center's preeminent location was reinforced by the convergence of the city's three most important avenues. Quoting Correia Lima, "within proper proportions, the monumental effect desired was the classical principle adopted at Versailles and later at Karlsruhe and Washington" (fig. 6).[19] Correia Lima's plan meshed with the intentions of Godói, who planned the arborization of the roads foreseeing "for the three avenues that converged on the administrative center, besides the arborization of the pathways, large central reserves also filled with leafy trees" (fig. 7).[20]

17. Yves Bruand, *Arquitetura contemporânea no Brasil* (São Paulo: Perspectiva, 1981), 349.

18. N. A. Cordeiro, *Goiânia, evoluções do plano urbanístico* (Goiânia: Instituto de Planejamento, 1989), 11.

19. The plan for Versailles was begun in 1661 with the enlargement of the royal palace under the direction of Louis Le Vau (1612–1670). The layout for the gardens was based on a system of radials and *rond-point*, in such a way that both parts were characterized by infinite perspective and had the palace as their center. Versailles represents the essence of a seventeenth-century city: authority and borders, dynamism and openness. The city of Karlsruhe, Germany, was conceived in 1715, with the palace situated at the distributive center of a system of radial streets. The development of the baroque palace was reinforced by projects of Balthasar Neumann. See Christian Norberg-Shulz, *Meaning in Western Architecture* (New York: Praeger, 1975).

20. Edgar A. Graeff, *1983—Goiânia: 50 anos* (Goiânia: Universidade Católica de Goiás, 1985), 12.

Fig. 6. Attílio Correia Lima, plan of Goiânia, 1933. Photograph from Edgar A. Graeff, *1983— Goiânia: 50 anos* (Goiânia: Universidade Católica de Goiás, 1985).

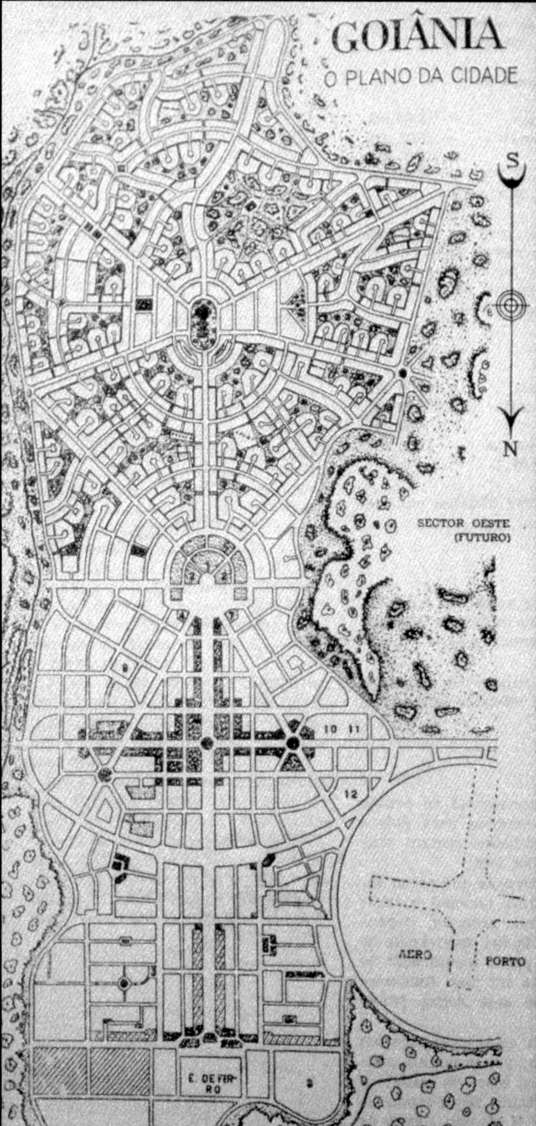

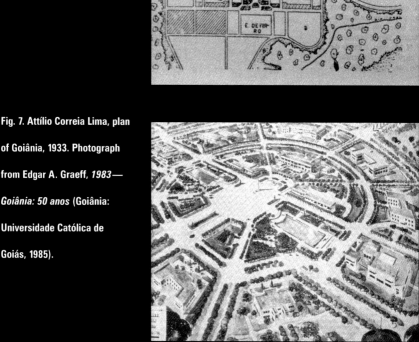

Fig. 7. Attílio Correia Lima, plan of Goiânia, 1933. Photograph from Edgar A. Graeff, *1983— Goiânia: 50 anos* (Goiânia: Universidade Católica de Goiás, 1985).

Along with these measures related to the environment, Correia Lima programed functions by sectors, integrating them into sanitation, water supply, and urban road systems. In terms of zoning, the urbanist foresaw the implantation of both a politico-administrative and a commercial center. The administrative center lay outside the densely traveled areas, providing a connection between commercial and residential sectors. Also, the city's functional organization into sectors was endowed with flexibility. This facilitated not only the interchange between areas but also the possibility of their expansion (fig. 8).

According to the above description, it can be seen that the plan for the city of Goiânia was characterized by a conjunction of modern tendencies in urbanism that recalled experiences occurring in Europe during the seventeenth, eighteenth, and nineteenth centuries, their basis being the revival of baroque perspective at Versailles. From Civic Square, center of state government, spring three main avenues that structure the spatial conception as a whole. This spatial organization, adopted in Washington and later in Belo Horizonte, takes as its focus the governing or administrative center. All these examples sought primarily to guarantee the monumental nature of the principal axis, in other words, the Governor's Palace (figs. 9 and 10). Though it was planned forty years after Belo Horizonte, some of the historical urbanistic references for Goiânia derive from the seventeenth century. In this way Goiânia superimposes two concepts, situating the plan historically at some distance from the ideas spreading among the modernists in São Paulo and Rio de Janeiro.

Alongside these neoclassical tendencies, the project of Goiânia under Godói derived its conclusive characteristics from the "garden cities" of Ebenezer Howard. These contained not just expressive landscaping but created bucolic environments that characterized the residential units. The outline evolving from the monumental axis had rings of ideal settings for the implantation of residential sectors or neighborhoods. The serenity facilitated by the landscape, as well as the natural geometry inherent in "garden cities" (like Letchworth and

Fig. 9. The Governor's Palace during construction, Goiânia, 1940s. Planning Institute archive, Goiânia.

Welwyn near London), are in contradiction to the baroque principal axis. The planting of trees, together with a non-monumental architecture, principally in public buildings, minimized the role of symbolic function, reducing the visual effect of urbanism at Versailles (fig. 11). While urbanists rejected this contradiction, formed by historicist fragments in the plan for Goiânia, they highlighted the benefits of modernization in the name of the future of the state: "[T]oday, thanks to social evolution and to the fact that humanity has entered fully into the industrial era, the modern city is a center for work, a great school in which to educate, develop, and improve the main elements of man's physical and spiritual nature, and a source for the powerful energies without which the people would not progress or prosper. It is from modern cities that vigorous collective impulses emanate and in which the movements and activities of a nation are coordinated."[21]

The city of Goiânia was based on these intentions, but its expansion was principally guided by the plan's initial contradictions. Thus, in terms of design, Goiânia represents the superimposition of temporalities, alternating between the neoclassical style and the preprogressivist and preculturalist models of the nineteenth century. Accidentally or not, these characteristics, taken together, did suit the tropical climate of Central Brazil.

Referring to the former capital, Lévi-Strauss commented that "it was all too small or too old. A completely virgin territory would have to be found for the establishment of the gigantic scheme that was now envisaged." But when he visited the new capital in 1937, he opined that Goiânia "was built on an endless plain, half vacant lot, half battlefield.... Nothing could be more barbaric or inhuman than this appropriation of the desert."[22] Given these circumstances, he indicated that the risk of Goiânia was greater than that of Belo Horizonte.

Despite the contradictions existent in the plan, and the testimony of the anthropologist, Goiânia corresponded to the aims of its creators,[23] performing the role of pioneer frontier for the Brazilian Central West. Combining tradition and artifice, the construction of Goiânia intensified the contrast between the interior and the city.

Before the creation of Goiânia, the modernist experiment in architecture and urbanism had not yet taken effect.[24] But soon after the inauguration of Goiânia and its repercussions, the modernist experience in Brazil struck a chord in the federal capital. The first manifestations of the modernist movement in architecture relate to the construction of the Ministry of Education and Public Health in Rio de Janeiro, under the direction of architect Lúcio Costa, and also the construction of the tourism and recreation complex in Pampulha, Belo Horizonte.

21. Lojkine, *Le marxisme*. We should note that when Godói adopts the idea of the "modern city," he is referring to urban industrial society. This concept was widely disseminated in Europe during the nineteenth century, when urbanism sought to solve the urban chaos generated principally by the industrial revolution. See Françoise Choay, *L'urbanisme, utopie et realités: une anthologie* (Paris: Editions Seuil, 1965).

22. Lévi-Strauss, *Tristes Tropiques*, 125–126.

23. Pedro Ludovico Teixeira signed the decree transferring the capital on 23 March 1937.

24. It is worth noting that when we speak of modern urbanism we are referring to nineteenth-century experiences based on neoclassical, preculturalist, and preprogressivist modern urbanisms. When we think of modernist architecture and urbanism, we situate this experiment created by the modernist vanguards in the twentieth century, after World War One. For more information consult Choay, *L'urbanisme*.

Fig. 11. View of Goiás Avenue, Goiânia, 1940s. Planning Institute archive, Goiânia.

With Juscelino Kubitschek in the city hall of Belo Horizonte, Minas Gerais had the chance to lead the modernist experiment so cultivated in the federal capital. The illustrious mayor understood that it was not enough to create an industrial park to direct his city toward the future. To this end, he assumed the heroic posture befitting modernist urbanists, seeking to modernize the famous "beautiful horizon." As history tells us, Belo Horizonte, created and planned as a symbol of progress, was again demanding innovations. The modern spirit that dominated the city, together with the interest of its dynamic mayor in defining his administration by bringing about modernization, found their principal goal in Pampulha.[25]

In 1938, in Pampulha, a dam and a water reservoir had been inaugurated. Mayor Kubitschek and Governor Benedito Valadares believed that the Pampulha area had greater potential, warranting the special attention of public authorities. Determined to modernize Belo Horizonte and reinject it with prosperity, they

25. At the beginning of the century, Pampulha was an agricultural area of farms and ranches. Located in the northern vector of Belo Horizonte, the area corresponding to Pampulha Velha (Old Pampulha) showed the first signs of urbanization at that time. Portuguese and Italian tenant farmers settled the area, calling it Santo Antônio da Pampulha. These settlers, upon acquisition of the land, formed one of the first supply points for Belo Horizonte. Pampulha is located eleven kilometers from the town center or original urban zone.

decided that Pampulha would delimit a new age in the capital. Considering intervention in urban space to be a strategic act of renewal, the mayor invited the French urbanist Alfred Agache to offer his diagnosis of the city and to evaluate the merits of Pampulha.[26] Agache determined that Belo Horizonte was an urban chaos, requiring expansion in order to solve a severe housing shortage.

Nonetheless, both leaders sought a design for Pampulha that would transform it into Belo Horizonte's principal center of tourism. Kubitschek invited architect Oscar Niemeyer[27] to plan the tourism and recreation complex. Niemeyer, who had just begun the design of a casino for Belo Horizonte, transferred this initiative to Pampulha. Along with the casino, Niemeyer proposed the development of a yacht and golf club, a dance pavilion, and the St. Francis of Assisi Church. In order to increase the stature of the projects, he invited landscape architect Roberto Burle Marx, painter Cândido Portinari, and sculptor Alfredo Ceschiatti to collaborate. Designed and built in a short period of time, the three buildings were completed in 1942. The inauguration of this complex announced not only the installation of a sophisticated center of tourism and recreation but also the innovative action of public authorities, crystallized in the daring modernist architecture of Niemeyer and his collaborators.

According to Niemeyer, Pampulha was what Belo Horizonte needed most. "The construction of the casino took place at the same time as the dance pavilion, the yacht and golf club, and the church; I remember them with particular affection because they were my first completed projects and those that made a decisive mark on my professional orientation."[28]

The architecture of Pampulha brings together certain rationalist principles, based on the experience of Le Corbusier. For example, the use of the independent structure created with reinforced concrete was crucial for Niemeyer to be able to manifest an expressive plastic imagination.[29] Additionally, the architect sought to reaffirm the modernist legacy left by Le Corbusier in the 1930s by means of the independent structure and the use of columns, glass walls, marquees, and *brize-soleil*. As we shall see, Niemeyer grasped the teachings of the rationalist master with ease, having explored thoroughly the plastic possibilities of reinforced concrete.

On the casino project (figs. 12 and 13) Niemeyer chose the juxtaposition and interpenetration of volumes. "The rigor of the straight lines that predominate in the structure is attenuated by the curved glass wall on the patio and by the irregular form of the marquee, whose apparent instability confers a dynamic element and a composition marked entirely by its equilibrium."[30] The casino was conceived out of energetic contrasts, based on the opposition of materials and of curved and plane volumes.

The yacht and golf club (fig. 14), as the principal recreation center of Pampulha, has an autonomy in relation to the casino based on its pure geometric forms. Niemeyer highlights oblique lines, beginning with the incline of

26. Known as "Professor Agache," the urbanist had been working in Rio de Janeiro since the end of the 1920s.

27. Oscar Niemeyer was born in Rio de Janeiro in 1907. He studied architecture at the National School of Fine Arts in Rio de Janeiro from 1929 to 1934.

28. Suzy de Mello, "Arquitetura moderna em Minas Gerais," in *I Seminário sobre cultura mineira* (Belo Horizonte: Imprensa Oficial, 1980), 46.

29. Yves Bruand, *Arquitetura contemporânea no Brasil* (São Paulo: Perspectiva, 1981), 109–115.

30. Ibid.

Fig. 12. Oscar Niemeyer, casino,

Pampulha, Belo Horizonte,

1942. Photograph by Ricardo

Nogueira, 1994.

the slab, facilitating movement in the facade. The longitudinal elevation, made up of two rectangular trapezoids interconnected by a smaller base, allows for spatial continuity between the exterior and the interior, strengthened by the glass walls. Out of this formal option is born the organization of internal space that is at the "same time unique and diversified in its essential elements."[31]

The restaurant and dance pavilion (fig. 15), a meeting and recreation center, was built on a small island. The conception of the project highlighted the island's natural gifts, and the neutrality of the space incorporates the beauty of lake and landscape. Nature was reinterpreted based on the curve and the concrete, highlighted in the circular building and the sinuous marquee. Both the glass wall and the outdoor marquee suggest lightness and transparency.

The project for the St. Francis of Assisi Church (fig. 16) was based on the configuration of four free spans distributed around a central parabolic dome. This dome is divided into two parts, covering the entire nave and altar. The spans cover the sacristy and the annexes. In the church's domed interior, a play of light juxtaposes the dark wood paneling of the nave and the fresco by Portinari, located in the presbytery. Externally, the building is carried by curved and oblique lines providing points of tension in space. "The systematic asymmetry and the flexibility of both the whole and the details translate into an extraordinary impression of lightness, harmony, and clarity of conception."[32] There is a distinct contrast between the dome and the tiled walls, situated opposite the main entrance, eliminating the transparency between interior and exterior. This is recaptured in the glass wall of the entrance and in the wooden latticework of the bell tower.

With reinforced concrete allowing flexibility of form, and "indifferent to criticism and veiled insinuations, such as gratuitous baroque," Niemeyer "penetrated confidently into the world of new forms, lyricism, and creative liberty that Pampulha opened for modern architecture." For the architect concrete suggested "something different," or rather, "an architecture made entirely of dream and fantasy, of curves, grand free spaces of extraordinary balances." Thus he chose an architecture that expressed "the boldness of new technique and the revolution that would mark the history of construction."[33]

Conceiving of architecture as esthetic object, shown by the purity of forms and the renowned landscape, Niemeyer sought in the baroque of Minas Gerais the "montage" of a tradition. The recuperation of a baroque vocabulary was decisive for the legitimation of the modernist scenario in Minas. This attitude did not mean a return to the past, as had occurred during the neoclassical and eclectic periods. The baroque was refigured, conceptually, by means of "a knowing play with the most essential characteristics of the free and rich composition of spaces, in the best and purest interpretation of the principles that can be recognized in baroque architecture in Minas...."[34]

Fig. 13. Oscar Niemeyer, interior of casino, Pampulha, Belo Horizonte, 1942. Photograph by Ricardo Nogueira, 1994.

31. Ibid.
32. Ibid.
33. Ibid.
34. Ibid.

Fig. 14. Oscar Niemeyer,

yacht and golf club, Pampulha,

Belo Horizonte, 1942.

Photograph from *L'Architecture*

D'Aujourd' Hui 18, no. 13/14

(September 1947).

Fig. 15. Oscar Niemeyer, restaurant and dance pavilion, Pampulha, Belo Horizonte, 1942. Photograph by

Ricardo Nogueira, 1994.

Fig. 16. Oscar Niemeyer,

St. Francis of Assisi Church,

Pampulha, Belo Horizonte,

1942. Photograph by

Cathy Leff, 1994.

In the opinion of Yves Bruand, the sculptural quality of Niemeyer's works in Pampulha shows a break with rigid rationalist vocabulary. The critic admits that there was simply a spiritual kinship; in other words, a formal imagination endowed with "features reminiscent of baroque taste." With this reasoning Bruand concludes that Niemeyer incorporates "spiritually a brilliant fusion of the great permanent tendencies of art history with the elements that inspired them: reason and intuition."[35]

The opinions of Mello and Bruand affirm that Niemeyer's inspiration from the eighteenth-century baroque experience of Minas Gerais was fundamental. In a detailed observation of the architectonic whole of Pampulha, we can discern a possible analogy with Heinrich Wölfflin's classic study of the baroque.[36] For Wölfflin the baroque devalued the line as outline, multiplying the edges and denoting pure visual movement. Niemeyer, with the parabolic curve of the church and the curved form of the dance pavilion and the casino, enriched and confirmed this analysis. Further considering the baroque esthetic, Wölfflin states that the curve is a plastic break with limits as such, creating an image in motion. Reaching the optical dimension, the walls vibrate, the space trembles in all its corners.[37] The vigorous and mysterious baroque spirit is also discernible internally because of the tension between points of brightness and points of depth. The mirrored walls and the glass panels enlarge spaces, creating depth and eliminating interruptions. The intentional luminosity both clarifies and

35. Ibid.
36. Heinrich Wölfflin, *Renaissance and Baroque*, trans. Kathrin Simon, intro. Peter Murray (Ithaca: Cornell University Press, 1966).
37. Heinrich Wölfflin, *Conceitos fundamentais da história da arte* (São Paulo: Martins Fontes, 1989).

obscures interior spaces, suggesting ambiguity, ordered disorder (fig. 13). All these characteristics were reinterpreted by Niemeyer's modernist architecture in which the search for movement, for the non-limit, and for beauty was transmuted through signs, in a stimulus to life. The search for the "always new" as a condition of the modernist attitude was actualized in the works of Pampulha. Niemeyer's modernist architecture was legitimized by finding in the baroque tradition a key to the present.

In conclusion, Pampulha signified the first step in the construction of a national identity in architecture. The success of the undertaking assured the next heroic step for the team of Oscar Niemeyer and Juscelino Kubitschek — the construction of Brasília. Alongside Belo Horizonte, Goiânia, and Pampulha, the plan of Brasília (figs. 17 and 18) represents the will to "construct" a modern country, which had consumed the Brazilian social imagination since the First Republic. The very plans for these cities and neighborhoods are a living archive of the progress from intention to realization. The arrival of modernism, allied with an effective program of modernization, showed an intention to construct a Brazil in accordance with a civilizing vision.[38] In that context, architecture and modern urbanism perfectly anticipated the future. Then the modernist experience, eliminating historical references from its corpus, opened a wide range of possibilities by means of the rationalization of functional principles. The real applicability of those principles corresponded in some cases to the dreams and goals of urban societies still in the process of development.

In Brazil's case, the idea of the modern was associated with values such as progress and civilization, constituting an "ideology of development." Today, the future hinted at by these cities is nothing more than a past. With their melancholy air, the planned cities, now aged by time, are visual remains of the intentions of those who dreamed of a different Brazil. □

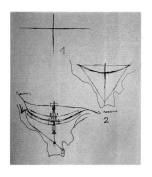

Fig. 17. Lúcio Costa, first design of Brasília, 1957. Photograph from *Módulo* (Rio de Janeiro), no. 18 (1960).

38. James Holston, *The Modernist City: An Anthropological Critique of Brasília* (Chicago: University of Chicago Press, 1989).

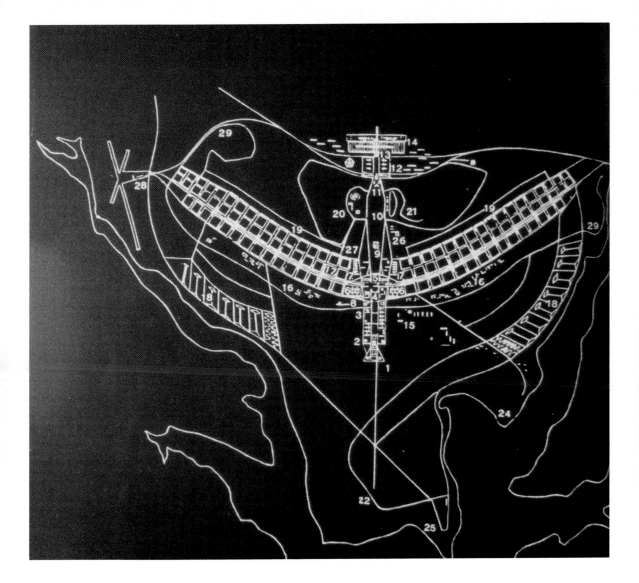

Fig. 18. Lúcio Costa, pilot plan
of Brasília, 1957.

1) Three Powers Square

2) Ministers Esplanade

3) Cathedral

4) Cultural Sector

5) Entertainment Sector

6) Service Sector

7) Commercial Sector

8) Hotel Sector

9) Radio and Television Tower

10) Sport Sector

11) City Hall Square

12) Military Quarters

13) Railroad Station

14) Light Industry and Warehousing

15) University City — Campus

16) Embassy Sector

17) Dwelling Sector

18) Mansion Sector

19) Horticulture and Floriculture

20) Botanic Park

21) Zoo

22) Golf Club

23) Bus Station

24) Yacht Club

25) Presidential Residence

26) Jockey Club

27) Open-Air Market

28) Airport

29) Cemetery

Photograph from *Módulo*

(Rio de Janeiro), no. 18 (1960).

Fig. 1 Amazon Theater, Manaus, walkway, Portuguese-style stone mosaic. Photograph by Jean Manzon.

The Jungle in Brazilian Modern Design

By Paulo Herkenhoff

Translated by Kim Mrazek Hastings

Paulo Herkenhoff is an art historian and an independent curator based in Rio de Janeiro. From 1985 to 1990 he was chief curator of the Museum of Modern Art in Rio, founding its collection of Brazilian design and illustrated books.

In the heart of the Amazon region, near the strategically situated city of Manaus, lies the confluence of the Negro and Solimões Rivers. At this meeting of the waters, the black current of the Negro and the clay-colored current of the Solimões form the Amazon River. For several kilometers, up to the final moment, nature guards this visual sign. Before the two rivers mix, areas of black water are seen as separate from areas of muddy water. This extraordinary phenomenon is the perfect metaphor of transformation in modern Brazil, of nature in art, and of the way the Amazon region molds the entire country.[1]

The meeting of the waters is the subject of the pavement in the plaza facing the Amazon Theater (1896) in Manaus (fig. 1). The pattern integrates the sinuous movement of black and white stripes, symbol of the birth of the Amazon River. It is a design of graphic synthesis; discourse is created by the reduction of its allegorical elements. The simple form evokes the elegant sensuality of the movement. Its construction recalls the Portuguese tradition of mosaic sidewalks in black and white stone, a tradition transported to coastal cities including Rio de Janeiro, Recife, and Salvador. The charming design of the Manaus sidewalk was adopted in the walkways along Copacabana Beach in Rio (fig. 2); there they symbolize the waves of the sea and have earned international fame. The Amazon Theater's sidewalks may well have been the first great modern Brazilian public monument. They reveal to us how Brazilian modernity has been constructed with bases in the jungle, considered as nature and native cultural territory.

The Amazon Theater also indicates how, at the turn of the century, the Amazon region thrived on the splendor of her fortune from the rubber monopoly. In Belém, Manaus, and other smaller cities, the rubber boom (1850–1910) shaped a culture in which nostalgia and desire for a Europe in the jungle were evident. French was heard in the cities' salons; the rich of Belém and Manaus sent their clothes to Europe to be cleaned. In a waiting room of the stately home built in Belém by Victor Maria da Silva during this

---

1. Allegorical representation of the Amazon began with the classical myth of the Amazons, who gave a name to the region and whose existence was reiterated throughout the centuries by travelers and scientists of all stripes. As recently as the end of the nineteenth century, Dom Pedro II, emperor of Brazil, commissioned a study by Gonçalves Dias to clear up doubts about the existence of tribes of warrior women. The study was published in *Revista do Instituto Histórico e Geográfico do Brasil* 18 (1885).

Fig. 2. Sidewalk at Copacabana

Beach, Rio de Janeiro,

Portuguese-style stone mosaic.

Photograph by Jean Manzon.

golden age, there are two *art-nouveau* panels in tile (A. Arnoux's design, executed by Boulanger). In the panels the flora of Europe represent spring and autumn. Nothing indicates better the artificiality of importing *art nouveau* to the Amazon. In Belém, located just south of the equator, only two seasons occur, "summer" and "winter"; and these periods are determined exclusively by the amount of daily rainfall.

In Belém the name of a small architectural folly—Paris na América (1906–1909) —conveys a certain dubious plan to construct a "tropical Paris," as Célia Bassalo stingingly summarized it.[2] Nearly all the materials with which this fabric shop was built were imported from Europe;[3] the architecture features inlays of *art-nouveau* details. There are no constructions in Belém with the structurally *art-nouveau* character of a Maison du Peuple (1896–1899) by Victor Horta, or that appear to sprout organically like Antoni Gaudí's projects. In the eclectic architecture of the Francisco Bolonha residence, a bathroom's European tiles

2. Célia Bassalo, *O 'art nouveau' em Belém* (Belém: Fundação Nacional de Arte/Universidade Federal de Pará, 1984), n.p.

3. Paris na América was built by engineer Raimundo Viana and foremen Salvador and Mesquita. Viana was the owner. The steel structure of the building was imported from Scotland; the tiles and stones from Portugal; the ceramic floor and the clock from Germany; windowpanes, chandeliers, mirrors, and the stairway from France.

were decorated with European water-lilies and dragonflies, basic natural themes of *art-nouveau* vocabulary. Amazonian flora is left out of the decoration. As for public works, among the constructions for which Francisco Bolonha was responsible are the São Braz Market, the Ver-o-Peso (See-the-weight) Markets, and the now defunct water reservoir, whose iron structure was imported from Walter MacFarlane and Company of Glasgow. The widespread use of iron architecture, exported to Belém and Manaus from Europe, is worth mentioning. In Belém Antonio Faciola's residence was decorated with ornamental details, including chandeliers and *plafonniers*, vases, china, and bronze sculptures, some signed by Émile Gallé, August and Antonin Daum, A. Larroux, and Félix Charpentier, acquired in Paris at the beginning of the century. With the Daum brothers and especially with Gallé, Faciola's preference was centered on the production of Nancy. As social history of the culture, *art nouveau*'s presence in Belém and Manaus is the result of the Amazon's integration into the international economy and signifies a capacity greater than that of many other Brazilian cities to assimilate a new international style.

One cannot speak of a singular and typically Amazonian *art nouveau*. Imported models were superimposed as status symbols, with no basis in the region's socio-economic situation. Amazonian urbanism and architecture of the turn of the century had little to do with the ecological needs of the tropics and its constructive knowledge, solidified over three centuries. In Belém Frenchified taste came face to face with a city of colonial Portuguese tradition coexisting with the *caboclo* (mestizo) universe. Furthermore, a nativist movement was beginning to take shape. Archaeological studies and findings by the Paraense Museum (the future Goeldi Museum) were establishing standards and measures of historicity with the ceramics of Marajó and the Tapajós River—and it is well-known that *art nouveau* intended to overcome historicism and academicism. This conflict between reference to national and foreign hegemonic centers and the strong character of native culture underlay the identity crisis suffered by the provincial lower middle class of the entire Amazon. The reorganization of the Philomathic Society into the Paraense Museum in Belém in 1894 propitiated the introduction of new scientific and museological bases, offering a stimulus that valued the material culture of Amazonian peoples, namely the Marajoaras.[4] For his role in this process, Swiss scientist Emílio Goeldi, among others, deserves special attention. In his studies of the Amazon, Goeldi brought Darwinism to Belém; he also sought to develop a nativist consciousness. In 1895 Goeldi wrote: "We covet neither the elephant of India nor the giraffe of Africa. We want what is ours, what is Amazonian, of Pará, and it isn't necessary for me (who wasn't born in this land and who today sees himself here for no reason other than love of science and the desire to create a solid stronghold in the Amazon) to show the people of Pará that the nature surrounding us has more than enough material to warrant filling a zoo as well as a botanical garden."[5]

4. The archaeology of Marajoara culture began in 1870 and has since attracted researchers from New York's American Museum of Natural History, the University of Pennsylvania, the British Museum, the Brooklyn Museum, and Berlin's Völkerkunde Museum, among many others. This ethnic group (i.e., the Marajoaras) lived on points of the large island of Marajó, at the mouth of the Amazon River, from A.D. 400 to 1350. They built artificial mounds for their homes and cemeteries, where objects from their material culture have been found. Prior to the arrival of Europeans in America, the group had disappeared. Its members were incapable of sustaining a large, permanent population because they failed to develop an intensive agricultural system to withstand the constant flooding of the island.

5. *Boletim do Museu Goeldi*, 2 January 1895.

Fig. 3. E. Torzo,

Emílio Goeldi's ex libris,

lithograph, 1902. Private

collection, Rio de Janeiro.

The cultural moment being lived by Belém — the need for scientific knowledge coexisting with a global view of the region as one of natural splendor — is reflected in Emílio Goeldi's own ex libris, designed in Belém in the *art-nouveau* style by E. Torzo (fig. 3). The *art nouveau* occurs in the typography and the sinuous adornment of the central image. Where the lines meander, two fleurs-de-lis confer a heraldic dimension on the bookplate. The scene is divided horizontally into two parts, a tribute to romanticism: in the background lies the "natural" space of the jungle; in the foreground the space of "civilization" is protected by a wall[6] that separates and at the same time permits the unveiling of nature's wonders. The Amazonian landscape shows a lone navigator in a *piragua* (dugout canoe). Above, a looming Indian crowned with a cockade of feathers is a clear model of otherness defined by science.

6. Two shields are engraved on the wall (Werdenberg and Hohensax) along with the scientist's name (Emil August Göldi v. T.) and academic title (Dr. phil.). Goeldi's coat of arms is at the center; that of his native Switzerland lies in the lower right corner. The wall is further decorated with flowers taken from the scientist's shield.

In modernist Brazil, nature was symbolized by the jungle. The writer José Graça Aranha observed in his *Estética da vida* (Esthetics of life) (1921) that, in Brazil, culture had been separated from nature by all three major ethnic groups — the Portuguese through "artificiality and melancholy," African slaves through a "cosmic fear," and the Indian through a "metaphysics of terror" that filled "the space between the human spirit and nature with apparitions and images."[7] Whatever prejudice we may find here, it is worth noting Graça Aranha's monist position for a culture that incorporates the "esthetic rhythm" of the cosmos. He encouraged the transformation of sensations into landscape — color, lines, planes, masses — the reunification in art of human nature with universal nature. In 1923 writer Mário de Andrade urged painter Tarsila do Amaral to return to national roots: "Tarsila, Tarsila, go back within yourself.... Leave Paris! Tarsila! Come to the virgin forest...."[8] Tarsila came — and invented a Brazil in modern painting. Brazilian modernism brought with it the attempt to recapture happiness by overcoming the "dread" that clouded the Brazilian gaze before nature. "Before the Portuguese discovered Brazil, Brazil had discovered happiness," poet Oswald de Andrade would later write in his *Manifesto antropófago* (Cannibal manifesto) (1928).

When he arrived in Rio in 1914, Portuguese Fernando Correia Dias (1893–1935) met the caricaturist Vieira da Cunha, with whom he founded a graphic arts studio. Cunha published the short essay "O nacionalismo na arte" (Nationalism in art), one of the first modern nationalist manifestos, illustrated with animals and tropical foliage by Correia Dias. Cunha advocated nationalism in art: "Brazilian society for the most part still suffers from a sophisticated and absurd artificiality, constantly revealed in all manifestations of life. It makes no sense to live in an environment that is not, nor could be, one's own. The excitement of civilization grabs, captivates, dominates, and [we] lose all sense of self."[9]

During the modernist period, two artists native to the Amazon region, Theodoro Braga (1872–1953) and Manoel Pastana,[10] developed the idea of decorative arts with nativist elements, along with Correia Dias. The traditions of rubber-boom Belém, with its *belle époque* social dimension, had consolidated an appreciation of decorative arts. Braga and Pastana were trained in this atmosphere and, by the 1920s, developed their nativist design plan. But there was a decline of the Amazon region following the 1906 entrance on the international market of rubber produced by the English in Asia. The Amazon could no longer support artists; thus Braga and Pastana produced in São Paulo and Rio, respectively.

Beginning in the 1920s, Correia Dias developed a graphic stylization of decorative Marajoara themes.[11] This particular artist did extensive ceramic work with

7. Eduardo Jardim de Moraes's work *A brasilidade modernista: sua dimensão filosófica* (Rio de Janeiro: Editora Graal, 1978) should also be mentioned in this regard.

8. Letter to Tarsila do Amaral on 15 November 1923, in Aracy Amaral, *Tarsila: sua obra e seu tempo* (São Paulo: Editora Perspectiva, 1975), 1, 110.

9. *Revista Nacional* (Rio de Janeiro) (August 1919).

10. Pastana was born in 1888; we can find no record of the year of his death.

11. At the beginning of the twentieth century, the National Museum in Rio and the Paraense Museum in Belém were the two primary sources of visual information on Marajoara ceramics for modernist artists and writers.

Fig. 4. Prentice and Floderep Architects, Itahy Building, main entrance, Nossa Senhora de Copacabana Avenue, Rio de Janeiro, ca. 1940s. Photograph by Vicente de Mello.

aboriginal motifs, in addition to tiles, rugs, bronze plaques, wrought-iron objects, and leather chests. He also designed a series of Marajoara motifs taken from the decoration of authentic vessels, destined for rug decoration and ceramics for architectural use. Upon visiting Correia Dias's studio in 1928, Paul Rivet, founder of the Musée de l'Homme in Paris, commented on the artist's nativist work that frequently centered on Marajoara stylization: "Among South America's indigenous arts, the art of the ancient inhabitants of the Island of Marajó and the lower Amazon remains one of the most mysterious. This art compares in beauty to the most perfect productions of the great Andean civilizations. To make this art be born again, to make it known

Fig. 5. Attributed to Theodoro Braga, *left*, vase with beetle motif, terra cotta, 8.5 cm, early 1920s; *right*, vase with alligator motif, terra cotta, 9.3 cm, early 1920s. Private collection, Rio de Janeiro. Photograph by Vicente de Mello.

in modern Brazil, [would] rejoin the past to the present in a beautiful esthetic tradition."[12] Correia Dias's ceramics are faithful to the shapes and materials of Marajoara vases and maintain the original symbols. This contrasts with Theodoro Braga's experimentation, his reduction of elements to compose a synthesis of design more appropriate to the tenets of art deco than to the static fidelity of early Marajoara ceramics.

Braga's production brought an intensity to the modernist universe of decorative arts where John Graz, Regina Gomide, and Antônio Gomide predominated in São Paulo with a more internationalist tendency.[13] The jungle is more generic in their work, as is true of the entrance to the Itahy Building in Rio (fig. 4). A number of terra cotta vases attributed to Theodoro Braga's early phase (fig. 5) are encrusted with series of animals, including beetles and alligators, emblematic of the fauna of the Amazon and the thematic object of Braga's studies as mentioned above. The animals' symbolic character is not well developed in these pieces; their employment does, however, serve as evidence of a nativist interest. The vase decorated with beetles is far from having the symbolic implications of insects present on Émile Gallé's glass. It fails to reach the level of "virgin symbol" potentially offered by science and nature.[14] "What is the decorative quality of a symbol?" inquired Gallé. On Braga's small vase a rigid order is created through the spacing of the beetles, again quite removed from the sensual flow of Gallé's decoration. On this particular vase, Braga does not explore the ornamental possibilities of the insect's anatomy in depth as would occur with an *art-nouveau* work; he treats the hind legs vaguely.

12. João Ribeiro Pinheiro, *História da pintura brasileira* (Rio de Janeiro: Casa Leuzinger, 1931), 47–48.

13. Antônio Gomide and John Graz each completed decorative projects (murals and stained-glass windows) with generic jungle themes that warrant separate treatment. J. Carlos, Hilda and Quirino Campofiorito, Karel Honzík, August Herborth, Antônio Paim Vieira, and Louis Rochet (who cast the monument to Emperor Pedro I [1862] in Rio) might also have been discussed if space had allowed.

14. In his lecture "Le décor symbolique," given at the Stanislas Academy on 17 May 1900, Émile Gallé developed ideas about symbolism in the decorative arts; see Philippe Garner's transcription in *Émile Gallé* (New York: Rizzoli, 1990), 157–162.

Fig. 6. Theodoro Braga, (1) *Yapoanã,* rug inspired by the *Victoria regia* (Amazonian water lily), executed by the Santa Helena Rug Manufacturer, São Paulo; (2) flowering mango tree, original plan for woven wall hangings; (3) *Caraná,* column with Amazonian palm theme, executed by Vicente Larocca; (4) and (5) covered jar and vase, *guatambu* wood, executed by Domenico Businelli; (6) plan for rug with Marajoara motifs. Maria Braga, (7) cushion, low relief, leather, decorated with Marajoara motifs. Photograph by Carlos Peruta, Rio de Janeiro, 1927.

In any case Braga's meticulously realistic treatment, albeit with a discreet *art-nouveau* accent, signals a premodernist moment. Were authorship confirmed, one might say that from here Braga went on to workmanship of a more elaborate nationalism, modeled on native cultural heritage and not merely on nature. Esthetically this would mean passage from verism to simplified geometry. Braga would head off in search of history and historicism. In 1896 he must have heard the opening lecture on mythology delivered by Francisco Inácio Homem de Mello at the National School of Fine Arts in Rio,[15] since the publication lists his name in the roster of students. Homem de Mello stressed the importance of mythology in ancient and modern production — understood as Western production since the Renaissance — but did not refer to Brazil's indigenous mythology. "In the realm of art, Mythology appears to us as perpetual renewal," Homem de Mello asserted. "We will study Mythology in the light of science, not as a mute page of the past, but as a precious document of the human spirit, full of light and movement. This is History's power. Past civilizations...resurface, restored to life." As the program at the former Imperial Academy of Fine Arts was entirely focused on Greco-Roman mythology, there was certainly exposure to mythology in Braga's formation.

The applied art section of the 1927 National Salon of Fine Arts in Rio presented a core of decorative and practical objects of Amazonian character designed by Theodoro and Maria Braga (fig. 6).[16] A more mature Theodoro Braga completed a series of vases in wrought metal (fig. 7) with details in enamel or distinctive metals, transforming the geometric motifs of Marajoara ceramics with their simple breaks and irregularities into a rigorous art-deco language. These vases, at least five of which are known to exist, form one of the key moments in Brazil's modernist decorative arts.[17] The small vase corresponds to a Marajoara ware (National Museum of the Quinta da Boa Vista, Rio de Janeiro) that served Braga in the formal design and decoration of his work; he also closely followed its proportions. The basic design is a detailed copy of the Marajoara original, even in the differences of color that Braga achieved through use of enamel paint. Vermilion is the predominant hue, as in the *tabatinga* (soft sedimentary clay) applied by the natives of the Amazon. In this case, in the general shape and decoration, Braga gives greater geometrical precision to the design but retains its motive force — the modular rhythm, the symmetries, the localization, and the way it dominates the entire rounded volume of the vase. This piece was reproduced in full detail by Manoel Pastana in gouache on paper. The large vase marks one of the most stylized moments in Braga's work, distanced from any Marajoara archaeological model, be it in terms of general shape or decoration. The geometric motifs are of yellow metal, a stripe, contrasting with the red body of copper. With this piece Braga sought to reproduce the chromatic differences on the surface of Marajoara ceramics using metals varying in color

Fig. 7. Theodoro Braga, vases, *left*, bronze and yellow metal, 41 x 30 cm; *right*, copper and brass, 18 x 19 cm, ca. 1930s. Museum of Modern Art, Rio de Janeiro, gifts of Lucien Correia and Fulvia and Adolpho Leirner, respectively. Photograph by Vicente de Mello.

15. "Aula de mythologia: anno letivo de 1896 discurso de abertura," Rio de Janeiro, twelve unnumbered pages.

16. Information from the photograph album *Salon 1927* by Carlos Peruta, with handwritten notes.

17. Rediscovered by Pietro Maria Bardi, the vases were reproduced in "Theodoro Braga, um art-déco brasileiro," in *Arte Vogue* 1, no. 1 (May 1977): 80–81. Five vases may be seen in the article on Theodoro Braga's home published in the June 1937 issue of *Illustração Brasileira*. At least four may be attributed to the artist; only one was among those published by Bardi, namely the large bronze piece (41 cm) belonging to the Museum of Modern Art in Rio.

Fig. 8. Manoel Pastana, plan for furniture with land turtle motif, gouache on paper, n.d. Pará State Museum, Belém. Photograph by Luiz Braga.

Fig. 9. Manoel Pastana, plan for lampshade with land turtle motif, in bronze and porcelain, gouache on paper, n.d. Pará State Museum, Belém. Photograph by Luiz Braga.

and sheen. Its structure is cylindrical, without seams or joints [*peça inteiriça*].[18] From the extremely pure stylization, one might take this to be a more mature work, from the 1930s.

Manoel Pastana, also born in Pará, left behind a vast corpus of decorative art projects and objects that remain to be studied. There are hundreds of watercolor and gouache paintings with plans for furniture and objects such as lamps, trays, a parasol, a coffee and tea set, and so on (figs. 8, 9, 10, 11, and 12), in which the artist alternately adopts decorative elements from the archaeological ceramics of Amazon tribes or from the material culture of contemporary Amazon tribes, then refers to the flora and fauna of the jungle, but without loss of the work's mythical dimension. Animals, plants, woven straw—symbolic details of the archaeological ceramics—are articulated in intricate spatial relation formulating the decorative object's body. There are many designs copied from pieces collected in Brazil's anthropological museums, the Goeldi Museum in Belém and the National Museum in Rio de Janeiro among them. In addition Pastana left countless decorative objects in bronze and yellow metal, many with zoomorphic motifs. Some are recreations, as occurred with Theodoro Braga, of pieces of Marajoara ceramics—vases and triangular plaques, in the style of indigenous *tangas* (loincloths). Others reconstruct symbols and legends—for example, the Icamiaba vases he made in yellow metal when he worked at the mint.[19]

The previous year, in Quirino Campofiorito's journal *Bellas Artes*,[20] Pastana developed several ideas in his article "O despertar da arte" (Art's awakening) regarding his nativism founded on the original cultures of the Amazon. "The indigenous peoples," he wrote, "decorated their instruments of war

18. *Illustração Brasileira* 15, no. 26 (June 1937): 29 mentions the employment of this technique by Theodoro Braga. The pieces were probably executed at São Paulo's Lyceum of Arts and Crafts.

19. *Icamiaba* refers to a tribe of women corresponding to a native version of the Amazons.

20. Number 43/44 (November/December 1938): 3.

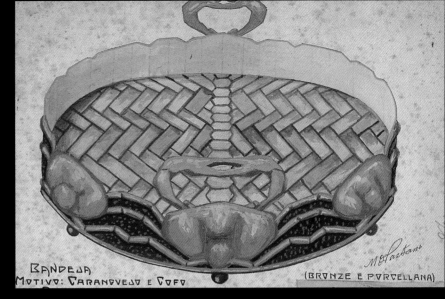

BANDEJA
MOTIVO: CARANGVEJO E COFO   (BRONZE E PORCELLANA)

Fig. 10. Manoel Pastana, plan for tray with crab and wicker basket motif, in bronze and porcelain, gouache on paper, n.d. Pará State Museum, Belém. Photograph by Luiz Braga.

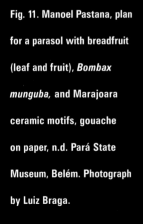

Fig. 11. Manoel Pastana, plan for a parasol with breadfruit (leaf and fruit), *Bombax munguba,* and Marajoara ceramic motifs, gouache on paper, n.d. Pará State Museum, Belém. Photograph by Luiz Braga.

APPARELHO PARA CAFÉ, LEITE E CHÁ
MOTIVO: TUCANO E ASSAHY
PASTANA.   PARÁ - BRASIL

Fig. 12. Manoel Pastana, plan for coffee and tea set with toucan and palm tree [*açaí*] motifs, gouache on paper, n.d. Pará State Museum, Belém. Photograph by Luiz Braga.

Fig. 13. J. Carlos,"Pororoca," illustration from *Fascinação* (Fascination) by Corrêa Pinto (Rio de Janeiro: Pongetti, 1943), India ink on paper, 23 x 30 cm, 1943. Luiz Carlos de Brito e Cunha collection.

and domestic use, irrefutable proof of their elevated degree of artistic sensibility.... There were tribes, such as those of Marajó and Santarém in Pará, who left their permanent mark on the art of sculpture, given the progressiveness of their decorative compositions."

By the end of the 1920s, the jungle had invaded Brazilian literature. "In a far corner of Northern Brazil, at an hour when so deep a hush had fallen on the virgin forest that the brawling of the Uraricoera River could be heard, an Indian woman of the Tapanhuma tribe gave birth to an unlovely son, sired by the Terror of the Night. This child was an oddity, his skin black as calcined ivory. They named him Macunaíma...." [21] This is the opening to *Macunaíma, o herói sem nenhum caráter* (Macunaíma, the hero with no character), Mário de Andrade's great rhapsodic novel about the Brazilian "race." From literature, the theme of the jungle would give impetus to some of the most important moments in twentieth-century Brazilian graphic arts. Generally speaking, there were graphic experimentations in editions of works by Ronald de Carvalho, Mário de Andrade, Oswald de Andrade, Guilherme de Almeida, Raul Bopp, Cassiano Ricardo, Murilo Mendes, and others. With the publication of Emiliano Di Cavalcanti's *Fantoches da meia noite* (Marionettes of midnight) (1921), plastic artists became sporadically involved in the design of book covers and book illustration (Tarsila do Amaral, Vicente do Rego Monteiro, Anita Malfatti, Victor Brecheret, Flávio de Carvalho, J. Carlos) and in book production, the richest example being the work of Oswaldo Goeldi (1895–1961). No artist of the period surpassed Goeldi in his fervent production of illustrations — engravings and especially drawings — for books, magazines, and journals.

21. Translation by E. A. Goodland (New York: Random House, 1984).

Fig. 14. *Above,* Fernando

Correia Dias, vignette,

Marajoara ceramic motif,

early 1920s.

Fig. 15. *Below,* Fernando

Correia Dias, vignette, toucan

motif, early 1920s. Photograph

by Vicente de Mello.

One of the defining traits of Brazilian modernism was the creation of the graphic design profession. Correia Dias was among the first to make a name for himself in this field. His production was extensive, diverse, and constant; furthermore, he developed his own graphic language. He was unquestionably the graphic artist most devoted to Amazonian themes. The greatest historian of Brazilian caricature, Herman Lima, considered Correia Dias's work at the end of the second decade of this century "the touchstone of a true renewal of his art among us" and felt his book covers "represent a beautiful effort in terms of plastic utilization of the fauna and flora of our land, with results only occasionally—in vignettes, with fish, butterflies, palms, and fern leaves—achieved in J. Carlos's comparably high art" (fig. 13).[22] After 1920, with a *Brazilian-American* cover, Correia Dias went on to employ Marajoara elements in graphic arts. Following an initial fascination with tropical nature, when his decorative motifs embraced the image of nature as paradise in the service of forming a Brazilian cultural identity, Correia Dias moved on with Marajoara ceramics to signs that bore witness to native history (figs. 14 and 15).

22. Herman Lima, *História da caricatura no Brasil* (Rio de Janeiro: José Olympio, 1963), vol. 4, 1380.

Fig. 16. Vicente do Rego Monteiro, book cover for *Légendes, croyances, et talismans des indiens de l'Amazone*, adapted by P. L. Duchartre (Paris: Editions Tolmer, 1923). Manoel Portinari Leão collection. Photograph by Vicente de Mello.

In 1923 the book *Légendes, croyances, et talismans des indiens de l'Amazone* (Legends, beliefs, and talismans of the Amazonian Indians), adapted by P. L. Duchartre and illustrated by Vicente do Rego Monteiro (1899–1970), was published in Paris (fig. 16). Printed in black and dark red, the graphic feel of the work is telluric, as if it were a piece of archaeological ceramic work from the Amazon. The book's cover, in black with two tones of brown and the white of the paper, foretell the palette that would define Monteiro's painting in the 1920s, his primary period of production. Despite all the problems of modernist appropriation of the esthetic patterns of tribal societies, frequently called "primitivism," Monteiro's work has another connotation. It represents an early corpus within Brazilian modernism, marked by nationalist intent, in an era of effort to overcome the culture's colonized status by incorporating native dimensions. Monteiro made a series of drawings with Indianist themes in Rio and São Paulo, where the works were exhibited in 1920.

As *Légendes, croyances, et talismans des indiens de l'Amazone* is profusely illustrated, including a cover, title page, friezes, and vignettes, it is possible to establish connections between Monteiro's drawing and some of the decorative and symbolic patterns of native ceramics. In one example, the crag that emerges from the waters in the illustration of the legend of the Maiandeua River (fig. 17) corresponds to anthropomorphic urns of the civilization of the Maracá River in

Fig. 17. Vicente do Rego Monteiro, "Maiandeua," illustration from *Légendes, croyances, et talismans des indiens de l'Amazone,* adapted by P. L. Duchartre (Paris: Editions Tolmer, 1923). Manoel Portinari Leão collection. Photograph by Vincente de Mello.

Fig. 18. Yan de Almeida Prado, book cover for *raça* (race) by Guilherme de Almeida (São Paulo: Tipografia Paulista, 1925). National Library, Rio de Janeiro. Photograph by Vicente de Mello.

Amapá, discovered in 1896. The reference is in the oval shape of the rock, the angular definition of its facial features, and the lateral line of its stylized top-knot.

If Vicente do Rego Monteiro initiated "archaism" in modern Brazilian art, Anita Malfatti's work, with the illustrative drawing *Índia* or *Moema* (1917), still falls within the rhetorical tradition of the nineteenth century, with no real relation to the native cultural universe. However, her work may be compared to the jungle invented by Henri Rousseau. Malfatti places a *Victoria regia*, an Amazonian plant, in the same landscape with several species of cactus, a plant traditionally associated with dry climates. The nature surrounding her *Moema* is more like that of a botanical garden—where plants of different ecosystems coexist—than a reference to the jungle. These facts and interpretations support the contention that it is Monteiro who inaugurates discovery of the culture of the jungle among the artists of the Week of Modern Art (11–18 February 1922). His painting is linked to the archaeology of Marajó by an ample visual vocabulary. Besides their hieratic, totemic presence, the figures in some paintings seem to surface as anthropomorphic ceramics. In Monteiro's pictorial work, figures acquire the "volume" of sculptures; lateral shadows create illusory mass in relief style. The earthy palette, his earth tones, are not merely a telluric message but also relate to the use of red clay in the ceramic work of Marajó. His jungle takes on added significance. It is the land of living legends, its soil the guardian of the history of past cultures, revealed by archaeology.

Ships travel through the text of Guilherme de Almeida's poem *raça* (race), symbolizing its ethnic dimension and social context. The Amazon River imposes its metaphorical force, conveying Brazilian history itself:

> amazonian rhythms of torrential waters with—
>   caravels
>   canoes
>   slave-ships

Using the symbolic dimension of the process of ethnic encounter between Portuguese (caravels), Indians (canoes), and Africans (slave-ships), Almeida's text turns to the image of three ships correlated in history's flow. The book's cover (fig. 18) has a discreet drawing by Yan de Almeida Prado (1898–1987). Its high point is its graphic structure, with three allegorical colors—the white paper, the black print, and the green in the drawing—referring to Brazil's ethnic groups.[23]

Oswaldo Goeldi, that great ethical paradigm of Brazilian art, was marked by the Amazon. He was born in Rio in 1895; the following year his family moved to Belém. His father, the scientist Emílio Goeldi (referred to above), was in charge of reorganizing the Paraense Museum, formerly the Philomathic Society (1866). The museum's gardens made an impression on the young Goeldi and were his most essential memory of the Amazon.

Goeldi's graphic work—his engravings, drawings, and illustrations—have an intense expressionist quality that fuses pathos and ethos. His light takes the anguished path of nocturnal light. This characteristic light led poet

23. A precedent for the graphic use of green to convey native Brazilianness appears in Gastão Cruls, *O embalo da rede* (The swaying hammock) (Rio de Janeiro: Livraria Castillo, 1923). The cover is by an unidentified author.

Carlos Drummond de Andrade to proclaim Goeldi Brazil's surveillant of the moral night that lies beneath the physical night. When remembering childhood, or while alone during somber evenings spent in an old Rio townhouse, Goeldi captured light that represents not only plastic elements but moral meaning (as in his masterpiece, the woodcut *O guarda-chuva vermelho* [The red umbrella]). His singularity, in the Brazilian modernist atmosphere and in his personal solitude, is linked to a rejection of the exotic and the literary, of caricatural nationalism and pamphletary social realism.

In 1937 Goeldi illustrated *Cobra Norato* (The snake Norato), Raul Bopp's book of forest legends. It came out in successive editions with covers by Brazilian expressionist Flávio de Carvalho (1931), Zoltan Kemeny (1947), and Joan Miró (1954). Here Goeldi's thematic agenda allowed for exploration into the possibilities of water: the dense waters of the forest and light weighted with humidity. The relation of the woodcuts to the structure of Bopp's book and the course of the text make *Cobra Norato* a unique work. Ant images migrate between the lines of the text as though constructing and deconstructing the language.[24] Goeldi also engraved the end papers, the title page, the chapter initials, vignettes, and large illustrations. Personally, I consider this work to be the finest moment in twentieth-century Brazilian graphics.[25]

In modernist architecture of the first half of this century, in various parts of Brazil — not only large cities like Rio and São Paulo but also smaller centers like Juiz de Fora[26] — there was a tendency to adopt Marajoara decorative motifs in certain constructions. There might be a theater with that architectural look. But, as with *art nouveau*, "Marajoara architecture" was merely decoration applied to a structure — a formalist attitude added as modernist taste to any kind of architecture. On the one hand, one might recall that there were no brick constructions by the Brazilian Indians — including the Marajó civilization. On the other hand, imported eclectic standards since the middle of the nineteenth century dispersed the knowledge developed by colonial Portuguese architecture, adapted to the tropical climate. A restored relationship with the environment was initiated along with intellectual events, including conferences. In 1924 the Brazilian Cultural Center announced a conference on art and thought, scheduling a 7 August session by José Mariano Filho on "O Jardim Tropical" (The tropical garden).[27] In 1933 the first International Exposition of Tropical Architecture, featuring a lecture by Frank Lloyd Wright, took place. Brazil's retropicalization was under way.

In 1930 in Rio, Correia Dias presented plans for a pool at Guilherme Guinle's residence (fig. 19). It was a garden with a tank for *Victorias regias*. Intended for an area of sloping ground, the plan included tiled benches and walls, fountains, stones in their natural form, vegetation, and steps. The tiles were

24. These ant images were almost certainly inspired by the edition of Blaise Cendrars's *Petits contes nègres pour les enfants des blancs* (Paris: Au sens pareil, 1929), illustrated with woodcuts of animals by Pierre Pinsard, since in 1937 (the year of the edition of *Cobra Norato*) the Swiss author gave a copy to Beatrix Reynal with whom Goeldi was living at the time. (This copy is at the National Library in Rio.) However, the animals in the European book occupy reserved space, a vignette for example; Goeldi's ants invade and wander through the text.

25. [An illustration from *Cobra Norato* may be found on page 80 of this journal. Ed.]

26. According to information from Piedade Epstein Grinberg.

27. *Terra do Sol* (Rio de Janeiro), no. 6 (June 1924): 424.

Fig. 19. Fernando Correia Dias, plan for pool with decoration in the style of Marajoara ceramics, Guilherme Guinle's residence, Rio de Janeiro, 1930. Photograph from João Ribeiro Pinheiro, *História da pintura brasileira* (Rio de Janeiro: Casa Leuzinger, 1931).

decorated with a modular graphic design in the Marajoara style. With this work Correia Dias continued the Portuguese tradition, widely transported to Brazil's coastal cities, of using tiles in the decoration of buildings; and he anticipated the incorporation of large painted tile panels by Cândido Portinari into the exterior walls of the Ministry of Education and Public Health in Rio. Vases in the Marajoara style, containing living plants, were strategically placed along walls and on benches. Atop the fountain, a large hieratic sculpture in the form of a *muiraquitã*,[28] approximately fifty centimeters in height, seemed to preside over the water's flow. By integrating natural elements such as stone, Correia Dias's plan simultaneously created an intimate space within a more ample and theatrical garden.

In São Paulo in the 1930s, Theodoro Braga built his Retiro Marajoara (Marajoara retreat)[29] (fig. 21), a house based on an architectural plan by Eduardo Kneese de Mello.[30] The construction of this manor house was in keeping with the colonial style permeating a certain type of twentieth-century

28. *Muiraquitãs* are stone pendants in the shape of frogs and toads, belonging to the Tapajós-Trombetas culture, and today popularly considered amulets.

29. "At the villa he built in São Paulo—the Retiro Marajoara—the artist contemplates with simplicity and justified pride his magnificent body of work, spread to the four corners of the land he so loves." Sociedade Brasileira de Bellas Artes, *Boletim de Bellas Artes* (Rio de Janeiro) 7 (July 1945): 50.

30. "A casa marajoara de Theodoro Braga," *Illustração Brasileira* 15, no. 26 (June 1937): 28–29. Descriptions of Theodoro Braga's house are based on this anonymous text and five accompanying photographs.

Fig. 20. Eduardo Kneese de Mello, Theodoro Braga's residence, interior of first floor, access stairway to studio, decorated with Marajoara motifs. Photograph from *Illustração Brasileira* 15, no. 26 (June 1937): 28–29.

◀

Fig. 21. Eduardo Kneese de Mello, Theodoro Braga's residence, main facade decorated with Marajoara motifs. Photograph from *Illustração Brasileira* 15, no. 26 (June 1937): 28–29.

Brazilian architecture, but quite distant from the Portuguese-style constructions of Belém and more especially from the Amazonian vernacular. What characterizes Braga's house is the plan for Marajoara decoration in the adornment of exterior walls, floors, and wrought-iron works — in sum, the details. All the ornamental motifs were fully executed by Braga, who realized a translation of the Marajoara style (with art-deco references) to the elements of colonial architecture: windows, tiles, balconies. The top floor is defined by two iron balconies, a further reminder of Belém. Four suspended arms, all iron, support globe lights over the balconies, a concept from the days of gas lanterns. Each balcony is held on the underside in simulated support by two wrought-iron brackets. In the colonial baroque style, the balcony doors are topped by a cornice in relief simulating an elevated lintel or "yoke." The contour of these doors and of the windows follows the same general decorative style. The exterior window treatments are shutters with their characteristic trellises. Tiles along the edge of the roof, in the style of colonial glazed ceramic tiles, are decorated on the lower part with the same Marajoara motifs. As with the ceramics of Marajó, in which some designs were carved into clay, the Marajoara motifs in white high relief, with their precise geometry, are applied to exterior walls that are also white. The ornament's design reveals itself in the play of shadows beneath the sun's light, perhaps best at the zenith. This effect is reminiscent of the white facade of the eighteenth-century St. Alexander's Church in Belém with its geometric decorations and rosaces, probably the work of indigenous peoples.

Inside Braga's Marajoara home (figs. 20 and 22), the parquet floor of two different color woods follows a simple pattern of straight lines. The resulting contrast is visually appealing and very much to the Amazonian taste. In the main room, a tempera mural reproduces the decorative background of an

Fig. 22. Eduardo Kneese de Mello, Theodoro Braga's residence, interior of the first floor, social area, decorated with Marajoara motifs. Photograph from *Illustração Brasileira* 15, no. 26 (June 1937): 28–29.

▶

Fig. 23. Carnival costumes, Municipal Theater dance, Rio de Janeiro, 1942. Photograph from *Illustração Brasileira* 20, no. 83 (March 1942): 29.

"*igaçaba* (funeral urn) from Brazil's prehistoric age,"[31] in two tones. Furniture carved with Marajoara motifs, and vases — possibly of metal and made by Braga himself — are distributed throughout the house. Other elements decorated in the Marajoara style are the wrought-iron railing along the indoor stairway, stairway risers with mosaic images of human faces, and the consoles of the exterior balconies. Between the three spaces of the plinth there are other ornamental motifs; the central space is filled by a stylized decoration of a *jaboti* (land turtle) — symbol of the vanished indigenous nation. Another distinguishing feature is two large arched iron doors opening from the living room onto the adjoining terrace. The space between the two areas is decorated with a complex of lines, forming a human figure in the Marajoara style, as though taken from a ceramic vase. An open arch, closed by an iron grate with Marajoara motifs, joins the living room and the dining room, giving a certain open feel to the social area. The grate is crowned by an anthropomorphic element, a stylized human face topping motifs of Marajoara women's *tangas*, all taken directly from decorations on Marajoara ceramics. The lights were designed by Braga, their copper structure made to stand out by filigreed design elements. This space is perhaps the most internationalist, as minimal Marajoara details give way to the volume and art-deco design of the objects.

From the 1920s to the 1940s the Marajoara style was widely adopted, refashioning the Brazilians' world as it moved from ceramic vases to rugs, lights, cushions, furniture, leather bags, shawls — even to carnival costumes (fig. 23). But the incorporation of elements of indigenous culture did not mean arbitrary appropriation of the Other's values. On the contrary, there was research into the self, an effort to establish a profile of this social being, the Brazilian, who had been given a name: Macunaíma. The basic patterns belonged to the pre-Columbian civilizations of the Amazon, which produced the most complex ceramic artifacts of the entire Brazilian territory. Thus the jungle, a space outside of history according to Hegel's philosophy, became the only native historical reference possible for symbolic modernist Brazilian production. □

31. Ibid.

Note

This article was made possible by a grant from the John Simon Guggenheim Memorial Foundation.

Ars Longa, Vita Brevis.

Burle Marx, Panel and floor. Entrance hall of Banco Safra's head office in São Paulo.

Art endures... throughout time.

At Safra, art has become an important

part of our entire business philosophy.

Art is reflected in everything from

the architecture of our offices and

branches, to the manner in which

services are extended to our

customers. Because, as art searches

for beauty and perfection, we've done

the same, creating good business

practices that are... enduring.

Banco Safra
Head Office - Avenida Paulista 2100
São Paulo - Brazil

The *Journal of Design History* plays an active role in the development of design history (including the history of crafts and applied arts), by publishing new research, by providing an international forum for dialogue and debate, and by addressing current issues of interest. The *Journal* also seeks to promote links with other disciplines which explore visual and material culture. In addition, it is the editors expressed wish to encourage contributions on design in preindustrial periods in non-European societies, as well as on hitherto neglected or unfamiliar areas, periods or themes.

In addition to full-length articles, the *Journal of Design History* publishes shorter case studies, carries regular book reviews, and reports on new educational initiatives, and on resources for design history, including the application of new technology.

RECENT AND FORTHCOMING ARTICLES

Roann Barris on Rodchenko's designs for Glebov's *Inga*

Paula Baxter on cross-cultural issues in the history of southwestern American Indian jewellery

Christine Boydell on freelance textile designers in Britain in the 1930's

Cheryl Buckley on the work of Susie Cooper

Kathleen Burnett on Herbert Bayer's exhibition design

David Crowley on design in Stalinist and post-Stalinist Poland

Darron Dean on Samuel Malkin and English eighteenth-century vernacular ceramics

Kathryn Dethier on an 'ideal homes' series in the *Ladies Home Journal*

Avi Friedman on postwar suburban housing in America

Pauline Madge on the literature of 'green design'

Margaret Maynard on the 'new look' in Australia

Kevin Nute on Frank Lloyd Wright and Japan

Journal of Design History

Volume 8   1995

**Edited by
Jeremy Aynsley;
Christopher Bailey;
Charlotte Benton;
Anthony Coulson; Pat Kirkham;
Pauline Madge; Tim Putnam;
Jonathan Woodham**

1995 ORDER FORM

☐ Please enter my subscription to
Journal of Design History
Subscription rates volume 8 (four issues)
☐ Institutional   US$115 / £62
☐ *Personal   US$55 / £30
☐ *Student   US$50 / £25
* Rate includes the cost of membership to the Society of Design History
(Please note: £ Sterling rates apply in United Kingdom and Europe, US$ rates elsewhere. Customers in the EC, and in Canada are subject to their local sales tax.)

☐ Please send me a free sample copy
☐ I enclose the correct remittance
Name..
Address...
....
City/State ....
Zip code ....
Please charge my American Express/
Visa/Diners/Mastercard card number:

☐☐☐☐ ☐☐☐☐ ☐☐☐☐ ☐☐☐☐
☐☐☐☐   Exp. date: ☐☐☐☐

For further subscriptions information please contact:
Oxford University Press,
Journals Marketing (X95),
2001 Evans Road,
Cary, NC 27513, USA.
Fax: +1 919 677 1714

**OXFORD
JOURNALS**

SOFA
SCULPTURE OBJECTS FUNCTIONAL ART
CHICAGO
EXPOSITION 1995
ART & DESIGN FOR LIVING
NOVEMBER 2-5 1995

The
International
Exposition
of
Sculpture
Objects
and
Functional
Art

For more information:

Mark Lyman

SOFA

210 W. Superior

Chicago, IL 60610

T: 1.800.551.SOFA

F: 616.469.6356

A Project of

Expressions of Culture, Inc.

Expressions of Culture Florida, Inc.

SOFA
SCULPTURE OBJECTS FUNCTIONAL ART
MIAMI
EXPOSITION 1996
ART & DESIGN FOR LIVING
MARCH 1996

If you thought Brazil was just Sugarloaf,

you're in for a sweet surprise!

The diversity and beauty that is this vast and fascinating land has been attracting settlers and visitors for over 300 years.

Of course there's the special magic of Rio de Janeiro with its well known

Sugarloaf mountain, fan beaches and gorgeous sun worshippers.

But there is also Bahia Brazil's oldest city, where the soul of Africa still bea in the generous hearts c its unique people. Or fly the charming colonial ci of Ouro Preto declared I UNESCO to be an inter tional monument. Visit th Pantanal, the largest natu reserve in all of South America. See astoundin Iguassu Falls roaring its dominance over the sur rounding countryside.

So by all means have your taste of Rio's Sugar loaf, the appetizer for a memorable Brazilian fea served up as only VARIC Brazilian Airlines can.

Brazil. A great idea whose time has come.

VARIG

The World Class Airline of Brazil.
Since 1927.

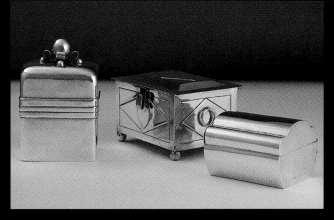

MIAMI Modernism

ART DECO ■ MODERNE ■ ART NOUVEAU ■ CUBISM ■ W.P.A.
■ MACHINE AGE ■ BAUHAUS ■ 50'S & 60'S ■ ARTS & CRAFTS ■

January 12-14,1996
James L. Knight Center
400 S.E.Second Avenue
Miami, Florida

PC AUSSIN PRODUCTIONS
12150 EAST OUTER DRIVE
DETROIT, MICHIGAN 48224
PHONE (313) 886 3443
FAX (313) 886 1067

■ Art & design 1900-1970, Sixty -five nationwide dealers.

■ A show that combines design scholarship with the casual elegance,hipness,& spirit of discovery that characterize the Twentieth Century collecting field.

■ Preview: Friday, January 12, 6:00pm - 10:00pm to benefit the Wolfsonian. For preview information call (305) 531 1001.

■ FREE shuttle bus from the Wolfsonian, at 10th and Washington Streets, Miami Beach, near the heart of the ART DECO WEEKEND® festivities along Ocean Drive, and the Knight Center.

THE PICCADILLY GALLERY LTD

16 Cork Street, London W1X 1PF
Tel: 0171-629 2875 Fax: 0171-499 0431

20th Century European Works on Paper

Symbolists, Klimt & Vienna Secession

Gill, Spencer & Other British Individualists

Exhibitions Changing Monthly
Monday–Friday 10–5.30
Saturdays By Appointment

Right; Marius de Zayas (1866–1947)

WILD FLOWER MODEL - Motif: Wild Flowers. (10.8' x 7.5')

Tropical Flowers and Colors in Izabel's Handmade Tapestries and Rugs.

By: Maria Graziela Peregrini (*).

ANTIQUE VASE MODEL
Motif: Brazilian Flora.
(6' x 41/2')

ADDRESS:
Rua: Dias D'Avila, nº 260
Várzea - Recife - PE - Brazil
CEP - 52.500-330
PHONE/FAX
55 (081) 271-2109

For several years I have been visiting and revisiting the spaces of Izabel's home, poetically extending themselves in the tapestries and rugs permanent exhibition rooms, located in the picturesque area of Recife suburbs, Várzea.

I have been to the very cozy home of Izabel surrounded by tropical vegetation and singing birds, freely roaming the fields.

I have also been there with friends, friends who are sensitive enough to discover the beauty of the place.

I could never forget the warm words of praise of the outstanding Professor and French artist Mme Aimée Humbert, former world president of the "International Society For Education through Art", nor the praise of the North-American Art Professor from Atlanta, Joe Perrin, in the long visits that I paid with them to Izabel's home. I think it's better suited to call her place "home" than "show-room", because in the environment in which they are exhibited, on the flooring of the rooms or hung on the walls, the tapestries and rugs seem to integrate the stately home. They are as members of a great family, personalized in each piece through the original features that identify and mark each one of them. Without the repetition of industrialized tapestries and rugs which lead the viewer to the tedious monotony of standardization.

Thus, the fertile imagination of Izabel is present in the countless formats of original concepts reflected in her own personal genius of depicting flowers, foliage, birds, butterflies, frames and symbolic figures which through her feminine sensitivity she pursues incessantly.

So, it is difficult to categorize Izabel's work as per influences, oriental of other, because her spontaneous inventiveness is not bound by schools or schemes, it flows in the torrent of emotion and feelings. This is her way of absorbing, unaware, the colors, luminosity and exuberance of the Tropics, drawn from the vegetation and animals that Izabel elaborates on, using figures and symbols in the context of her tapestry.

Izabel's personal creativity is represented in each one of her tapestries and rugs, as if each one of the them possessed a "lifetime story" to tell the visitors through the thousands of points and mark, the colors and the designs which fills with wonder those who appreciate them with sensitivity.

Tapestries and rugs that were conceived in the first place by the creative genius of Izabel and then materialized through the delicate work of her own and other Northeastern craft artists anonymous hands who together with Izabel are creating the history of beauty and community work through the production of countless craft tapestries and rugs.

A most unique figure representative of the Brazilian women, who was able to create with both originality and art such as Maria Izabel Goberto e Silva, or simply Izabel, this very talented Northeastern woman.

(*) Researcher of the Fundação Joaquim Nabuco, Recife, PE, Brazil, Recife, Dec.1994.

R E F E R E N C E S
D
S
I
G
N

BOOKSELLERS SPECIALIZING in OUT-OF-PRINT &

PERIOD MATERIALS on the PROGRESSIVE & RETROGRESSIVE

IDEAS of MODERNISM and **POST-MODERNISM** in

DECORATIVE ARTS and ARCHITECTURE, INDUSTRIAL and STUDIO

ARTS as well as DESIGN CRITICISM of the 19TH & **20TH CENTURIES**

(716) 889-7848

P.O. BOX 92305, ROCHESTER, NEW YORK, 14692

CATALOGUE AVAILABLE

I like to paint over any bi- or tridimensional ground that attracts me or says something
to me, answering to the touch of my brush stroke with beauty and harmony.

Maria Adair

"POR DO SOL NO PORTO DA BARRA," an art installation including painted walls, canvases, a glass
top table, chairs, a little wooden truck, ceramic plates, silverware, and sandblasted glasses and plates.

ATELIER MARIA ADAIR . RUA J. CASTRO RABELO, 02 PELOURINHO
40025-050 . SALVADOR . BAHIA . BRAZIL
TELEFAX . (55) . (71) . 321-3363

Larry Bell
Sumerian Figures

Limited Edition Ceramics

8306 Wilshire Boulevard Suite 39
Beverly Hills, California 90211
213 931 1102

Boo
sterling children's fork and spoon

classically designed flatware & china

bissell & wilhite co.
8306 Wilshire Boulevard, Suite 39, Beverly Hills, CA 213 931 1101

Zodiac 12

Rivista internazionale
di architettura
International
Review of Architecture

Full text in Italian and English

è in libreria
is now on sale
in major bookshop

Manfredo Tafuri (1935-1944)

Guido Canella
Premiata Architettura Contemporanea

**The Pritzker Architecture Prize
Laureates, 1979-94
Jay A. Pritzker**
Origins and Evolution of Pritzker
Architecture Prize

Francesco Dal Co
Il migliore architetto
del mondo

Philip Johnson, 1979
United States
Luis Barragán, 1980
Mexico
James Stirling, 1981
Great Britain
Kevin Roche, 1982
United States
Ieoh Ming Pei, 1983
United States
Richard Meier, 1984
United States
Hans Hollein, 1985
Austria
Gottfried Böhm, 1986
Germany
Kenzo Tange, 1987
Japan
Gordon Bunshaft, 1988
United States
Oscar Niemeyer, 1988
Brazil

Frank O. Gehry, 1989
United States
Aldo Rossi, 1990
Italia
Robert Venturi, 1991
United States
Alvaro Siza, 1992
Portugal
Fumihiko Maki, 1993
Japan
Christian de Portzamparc, 1994
France

editriceAbitareSegesta

The Journal of Decorative and Propaganda Arts

Founded in 1986 and published annually by the Wolfson Foundation of Decorative and Propaganda Arts, the Journal fosters scholarship in the period 1875–1945.

For further information on current and back issues, contact the Journal office:

2399 NE 2nd Avenue
Miami, FL 33137 USA
305.573.9170 Phone
305.573.0409 Fax

MARCIO ROITER

20th century decorative arts

At the turn of the century, Rio de Janeiro was a town of cultural importance, and one of Émile Gallé's greatest retail outlets.

Gallé created a series of vases depicting Rio. The views include Sugarloaf Mountain, Guanabara Bay, Corcovado, Gavea Mountain, and São Conrado Beach.

We can say that these pieces date to the very beginning of the century because the Sugarloaf cable car, inaugurated in 1910, is not shown.

Rua Pacheco Leão, 110 / CEP 22460.030 / Rio de Janeiro / RJ / Brazil /

The Design Movement 1870 to Present Studio Ceramics Latin American American Modernist Paintings Arts and Crafts

Maija Grotell . c. 1951 . 18"(H) x 11"(D)

Bryce Bannatyne
Gallery
604 Colorado Avenue . Santa Monica . CA 90401 . 310.396.9668

Joel Edelstein
arte contemporânea

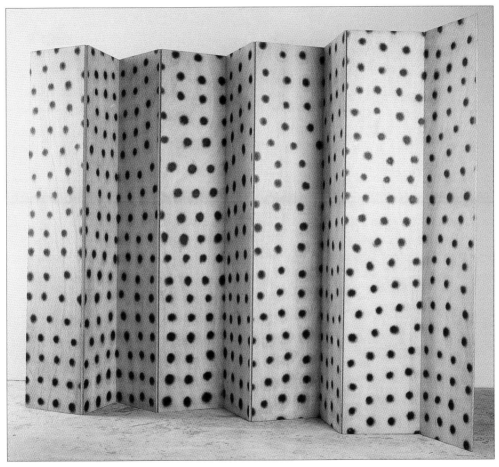

BENJAMIM
Wood stamped with fire
63" X 106"
1992

Rua Jangadeiros, 14 - B - Ipanema - Rio de Janeiro - Brasil - CEP 22420-010
Tel.: (55 21) 267-2549   Fax: (55 21) 267-1254

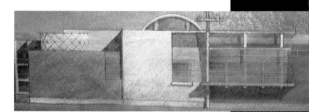

MODERNE

ART DECO

MODERNE
111 NORTH THIRD STREET • PHILADELPHIA, PENNSYLVANIA 19106 • 215-923-8536

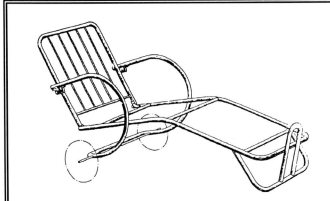

VITAE is a grant-making institution which supports cultural, educational and social projects in Brazil. As are its sister institutions, Fundación Antorchas in Argentina and Fundación Andes in Chile, *VITAE* is fully maintained by the Lampadia Foundation.

VITAE carries out projects initiated by itself and assists institutional projects submitted by other non-profit organizations, public or private. Priority is given to projects which clearly display multiplying and catalytic potential, which may set new patterns of quality and which hold good prospects of continuity after the financial support of *VITAE* has ended. Applications from individuals are considered only within the frame of existing fellowship programs sponsored by *VITAE*. *VITAE* supports and welcomes joint projects with other foundations working in Brazil.

The support of *VITAE* for this issue of
The Journal of Decorative and Propaganda Arts
is a contribution towards the international diffusion
of Brazilian Arts and Culture.

Vitae Apoio à Cultura, Educação e Promoção Social
Rua Oscar Freire, 379 - 5º andar
CEP 01426-001 - São Paulo - SP - Brazil
Phone # (55.11) 851.5299 - Fax # (55.11) 883.6361
E-Mail vitae@fpsp.fapesp.br   vitae@brfapesp.bitnet

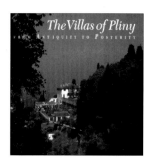

THE VILLAS OF PLINY

From Antiquity to Posterity

PIERRE DE LA RUFFINIÈRE DU PREY

"A charming and digressive essay that takes the reader on a memorable architectural excursion. Ostensibly about the villas of Pliny the Younger, the true subject of this amiable book is the imaginary world that architects make for themselves—and for us—when they dream."**—Witold Rybczynski**

Cloth $65.00 440 pages
48 color plates, 159 halftones,
29 line drawings

STYLE-ARCHITECTURE AND BUILDING-ART

Transformations of Architecture in the Nineteenth Century and Its Present Condition

HERMANN MUTHESIUS

This pivotal text is Muthesius's classic criticism of nineteenth century architecture. Now published for the first time in English, it represents one of the earliest attempts to define the elements of architecture according to modernist notions of realism and simplicity.

Paper $19.95 208 pages
7 illustrations Cloth edition available
Distributed for the Getty Center for the History of Art and the Humanities
Texts and Documents Series

MODERNISM AT MID-CENTURY

The Architecture of the United States Air Force Academy

**Edited by
ROBERT BRUEGMANN**

"This beautiful and informative book reflects in both its content and in its format the sturdy elegance of the International Style at the pinnacle of its influence in mid-twentieth-century America."
**—Thomas S. Hines,
University of California**

Cloth $70.00 200 pages
25 color plates, 79 halftones

NOW IN PAPER

MAKING THE MODERN

Industry, Art, and Design in America

TERRY SMITH

"*Making the Modern* is a vast undertaking covering often in close detail a crucial period in the history of modern culture....Smith's book will be valued not only for its breadth and scholarly acumen but also for its sheer critical brilliance, for the insights that crowd its pages."

**—Alan Wallach,
College of William and Mary**

Paper $34.95 538 pages
156 halftones

DIMENSIONS OF THE AMERICAS

Art and Social Change in Latin America and the United States

SHIFRA M. GOLDMAN

"Essential reading for anyone interested in the often contradictory developments that have shaped Latin American and U.S. Latino art since the 1970s. The essays break new ground by establishing the basis for a social history of Latin American/Latino art. Goldman's multi-faceted role (pioneer researcher, art historian, teacher, cultural theoretician, implacable social critic) makes her work stand on its own, with no parallel in the field."**—Mari Carmen Ramírez,
Curator of Latin American Art,
University of Texas at Austin**

Paper $29.95 518 pages
95 halftones Cloth edition available

T H E   U N I V E R S I T Y   O F   C H I C A G O   P R E S S
5 8 0 1   S O U T H   E L L I S   A V E N U E ,   C H I C A G O ,   I L L I N O I S   6 0 6 3 7

Luis Barragan

Drawings
1928 - 1988

Max Protetch 560 Broadway New York, NY 212.966.5454

German Literature · Czech Avantgarde
Modern Illustrated Books · First Editions

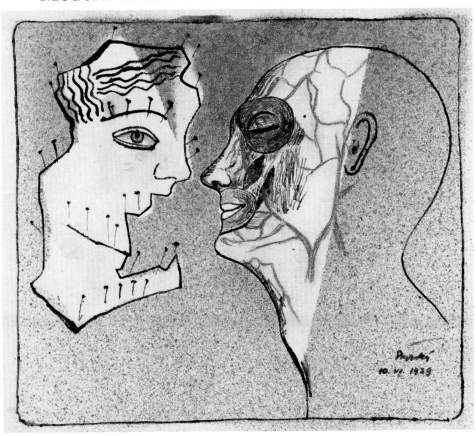

ŠTYRSKÝ, J. – DESNOS, Robert. Báseň. Manuscript on paper, no place, no date. Small oblong quarto. Four unnumbered pages. With an original drawing by Jindřich Štyrský, dated 10. VI. 1939. Original wrappers made with imitation snakeskin paper.

An exquisite small manuscript with a drawing from Štyrský's best time. The translation of Robert Desnos's poem is by Jindřich Hořejsí, the calligraphy of the poem in green ink, however, is by Štyrský. The drawing shows the fragment of a classical woman's head in opposition to a quasi-anatomical drawing of a man's head, executed in brown ink, heightened with blue and red, over a ground of light brown wash. The manuscript opens with a title page, showing the signature of the artist and the translator as well as the name of the dedicated person (M. Burešová).

BUCHANTIQUARIAT
"AM RHEIN"
GEORG J. BERAN

Kartausgasse 1 · Postfach 46
CH-4005 Basel · Switzerland

Tel. [+41] 061 / 692 62 84
Fax [+41] 061 / 692 62 63

ART HISTORY

Editor **Marcia Pointon**

Reviews Editor **Kathleen Adler**

Associate Editor **Paul Binski**

ARTICLES FORTHCOMING IN ART HISTORY 1995:

Robert E. Haywood, Heretical Alliance: *Clacs Oldenburg and the Judson Memorial Church in the 1960s.*

John Clark, Yoga in Japan: *Model or Exception ?*

Water Cahn, Foçillons Jongleur

Kate Winskell, the Art of Propaganda: *Herwarth Walden 1914-1919*

Zainab Bahrani: *the Fate of the Royal Image in the Ancient Near East*

SPECIAL ISSUES:

Representation and the Politics of Difference *September 1993*

The Image and the Ancient World *March 1994*

Psychoanalysis and Art History *September 1994,*
Guest Editor, M. Iversen

SUBSCRIPTION RATES 1995

INSTITUTIONS: UK/EUROPE £87.00 REST OF WORLD £98.00 N. AMERICA $152.00
INDIVIDUALS: UK/EUROPE £52.00 REST OF WORLD £64.00 N. AMERICA $98.00

MEMBERSHIP RATES 1995

UK £34.00 EUROPE £39.00 N. AMERICA $80.00/£45.00 REST OF WORLD £45.00

Membership of the Association of Art Historians is open to individuals who are art or design historians by profession or avocation. Members will receive four issues of **Art History** as well as four issues of the **Association of Art Historians Bulletin**. Applications for membership should be sent to:

**Kate Woodhead, Dog & Partridge House, Byley, Cheshire, CW10 9NJ.
Telephone: 0606 835 517 Fax: 0606 834 799.**

To subscribe to *Art History* or to order a sample copy,
please write to:
Journals Marketing Department, Blackwell Publishers,
108 Cowley Road, Oxford OX4 IJF, England

**ART HISTORY IS PUBLISHED FOR THE ASSOCIATION OF ART HISTORIANS BY:
BLACKWELL PUBLISHERS, OXFORD, UK AND CAMBRIDGE, USA.**

ommi, Enio
Espacialidad en los planos" 1969
luminium and wood, 97 cm high

LATIN AMERICAN ART : ARTE CONCRETO INVENCION, ARTE MADI

GALERIE von BARTHA

SCHERTLINGASSE 16, 4051 BASEL, SWITZERLAND
TEL: 41-61-271 63 84, FAX: 41-61-271 03 05

GRAFICA Magazine

GRAFICA

PROPAGANDA

1907   A / TO   1995

COMMERCIAL ART

CASA DE IDÉIAS
Editora

AV. CÂNDIDO DE ABREU, 526
16º/1602/1603 - TORRE B
CURITIBA / PARANÁ /
BRASIL CEP 80530-905
- FONE: (041) 253-1276
FAX: (041) 252-1365
EDITA AS PUBLI-
CAÇÕES: GRÁ-
FICA/OZONE
E REK
LAME

!

CASA DE IDÉIAS / AV.CÂNDIDO DE ABREU, 526 / TORRE B / 16º 1602-603 CURITIBA / PR / BRASIL / 80530-905

Charles Cowles Gallery

420 West Broadway
New York 10012
Tel (212) 925-3500
Fax (212) 925-3501

Charles Arnoldi	Jim Martin
Don Bachardy	Sylvia Martins
David Bates	Wilhelm Moser
Howard Ben Tré	Ron Nagle
Marsha Burns	Manuel Neri
Dale Chihuly	Beverly Pepper
Caio Fonseca	Ken Price
Tom Holland	Peter Schlesinger
Patrick Ireland	Daniel Senise
Harry Kramer	Toshiko Takaezu
Terence La Noue	Peter Voulkos
Doug Martin	Darren Waterston

THE MAKSOUD PLAZA
São Paulo • Brazil

A Landmark of Hospitality and Elegance.

LOCATION: Perfectly located in the heart of São Paulo, just off fashionable Avenida Paulista • 40 minutes from International Airport (Guarulhos) • 15 minutes from Congonhas Airport, for air shuttle service to/from Rio de Janeiro • Limousine service on request.

ACCOMODATIONS: Perfect air conditioning in 420 elegantly furnished rooms including 34 Studio Demi-suites, 20 King Corner Rooms, 38 Brasiliana and Paulistana deluxe suites and 7 Presidential suites • Two Presidential floors with Butler service • All rooms with king size or two queen sized beds • New state of the art IDD phone system with voice mail and two-line speakerphones with data/fax port.

SPECIAL AUDIO AND VIDEO FEATURES: Remoto controlled Stereo color TVs linked to our exclusive private cable system with 25 channels, with four 24 hour movie channels including HBO • Seven channels with news in English, Spanish, French, German and Italian, also CNN International. Special International programming throught satelitte antennas • Six music and radio channels.

BUSINESS: Fully-equipped 24 hours Executive Service Center with Personal Computers and Modems, Fax, Telex, Copying equipment • Secretarial services, translation and interpreter services • Several board rooms and offices for rent.

SPECIAL FEATURES: Magnificent Atrium Lobby with fountains, plants, panoramic elevators, shops and works of art • Multi-lingual staff • Valet Parking • Complete Health and Fitness Center with year-round heated pool, exercise equipment with instructors, solarium, game room, sauna, massage parlor and a comprehensive Physiotherapy and Rehabilitation Center. • Also: 24 hours full room-service menu • Same day laundry (7 days a week) with express service and 24-hr housekeeping. • Check-in: 3;00 pm - Check-out: 12:00 (noon).

DINING AND ENTERTAINMENT: Six of São Paulo's finest Restaurants: *La Cuisine du Soleil*, the best cuisines of the World; *Brasserie Belavista* that never closes; *The Seafood Mezzanino*, griddle and grill lobster, shrimps, fish and other fruits from the sea and brazilian rivers; *Arlanza Grill*, specialty steakhouse; *Vikings*, for Scandinavian smorgasbord; *Pizzeria Belavista*, that also never closes. **Also:** *Trianon Piano Bar, Atrium Lobby Bar, Amaryllis Bar, Batidas & Petiscos Bar*, with live music and entertainment.

• **We take special care in the low-fat, low-cholesterol and nutrition features of all our food products and delicious cooking.**

MEETING FACILITIES: 21,000 square feet of meeting and banquet space for up to 2,000 participants • Several boardrooms • Theatre for 500 people • All facilities fully-equipped for simultaneous translation and audio-visual capabilities • Vip Club with five private dining rooms • Complete catering and banquet services.

RATES: Singles from US$ 245.00 Doubles from US$ 250.00 Suites from US$ 410.00 • Breakfast not included in room-rate. • No taxes and service charges. • 10% Travel Agent commission paid promptly.

RESERVATIONS:
• USA and Canada: (800) 223.6800 Toll Free
• New York City: (212) 838.3110 - Fax (212) 758-7367
• Europe & Elsewhere - Any Leading Hotels of The World office.

Use the following codes for: Amadeus - LW SAO 077
• Apollo - LW 8477 • Datas II - LW 7007 • Pars - LW 07007
• Sabre - LW 4790 • SystemOne - LW SAO 077
• Sita/Sahara - LW SAO 7007

MAKSOUD PLAZA
SÃO PAULO
one of The Leading Hotels of the World ®

THE MAKSOUD PLAZA
Alameda Campinas, 150
01404-900 - São Paulo, SP - Brazil
Phone: (55) (11) 253-4411 - Fax: (55) (11) 253-4544
Telex: (*) (11) 30026 MAKS BR
(*) The telex access code to Brazil is different from country to country. Please refer to your telex catalog.
Cable Address: MAKSOUD PLAZA

RARE BOOKS
ART REFERENCE
ILLUSTRATED BOOKS
CATALOGUES ISSUED

WILLIAM + VICTORIA DAILEY

8216 MELROSE AVENUE, P.O. BOX 69160, LOS ANGELES CA 90069 ≋ 213 658-8515